W9-BHM-722

G-8750

SINGING OURFAITH

SECOND EDITION

A HYMNAL FOR YOUNG CATHOLICS

GIA PUBLICATIONS, INC.
CHICAGO

G-8750
Copyright © 2014 by GIA Publications, Inc.
7404 South Mason Avenue, Chicago, Illinois 60638
www.giamusic.com

Cover design and art by Andrew Schultz.

Book design based upon *Worship — Third Edition* by Michael Tapia.

Published with the approval of the Committee on Divine Worship, United States Conference of
Catholic Bishops.

ISBN 978-1-62277-111-0

1 2 3 4 5 6 7 8 9 10 11 12 13 14 15 16 17 18 19 20

PREFACE

GIA Publications, Inc., is pleased to release *Singing Our Faith—Second Edition*. As was the case with the first edition (published in 2001) and our *Hymnal for Catholic Students* (published in 1988), we at GIA have sought to create music resources for children and young people that are broad in content and scope. It has been our intent to offer children songs that they can grow with, and not out of; to provide young people, specifically in grades K through 8, with music that will accompany them on their faith journey to Christian adulthood.

This volume represents the spectrum of styles and types of music used in Catholic liturgy and worship. Many of the titles are from the common repertoire of the adult faith community. Chant, spirituals, world church music, selections from the Taizé and Iona Communities, praise & worship songs, canons, refrains, and shorter songs augment a sizeable collection of metrical hymns. While not a specifically bilingual resource, we felt it very important to include many of the pieces with English and Spanish texts.

The Service Music section of *Singing Our Faith* contains three complete Mass settings, all of which include the additional musical acclamations found in *Eucharistic Prayers for Masses with Children*. A generous assortment of other service music items—selections children are likely to encounter at Sunday worship—is also included in this volume.

As with the previous edition, an order for Morning Prayer and Prayer to the End the Day has been included. Numerous psalm settings are found within this resource; some are well known psalm paraphrases, while others use the 2010 translation of *The Revised Grail Psalms*.

New to this edition are simple outlines both for the Stations of the Cross and for the Exposition and Adoration of the Blessed Sacrament.

Music is a doorway to the experience of the sacred. It is our hope that *Singing Our Faith* will help children and young people grow in their knowledge and understanding of their faith through song.

Special thanks and acknowledgement go to Wendy Barton Silhavy and Robert Wolf for consulting on this project.

We also wish to acknowledge Jeffry Mickus, production coordinator, book layout, and music engraver; Gail Gillispie, music engraver; Clarence Reiels, proofreader; Andrew Schultz, cover art; and Michael Boschert, copyright permissions.

David Anderson
Senior Editor

Michael Silhavy
Associate Senior Editor

Contents

Daily Prayer

1   Prayer to Begin the Day
5   Prayer to End the Day
9   Psalms

44   Service Music

Hymns and Songs

109   Advent
120   Christmas
132   Christmas / Epiphany
135   Lent
147   Lent / Holy Week
151   Easter
167   Pentecost and Holy Spirit
175   Trinity
178   Jesus Christ
183   Praise and Thanksgiving
209   Creation
216   Light
221   Christian Life
246   Comfort
255   Grace and Mercy
257   Peace
263   Unity
266   Prayer and Petition
275   Gathering
282   Morning and Evening
286   Angels and Saints
293   Exaltation of the Holy Cross
294   Blessed Virgin Mary
305   Eternal Life and Heaven
309   Sacraments and Initiation
314   Eucharist
330   Eucharistic Exposition and Benediction
332   Forgiveness and Healing
334   Blessing

Indexes

339   Acknowledgments
340   Scripture Passages Related to Hymns*
341   Liturgical Index*
342   Topical Index*
343   Index of Composers, Authors and Sources*
344   Metrical Index*
345   Tune Index*
346   Index of Service Music*
347   Psalm Refrains Set to Music*
348   Index of First Lines and Common Titles

These indexes only appear in the Cantor/Guitar and Accompaniment editons.

Daily Prayer

PRAYER TO BEGIN THE DAY

We make the sign of the cross as the leader begins:
Lord, open my lips.

Assembly: **And my mouth will proclaim your praise.**

MORNING HYMN

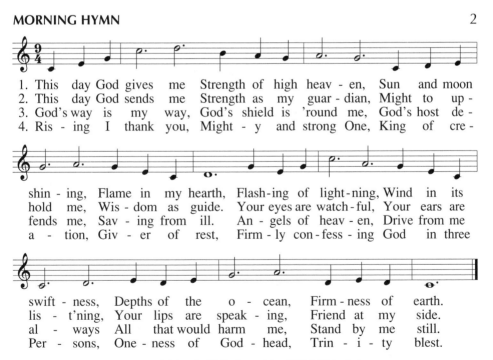

1. This day God gives me Strength of high heav - en, Sun and moon
2. This day God sends me Strength as my guar - dian, Might to up -
3. God's way is my way, God's shield is 'round me, God's host de -
4. Ris - ing I thank you, Might - y and strong One, King of cre -

shin - ing, Flame in my hearth, Flash-ing of light-ning, Wind in its
hold me, Wis - dom as guide. Your eyes are watch-ful, Your ears are
fends me, Sav - ing from ill. An - gels of heav - en, Drive from me
a - tion, Giv - er of rest, Firm - ly con-fess-ing God in three

swift - ness, Depths of the o - cean, Firm-ness of earth.
lis - t'ning, Your lips are speak - ing, Friend at my side.
al - ways All that would harm me, Stand by me still.
Per - sons, One-ness of God - head, Trin - i - ty blest.

Text: Ascribed to St. Patrick; James Quinn, SJ, 1919–2010, © 1969. Used by permission of Selah Publishing Co., Inc.
Tune: BUNESSAN, 5 5 5 4 D; Gaelic melody; acc. by Robert J. Batastini, b.1942, © 1999, GIA Publications, Inc.

PSALMODY

3 PSALM 146

Refrain

I will praise the Lord all my days, make

mu - sic to my God while I live, make

mu - sic to my God while I live.

Verses

1. Put no trust in the powerful, mere mortals in whom there is no help.
   Take their breath, they return to clay, and their plans that day come to nothing.
   They are happy who are helped by Jacob's God, whose hope is in the Lord their God,
   who alone made heaven and earth, the seas and all they contain.

2. It is the Lord who keeps faith for ever, who is just to the oppressed.
   It is God who gives bread to the hungry, the Lord, who sets prisoners free.
   It is the Lord who gives sight to the blind, who raises up those who are bowed down,
   the Lord who protects the stranger, and upholds the widow and orphan.

3. It is the Lord who loves the just but thwarts the path of the wicked.
   The Lord will reign for ever, Zion's God from age to age.

Text: Psalm 146; © 1963, 1993, The Grail, GIA Publications, Inc., agent
Music: Michael Joncas, © 1990, GIA Publications, Inc.

Other psalms may be substituted, especially Psalm 63 or Psalm 100. Psalm 51 is commonly used on Fridays.

PSALM PRAYER

Leader: O God,
maker of the heavens and the earth,
maker of night and of day,
we sing and pray to you.
Help us to walk together in your path
and to care for one another
all through this day.
Hear our prayer through Jesus Christ our Lord.

All: **Amen.**

WORD OF GOD

The reading is from the Bible. One of the texts below may be read, or one chosen especially for this day.

Reader: A. Listen to the words of Paul.
Whatever you do, in word or in deed,
do everything in the name of the Lord Jesus,
giving thanks to God the Father through him.
Colossians 3:17

B. Listen to the words of the second letter of Peter.
Grow in grace and in the knowledge of our Lord and Savior
Jesus Christ. To him be glory now and to the day of eternity.
2 Peter 3:18

C. Listen to the words of Paul.
Rejoice with those who rejoice, weep with those who weep.
Do not repay anyone evil for evil; be concerned for what is noble
in the sight of all. If possible, on your part, live at peace with all.
Do not be conquered by evil but conquer evil with good.
Romans 12:15, 17, 18, 21

D. Listen to the words of the book of Tobit.
Do to no one what you yourself dislike. Give to the
hungry some of your bread, and to the naked some of
your clothing. At all times bless the Lord God, and ask
him to make all your paths straight and to grant success
to all your endeavors and plans.
Tobit 4:15, 16, 19

E. Listen to the words of the gospel of Luke.
There was a scholar of the law who stood up to test
Jesus and said, "Teacher, what must I do to inherit
eternal life?" Jesus said to him, "What is written in the
law? How do you read it?" He said in reply, "You shall
love the Lord, your God, with all your heart, with all
your being, with all your strength, and with all your
mind, and your neighbor as yourself." He replied to
him, "You have answered correctly; do this and you
will live."
Luke 10:25–28

The reader concludes: The Word of the Lord.
All: **Thanks be to God.**

4   CANTICLE OF ZACHARY (BENEDICTUS)

1. Now ✠ bless the God of Is - ra - el, Who
2. Re - mem - ber - ing the cov - e - nant, God
3. In ten - der mer - cy, God will send The

comes in love and pow'r, Who rais - es from the
res - cues us from fear, That we might serve in
day - spring from on high, Our ris - ing sun, the

roy - al house De - liv - 'rance in this hour. Through
ho - li - ness And peace from year to year; And
light of life For those who sit and sigh. God

ho - ly proph - ets God has sworn To
you, my child, shall go be - fore To
comes to guide our way to peace, That

free us from a - larm, To save us from the
preach, to proph - e - sy, That all may know the
death shall reign no more. Sing prais - es to the

heav - y hand Of all who wish us harm.
ten - der love, The grace of God most high.
Ho - ly One! O wor - ship and a - dore!

Text: *Benedictus,* Luke 1:68–79; Ruth Duck, b.1947, © 1992, GIA Publications, Inc.
Tune: FOREST GREEN, CMD; English; harm. by Michael Joncas, b.1951, © 1987, GIA Publications, Inc.

INTERCESSIONS

Leader: That we may walk in the light of Christ this day,
let us pray to the Lord.

All: **Lord, hear our prayer.**

Leader: That our day may be filled with charity,
eagerness and peace,
let us pray to the Lord.

All: **Lord, hear our prayer.**

Leader: That our work and our play may bring glory to God,
let us pray to the Lord.

All: **Lord, hear our prayer.**

Leader: For the poor, the sick, and all who suffer;
for prisoners and all who are in danger,
let us pray to the Lord.

All: **Lord, hear our prayer.**

Other petitions may be offered aloud or in silence.

THE LORD'S PRAYER

Leader: Now let us pray as Jesus taught us:

All: **Our Father, who art in heaven,
hallowed be thy name;
thy kingdom come;
thy will be done on earth as it is in heaven.
Give us this day our daily bread;
and forgive us our trespasses
as we forgive those who trespass against us;
and lead us not into temptation,
but deliver us from evil.**

CONCLUDING PRAYER

Leader: God of light,
yours is the morning
and yours is the evening.
May Jesus, the Sun of Justice,
shine for ever in our hearts
and in all that we do.
We ask this through Christ our Lord.

All: **Amen.**

BLESSING

Leader: May the Lord bless us,
protect us from all evil
and bring us to everlasting life.

All: **Amen.**

PRAYER TO END THE DAY 5

We make the sign of the cross as the leader begins:
God, come to my assistance.

> *Assembly:* **Lord, make haste to help me.**

> *All:* **Glory to the Father, and to the Son, and to the Holy Spirit:**
> **as it was in the beginning, is now and will be for ever. Amen.**

(*Outside Lent:* **Alleluia.**)

EVENING HYMN 6

1. Day is done, but love un-fail-ing Dwells ev-er
2. Dark de-scends, but light un-end-ing Shines through our

here; Shad - ows fall, but hope, pre-vail-ing,
night; You are with us, ev - er lend-ing

Calms ev - 'ry fear. God, our Mak-er, none for-sak-ing,
New strength to sight: One in love, your truth con-fess-ing,

Take our hearts, of Love's own mak-ing, Watch our sleep-ing,
One in hope of heav - en's bless-ing, May we see, in

guard our wak-ing, Be al - ways near.
love's pos-sess-ing, Love's end - less light!

Text: James Quinn, SJ, 1919–2010, © 1969. Used by permission of Selah Publishing Co., Inc.
Tune: AR HYD Y NOS, 8 4 8 4 888 4; Welsh melody

PSALMODY

7   PSALM 121

Refrain

Guid - ing me,   guard - ing me,   the Lord is   by   my side;

guid - ing me,   guard - ing me,   the Lord up - holds my   life.

Verses

1. I lift up my eyes to the mountains;
   from where shall come my help?
   My help shall come from the Lord my God
   who made heaven and earth.

2. May he never allow you to stumble!
   Let him sleep not, your guard.
   No, he sleeps not nor slumbers,
   he, Israel's guard.

3. The Lord is your guard and your shade;
   at your right side he stands.
   By day the sun shall not smite you
   nor the moon in the night.

4. The Lord will guard you from evil,
   he will guard your soul.
   The Lord will guard your going and coming
   both now and for ever.

5. Praise the Father, the Son and Holy Spirit,
   both now and for ever,
   the God who is, who was and who will be,
   world without end.

Text: Psalm 121, Michael Joncas
Music: Michael Joncas
© 1988, GIA Publications, Inc.

Other psalms may be substituted, especially Psalms 23, 27, and 129.

PSALM PRAYER

Leader: Lord God,
every day and every night
you watch over our coming and our going.
Protect us from danger
and lead us safely home to you.
You are good and you love us for ever and ever.

All: **Amen.**

WORD OF GOD

The reading is from the Bible. One of the texts below may be read, or one chosen especially for this day.

Reader: A. Listen to the words of the gospel of Luke.
As they approached the village to which they were
going, Jesus gave the impression that he was going on
farther. But they urged him, "Stay with us, for it is
nearly evening and the day is almost over." So he went
in to stay with them.
Luke 24:28–29

B. Listen to the words of Paul.
Be on your guard, stand firm in the faith,
be courageous, be strong. Your every act should be
done with love. The grace of the Lord Jesus be with
you. My love to all of you in Christ Jesus.
2 Peter 3:18

C. Listen to the words of the gospel of Matthew.
Jesus said, "Love your enemies, and pray for those who
persecute you, that you may be children of your heavenly
Father, for he makes his sun rise on the bad and the good,
and causes rain to fall on the just and the unjust."
Matthew 5:44–45

D. Listen to the words of the prophet Micah.
You have been told what is good,
and what the LORD requires of you:
Only to do the right and to love goodness,
and to walk humbly with your God.
Micah 6:8

The reader concludes: The Word of the Lord.
All: **Thanks be to God.**

8   CANTICLE OF MARY (MAGNIFICAT)

1. My ✠ heart sings out with joy - ful praise To
2. The arm of God is strong and just To
3. The prom - ise made in a - ges past At

God who rais - es me, Who came to me when
scat - ter all the proud. The ty - rants tum - ble
last has come to be, For God has come in

I was low And changed my des - ti - ny. The
from their thrones And van - ish like a cloud. The
pow'r to save, To set all peo - ple free. Re -

Ho - ly One, the Liv - ing God, Is al - ways
hun - gry all are sat - is - fied; The rich are
mem - b'ring those who wait to see Sal - va - tion's

full of grace To those who seek their
sent a - way. The poor of earth who
dawn - ing day, Our Sav - ior comes to

Mak - er's will In ev - 'ry time and place.
suf - fer long Will wel - come God's new day.
all who weep To wipe their tears a - way.

Text: *Magnificat*, Luke 1:46–55; Ruth Duck, b.1947, © 1992, GIA Publications, Inc.
Tune: KINGSFOLD, CMD; English traditional; harm. by Ralph Vaughan Williams, 1872–1958

INTERCESSIONS

Leader: For the Church,
let us pray to the Lord.

All: **Lord, hear our prayer.**

Leader: For all who serve in government,
let us pray to the Lord.

All: **Lord, hear our prayer.**

Leader: For the poor, the sick, the lonely, and the sorrowful,
let us pray to the Lord.

All: **Lord, hear our prayer.**

Leader: For peace in the world,
let us pray to the Lord.

All: **Lord, hear our prayer.**

Other petitions may be offered aloud or in silence, always concluding:

Leader: For all who have died,
let us pray to the Lord.

All: **Lord, hear our prayer.**

THE LORD'S PRAYER

Leader: Now let us pray as Jesus taught us:

All: **Our Father, who art in heaven,**
hallowed be thy name;
thy kingdom come;
thy will be done on earth as it is in heaven.
Give us this day our daily bread;
and forgive us our trespasses
as we forgive those who trespass against us;
and lead us not into temptation,
but deliver us from evil.

CONCLUDING PRAYER

Leader: Be our shining light, O Lord,
during the rest of the day
and all through the night.
Show us the good that surrounds us
so that we might praise you.
Protect us from all dangers
that we might give you thanks
through Jesus, who is Lord for ever and ever.

All: **Amen.**

BLESSING

Leader: May the Lord bless us,
protect us from all evil
and bring us to everlasting life.

All: **Amen.**

Psalm Refrains

Psalm 23: My Shepherd Is the Lord (JG) 9

My shep-herd is the Lord, noth-ing in-deed shall I want.

Psalm 23: The Lord Is My Shepherd (RP) 10

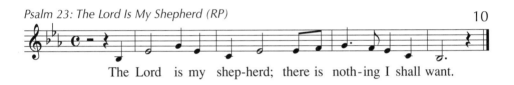

The Lord is my shep-herd; there is noth-ing I shall want.

Psalm 24: We Long to See Your Face (KK) 11

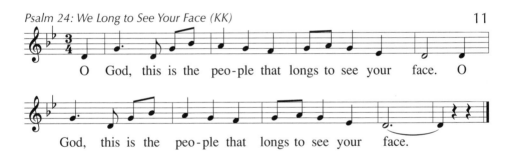

O God, this is the peo-ple that longs to see your face. O

God, this is the peo-ple that longs to see your face.

Psalm 24: Open Wide Your Gates (KK) 12

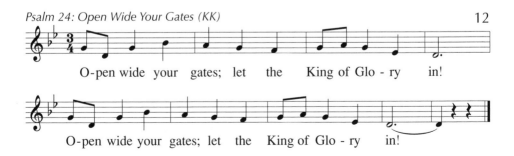

O-pen wide your gates; let the King of Glo - ry in!

O-pen wide your gates; let the King of Glo - ry in!

13 *Psalm 25: To You, O Lord / A Ti, Señor (MH)*

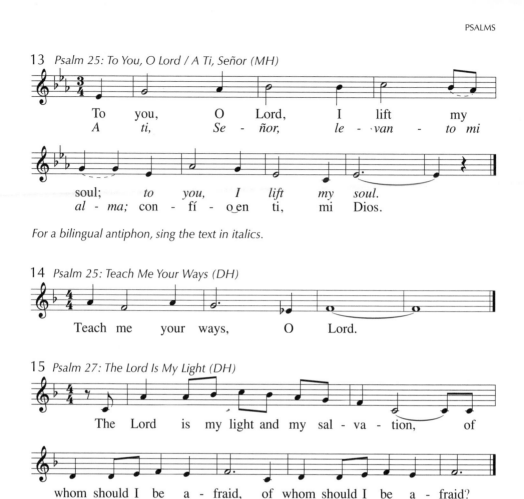

To you, O Lord, I lift my
A ti, Se - ñor, le - van - to mi

soul; to you, I lift my soul.
al - ma; con - fí - o en ti, mi Dios.

For a bilingual antiphon, sing the text in italics.

14 *Psalm 25: Teach Me Your Ways (DH)*

Teach me your ways, O Lord.

15 *Psalm 27: The Lord Is My Light (DH)*

The Lord is my light and my sal - va - tion, of

whom should I be a - fraid, of whom should I be a - fraid?

16 *Psalm 33: Lord, Let Your Mercy (MG)*

Lord, let your mer-cy be on us, as we place our trust in you.

17 *Psalm 34: Taste and See (MG)*

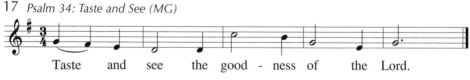

Taste and see the good - ness of the Lord.

18 *Psalm 51: Be Merciful, O Lord / Señor, Misericordia (PC)*

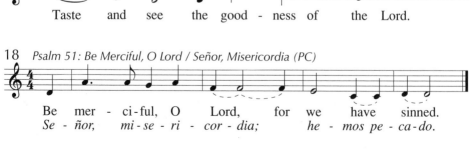

Be mer - ci - ful, O Lord, for we have sinned.
Se - ñor, mi - se - ri - cor - dia; he - mos pe - ca - do.

Psalm 63: My Soul Is Thirsting (RP) — 19

My soul is thirst-ing for you, O Lord, thirst-ing for you my God.

Psalm 63: In the Morning I Will Sing (DCI) — 20

In the morn - ing I will sing, will sing glad songs of praise to you.

Psalm 78: The Lord Gave Them Bread (MG) — 21

The Lord gave them bread from heav - en.

Psalm 78: Do Not Forget (RJB) — 22

Do not for - get the works of the Lord!

Psalm 89: For Ever I Will Sing (JRC) — 23

For ev - er I will sing the good - ness of the Lord.

Psalm 91: Be with Me / Acompáñame (MH) — 24

Be with me, Lord, when I am in trou - ble,
A - com - pá - ña - me en la tri - bu - la - ción.

be with me, Lord, I pray.
A - com - pá - ña - me, Se - ñor.

For a bilingual antiphon, sing the text in italics.

25 *Psalm 96: Proclaim to All the Nations (DH)*

Pro-claim to all the na-tions the mar-vel-ous deeds of the Lord.

Pro-claim to all the na-tions the mar-vel-ous deeds of the Lord.

26 *Psalm 98: All the Ends of the Earth (DH, MH)*

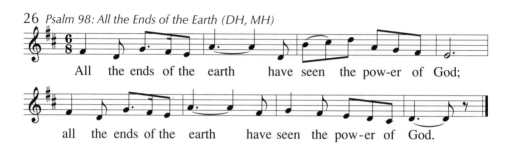

All the ends of the earth have seen the pow-er of God;

all the ends of the earth have seen the pow-er of God.

27 *Psalm 98: Sing to the Lord a New Song (MG)*

Sing to the Lord a new song, for he has done mar-vel-ous deeds.

28 *Psalm 100: We Are God's People (DH)*

We are God's peo - ple, the flock of the Lord.

29 *Psalm 103: The Lord Is Kind and Merciful / El Señor Es Compasivo (MH)*

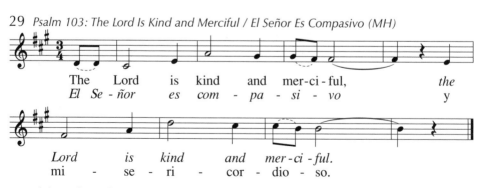

The Lord is kind and mer-ci-ful, *the*
El Se - ñor es com - pa - si - vo y

Lord is kind and mer-ci-ful.
mi - se - ri - cor - dio - so.

For a bilingual antiphon, sing the text in italics.

Psalm 104: Lord, Send Out Your Spirit / Señor, Envía Tu Espíritu (PL)   30

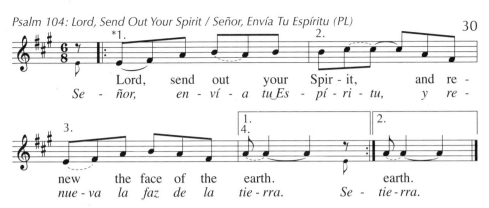

Lord, send out your Spir - it, and re -
Se - ñor, en - ví - a tu Es - pí - ri - tu, y re -

new the face of the earth.
nue - va la faz de la tie - rra. Se - tie - rra.

May be sung as a canon. For a bilingual antiphon, sing the English through the first ending, followed by the Spanish on the repeat.

Psalm 117: Go Out to All the World (AP)   31

Go out to all the world and tell the Good News.

Psalm 118: Let Us Rejoice (MH)   32

This is the day the Lord has made, let us re -
Or: Al - le - lu - ia, al - le - lu - ia! Al - le -

joice and be glad; let us re - joice and be glad!
lu - ia! Al - le - lu - ia!

Salmo 118: Éste Es el Día (MH)

És - te es el dí - a que hi-zo el Se - ñor: sea nues-tra a-le-grí-a y

go - zo. nues-tra a-le - grí - a y go - zo.

For a bilingual antiphon, sing the English through the first ending, followed by the Spanish with the second ending.

33 *Psalm 119: Blessed Are They (RG)*

Bless-ed are they who fol-low the law of the Lord.

34 *Psalm 121: Our Help Comes from the Lord (MJ)*

Our help comes from the Lord, the mak-er of heav-en and earth.

35 *Psalm 122: Let Us Go Rejoicing / Vamos Todos Alegres (MJ)*

Let us go re - joic-ing to the house of the Lord.
Va - mos to - dos a - le - gres a la ca - sa del Se - ñor.

Let us go re - joic-ing to the house of the Lord.
Va - mos to - dos a - le - gres a la ca - sa del Se - ñor.

For a bilingual antiphon, sing the text in italics.

36 *Psalm 126: The Lord Has Done Great Things (RP)*

The Lord has done great things for us;

we are filled with joy, we are filled with joy.

37 *Psalm 138: In the Sight of the Angels (JRC)*

In the sight of the an-gels I will sing your prais-es, Lord.

Psalm 138: Lord, On the Day I Called (RV)   38

Lord, on the day I called for help, you an-swered me.

Psalm 139: I Praise You, O Lord (MG)   39

I praise you, O Lord, for I am won-der-ful-ly made.

Psalm 145: I Will Praise Your Name for Ever (LR)   40

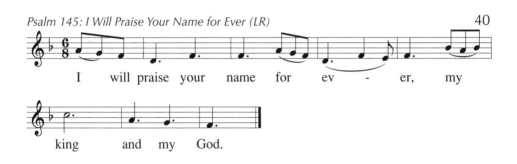

I will praise your name for ev - er, my

king and my God.

Psalm 146: Praise the Lord, My Soul (MG)   41

Praise the Lord, my soul! Praise the Lord!

Judith 13: You Are the Highest Honor (KC)   42

You are the high - est hon - or of our race.
Tú e - res el or - gu - llo de nues - tra ra - za.

Isaiah 12: You Will Draw Water (MG)   43

You will draw wa-ter joy-ful-ly from the springs of sal - va-tion.

Service Music

44 SPRINKLING SONG

Refrain

Springs of wa-ter, bless the Lord! Sing your glo-ry and praise for ev-er!

Verses

Cantor:

1. O - ceans of earth, sing glo-ry to God! Praise to the one who
2. Riv - ers and lakes, sing glo-ry to God! Praise, all you ponds and
3. Brooks of the hills, sing glo-ry to God! Praise to the source of
4. Show - ers and springs, sing glo-ry to God! Praise, all you liv - ing

formed you!   Sound from your depths a   hymn that tells the
bogs!   Rich with the life that   God cre - ates, now
life!   Danc - ing with joy from   peak to val - ley,
wa - ters!   Show - er the earth with   life and good-ness,

won - ders God has done!
let your song be heard!
laugh-ing and clear your song!
show - er the grace of God!

Oh, bless-ed be God for

All: **D.C.**

ev - er!   Bless - ed be God for ev - er!

Text: Marty Haugen
Music: Marty Haugen
© 1994, GIA Publications, Inc.

KYRIE ELEISON 45

Lord, have mer - cy. Lord, have mer - cy.

Christ, have mer - cy. Christ, have mer - cy.

Lord, have mer - cy. Lord, have mer - cy.

Music: Traditional chant; acc. by Richard Proulx, © 1971, GIA Publications, Inc.

Or:

Ký - ri - e, e - lé - i - son. Ký - ri - e, e - lé - i - son.

Chri - ste, e - lé - i - son. Chri - ste, e - lé - i - son.

Ký - ri - e, e - lé - i - son. Ký - ri - e, e - lé - i - son.

Music: Traditional chant; acc. by Richard Proulx, © 1971, GIA Publications, Inc.

KYRIE ELEISON 46

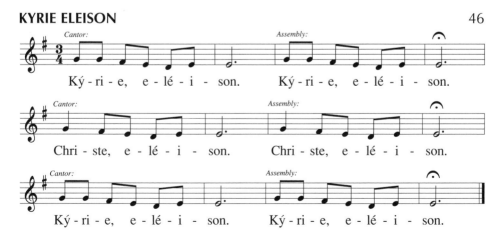

Ký - ri - e, e - lé - i - son. Ký - ri - e, e - lé - i - son.

Chri - ste, e - lé - i - son. Chri - ste, e - lé - i - son.

Ký - ri - e, e - lé - i - son. Ký - ri - e, e - lé - i - son.

Music: *Mass of Light,* David Haas, © 1988, GIA Publications, Inc.

47 GLORIA

Refrain

Glo - ry to God in the high - est, and on
Glo - ria_a Dios en el cie - lo, y_en la

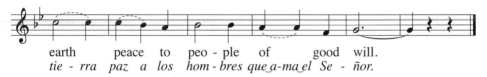

earth peace to peo - ple of good will.
tie - rra paz a los hom - bres que_a-ma_el Se - ñor.

Verses

1. We praise you,
   we bless you,
   we adore you,
   we glorify you,
   we give you thanks for your great glory,
   Lord God, heavenly King,
   O God, almighty Father.

2. Lord Jesus Christ, Only Begotten Son,
   Lord God, Lamb of God, Son of the
      Father,
   you take away the sins of the world,
   have mercy on us;
   you take away the sins of the world,
   receive our prayer;
   you are seated at the right hand of the
      Father,
   have mercy on us.

3. For you alone are the Holy One,
   you alone are the Lord,
   you alone are the Most High,
   Jesus Christ,
   with the Holy Spirit,
   in the glory of God the Father.
   Amen.

1. *Por tu_inmensa gloria te_alabamos,*
   te bendecimos,
   te_adoramos,
   te glorificamos,
   te damos gracias,
   Señor Dios, Rey celestial,
   Dios Padre todopoderoso.

2. *Señor, Hijo único, Jesucristo,*
   Señor Dios, Cordero de Dios, Hijo
      del Padre;
   tú que quitas el pecado del mundo,
   ten piedad de nosotros;
   tú que quitas el pecado del mundo,
   a tiende nuestra súplica;
   tú que_estás sentado_a la derecha
      del Padre,
   ten piedad de nosotros.

3. *Porque sólo tú_eres Santo,*
   sólo tú Señor,
   sólo tú Altísimo,
   Jesucristo,
   con el Espíritu Santo
   en la gloria de Dios Padre.
   Amén.

Text: English, ICEL, © 2010
Music: *Mass of Creation*, Marty Haugen; adapt. by Tony E. Alonso, © 1984, 1985, 2010, 2013, GIA Publications, Inc.

GLORIA

Refrain

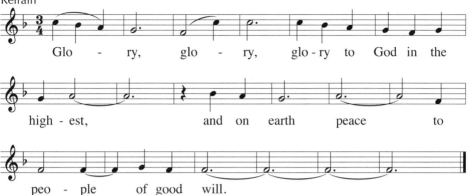

Glo - ry, glo - ry, glo - ry to God in the high - est, and on earth peace to peo - ple of good will.

Verses

1. We praise you,
   we bless you,
   we adore you,
   we glorify you,
   we give you thanks for your great glory,
   Lord God, heavenly King,
   O God, almighty Father.

2. Lord Jesus Christ, Only Begotten Son,
   Lord God, Lamb of God, Son of the
       Father,
   you take away the sins of the world,
   have mercy on us;
   you take away the sins of the world,
   receive our prayer;
   you are seated at the right hand of the
       Father,
   have mercy on us.

3. For you alone are the Holy One,
   you alone are the Lord,
   you alone are the Most High,
   Jesus Christ,
   with the Holy Spirit,
   in the glory of God the Father.
   Amen.

Text: ICEL, © 2010
Music: *Mass of Christ, Our Hope*, David Haas, © 2014, GIA Publications, Inc.

49 GOSPEL ACCLAMATION

Al - le - lu - ia,   al - le - lu - ia,   Al - le - lu - ia,   al - le - lu.

Al - le - lu - ia,   al - le - lu - ia,   Al - le - lu - ia,   al - le - lu.

Al - le - lu - ia,   al - le - lu.   Al - le - lu - ia,   al - le - lu.

Al - le - lu - ia,   al - le - lu - ia,   Al - le - lu - ia,   al - le - lu.

Music: Palestinian traditional; acc. by Robert N. Roth, © 2000, GIA Publications, Inc.

50 GOSPEL ACCLAMATION

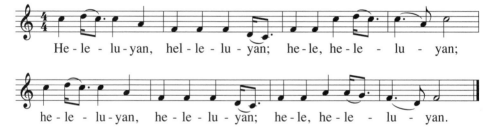

He - le - lu - yan,   hel - le - lu - yan;   he - le, he - le - lu - yan;

he - le - lu - yan,   he - le - lu - yan;   he - le, he - le - lu - yan.

Text: Traditional Muscogee Indian
Tune: Traditional Muscogee Indian; transcribed by Charles H. Webb, © 1989, The United Methodist Publishing House

51 GOSPEL ACCLAMATION

Hal - le, hal - le, hal - le - lu - jah!   Hal - le, hal - le, hal-

le - lu - jah!   Hal - le, hal - le, hal - le -

lu - jah!   Hal - le - lu - jah!   Hal - le - lu - jah!

Music: Traditional Caribbean, arr. by John L. Bell, © 1990, Iona Community, GIA Publications, Inc., agent; verses and acc. by Marty Haugen, © 1993, GIA Publications, Inc.

GOSPEL ACCLAMATION

Refrain

¡A-le - lu-ya, a-le-lu - ya! ¡A-le-lu-ya, a-le-lu - ya! ¡A-le -

lu - ya, a-le-lu - ya! ¡El Se - ñor re-su-ci-tó!

Verse

¡A-le - lu-ya! ¡A-le-lu-ya! ¡A-le - lu-ya! ¡A-le-lu-ya! ¡A-le -

lu-ya! ¡A-le-lu-ya! ¡A-le - lu-ya! ¡A-le-lu-ya! ¡A-le -

lu-ya! ¡A-le-lu-ya! ¡A-le - lu-ya! ¡A-le - lu-ya! ¡A-le -

D.C.

lu-ya! ¡A-le-lu-ya! ¡A-le - lu-ya! ¡A-le-lu - ya!

Gospel Acclamation Verses

1. Yo soy el buen pastor, dice el Señor.
   Yo conozco a mis ovejas y ellas me conocen a mí.

2. Yo soy el camino, la verdad y la vida.
   Solamente por mí se puede llegar al Padre.

3. Ven, Santo Espíritu, ilumina nuestra corazones.
   Enciende en nosotros el fuego de tu amor.

1. *I am the good shepherd, says the Lord;*
   I know my sheep, and mine know me.

2. *I am the way, the truth and life, says the Lord;*
   no one comes to the Father, except through me.

3. *Come, Holy Spirit, fill the hearts of your faithful*
   and kindle in all of them the fire of your love.

Text: English verses, *Lectionary for Mass*, © 1969, 1981, 1997, ICEL
Music: Traditional Honduran; arr. by Rob Glover, © 1997, GIA Publications, Inc.

53 GOSPEL ACCLAMATION

(Al - le - lu - ia) Al - le - lu - ia, al - le -
lu - ia, al - le - lu - ia! (hum)

Music: Alleluia II, Jacques Berthier, © 1984, Les Presses de Taizé, GIA Publications, Inc., agent

54 GOSPEL ACCLAMATION

1.   2.   3.
Al - le - lu - ia, al - le - lu - ia, al - le - lu - ia!

Music: *Mass of Remembrance*, Marty Haugen, © 1987, GIA Publications, Inc.

55 GOSPEL ACCLAMATION / ACLAMACIÓN ANTES DEL EVANGELIO

Al-le - lu - ia, al-le - lu - ia, al-le - lu-ia, al - le - lu - ia. Al-le -
A - le - lu - ya, a-le - lu-ya, a-le - lu-ya, a - le - lu - ya. A-le -

lu - ia, al - le - lu - ia, al - le - lu-ia, al - le - lu - ia.
lu - ya, a - le - lu ya, a - le - lu-ya, a - le - lu - ya.

Music: *Mass of Creation*, Marty Haugen; adapt. by Tony E. Alonso, © 1984, 1985, 2010, 2013, GIA Publications, Inc.

56 GOSPEL ACCLAMATION

Al - le - lu - ia, al - le - lu - ia, al - le - lu - ia.

Music: Chant Mode VI; acc. by Richard Proulx, © 1985, GIA Publications, Inc.

GOSPEL ACCLAMATION 57

Al - le - lu - ia, al - le - lu,
Al - le - lu - ia, al - le - lu - ia,
Al - le - lu - ia, al - le - lu - ia,

To repeat | Last time

al - le - lu - ia, al - le - lu - ia. ia.
al - le - lu - ia, al - le - lu - ia. ia.
al - le - lu - ia, al - le - lu - ia. ia.

Music: Abraham Maraire, © Verbum Forlong AB, Sweden

GOSPEL ACCLAMATION 58

Al - le - lu - ia, al - le - lu - ia.
Al - le - lu - ia, al - le - lu - ia.

Music: *Mass of Christ, Our Hope,* David Haas, © 2014, GIA Publications, Inc.

59 GOSPEL ACCLAMATION

Al - le - lu - ia!   Al - le - lu - ia!   Al - le - lu - ia!

Lent: Glo - ry to you,   O Word of God,   Lord Je - sus Christ!

Text: ICEL, © 1969
Music: *Mass of Light,* David Haas, © 1988, GIA Publications, Inc.

60 GOSPEL ACCLAMATION / ACLAMACIÓN ANTES DEL EVANGELIO

Al - le - lu - ia,   al - le - lu - ia,   al - le - lu - ia.
A - le - lu - ya,   a - le - lu - ya,   a - le - lu - ya.
Lent: Glo - ry to you,   Word of God,   Lord Je - sus Christ.
Cuaresma: Ho - nor a ti,   Cris - to Je - sús,   Rey de e - ter - na glo - ria.

Al - le - lu - ia,   al - le - lu - ia,   al - le - lu - ia.
A - le - lu - ya,   a - le - lu - ya,   a - le - lu - ya.
Glo - ry to you,   Word of God,   Lord Je - sus Christ.
Ho - nor a ti,   Cris - to Je - sús,   Rey de e - ter - na glo - ria.

Text: English Lenten refrain, ICEL, © 1969
Music: *Jubilation Mass,* James J. Chepponis, © 1999, GIA Publications, Inc.

61 LENTEN GOSPEL ACCLAMATION

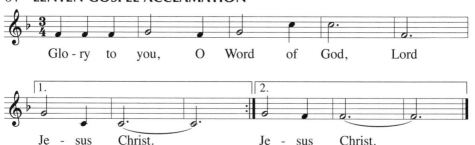

Glo - ry to you,   O Word of God,   Lord

1. Je - sus Christ.   2. Je - sus Christ.

Text: ICEL, © 1969
Music: *Mass of Christ, Our Hope,* David Haas, © 2014, GIA Publications, Inc.

LENTEN GOSPEL ACCLAMATION / ACLAMACIÓN ANTES DEL EVANGELIO DURANTE LA CUARESMA 62

Glo - ry and praise to you, Lord Je - sus Christ.
Ho - nor y glo - ria_a ti, Se - ñor Je - sús.

Text: English, ICEL, © 1969
Music: Marty Haugen, © 1995, GIA Publications, Inc.

LENTEN GOSPEL ACCLAMATION / ACLAMACIÓN ANTES DEL EVANGELIO DURANTE LA CUARESMA 63

Praise to you, Lord Je-sus Christ, King of end-less glo - ry!
A-la -ban-za_a ti, oh Cris - to, rey de_e-ter - na glo-ria.

Text: English, ICEL, © 1969
Music: *Mass of Creation*, Marty Haugen; adapt. by Tony E. Alonso, © 1984, 1985, 2010, 2013, GIA Publications, Inc.

PRAYER OF THE FAITHFUL 64

Ký - ri - e, Ký - ri - e, e - lé - i - son. (hum)

Music: Jacques Berthier, © 1980, Les Presses de Taizé, GIA Publications, Inc., agent

PRAYER OF THE FAITHFUL 65

Te ro - ga-mos, ó - ye-nos. Lord, hear our prayer.

Music: Peter M. Kolar, © 2001, World Library Publications

Mass of Creation

66 CHILDREN'S ACCLAMATION 1

Ho-san-na in the high-est, ho-san-na in the high-est.

Text: ICEL, © 1975
Music: Eucharistic Prayer for Children, *Mass of Creation,* Marty Haugen, adapt. by Rob Glover, © 1989, GIA Publications, Inc.

67 HOLY, HOLY, HOLY

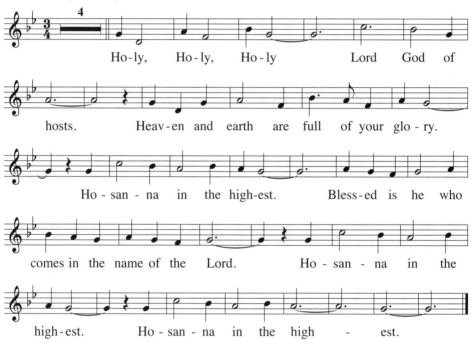

Ho-ly, Ho-ly, Ho-ly Lord God of

hosts. Heav-en and earth are full of your glo-ry.

Ho - san - na in the high-est. Bless-ed is he who

comes in the name of the Lord. Ho - san - na in the

high-est. Ho - san - na in the high - est.

Text: ICEL, © 2010
Music: *Mass of Creation,* Marty Haugen, © 1984, 1985, 2010, GIA Publications, Inc.

68 CHILDREN'S ACCLAMATION 2

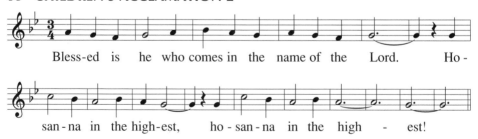

Bless-ed is he who comes in the name of the Lord. Ho -

san-na in the high-est, ho-san-na in the high - est!

Text: ICEL, © 1975
Music: Eucharistic Prayer for Children, *Mass of Creation,* Marty Haugen, adapt. by Rob Glover, © 1989, GIA Publications, Inc.

In Eucharistic Prayer 1, this acclamation precedes the Holy, Holy, Holy.

MEMORIAL ACCLAMATION A 69

We pro-claim your Death, O Lord, and pro-fess your Res-ur -

rec-tion un - til you come a - gain, un - til you come a - gain.

Text: ICEL, © 2010
Music: *Mass of Creation,* Marty Haugen, © 2010, GIA Publications, Inc.

MEMORIAL ACCLAMATION B 70

When we eat this Bread and drink this Cup, we pro -

claim your Death, O Lord, un - til you come a - gain.

Text: ICEL, © 2010
Music: *Mass of Creation,* Marty Haugen, © 2010, GIA Publications, Inc.

MEMORIAL ACCLAMATION C 71

Save us, Sav-ior of the world, for by your Cross and Res-ur -

rec-tion you have set us free, you have set us free.

Text: ICEL, © 2010
Music: *Mass of Creation,* Marty Haugen, © 2010, GIA Publications, Inc.

CHILDREN'S ACCLAMATION 3 72

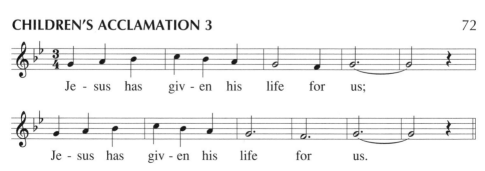

Je - sus has giv-en his life for us;

Je - sus has giv-en his life for us.

Text: ICEL, © 1975
Music: Eucharistic Prayer for Children, *Mass of Creation,* Marty Haugen, adapt. by Rob Glover, © 1989, GIA Publications, Inc.

73 CHILDREN'S ACCLAMATION 4

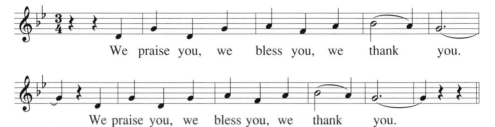

We praise you, we bless you, we thank you.

We praise you, we bless you, we thank you.

Text: ICEL, © 1975
Music: Eucharistic Prayer for Children, *Mass of Creation,* Marty Haugen, adapt. by Rob Glover, © 1989, GIA Publications, Inc.

74 AMEN

A - men, a - men, a - men!

Music: *Mass of Creation,* Marty Haugen, © 1984, 1985, GIA Publications, Inc.

Mass of Creation   Misa de la Creación

75 SANTO, SANTO, SANTO   HOLY, HOLY, HOLY

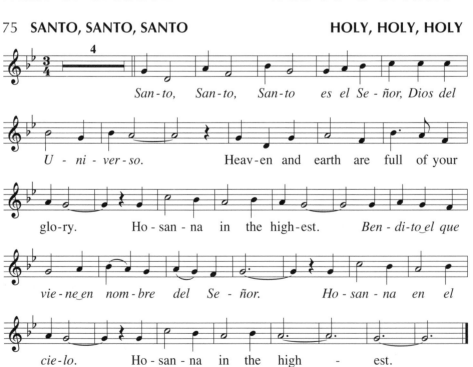

San-to, San-to, San-to es el Se - ñor, Dios del
U - ni - ver-so. Heav-en and earth are full of your
glo-ry. Ho - san - na in the high-est. Ben - di-to el que
vie-ne en nom-bre del Se - ñor. Ho - san - na en el
cie-lo. Ho - san - na in the high - est.

Text: English, ICEL, © 2010
Music: *Mass of Creation,* Marty Haugen; adapt. by Tony E. Alonso, © 1984, 1985, 2010, 2013, GIA Publications, Inc.

MEMORIAL ACCLAMATION A   ACLAMACIÓN AL MEMORIAL A   76

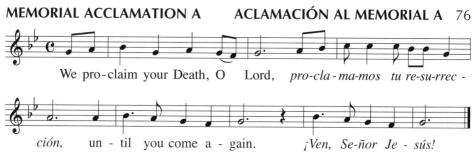

We pro-claim your Death, O Lord, *pro-cla-ma-mos tu re-su-rrec-ción,* un-til you come a-gain. *¡Ven, Señor Je-sús!*

Text: English, ICEL, © 2010
Music: *Mass of Creation*, Marty Haugen; adapt. by Tony E. Alonso, © 2010, 2013, GIA Publications, Inc.

MEMORIAL ACCLAMATION B   ACLAMACIÓN AL MEMORIAL B   77

When we eat this Bread and drink this Cup, *a-nun-cia-mos tu muer-te, Se-ñor,* *has-ta que vuel-vas,* un-til you come a-gain.

Text: English, ICEL, © 2010
Music: *Mass of Creation*, Marty Haugen; adapt. by Tony E. Alonso, © 2010, 2013, GIA Publications, Inc.

MEMORIAL ACCLAMATION C   ACLAMACIÓN AL MEMORIAL C   78

Save us, Sav-ior of the world, *por tu cruz y re-su-rrec-ción nos has sal-va-do, Se-ñor,* you have set us free.

Text: English, ICEL, © 2010
Music: *Mass of Creation*, Marty Haugen; adapt. by Tony E. Alonso, © 2010, 2013, GIA Publications, Inc.

AMÉN   79

A - mén, a - mén, a - mén!

Music: *Mass of Creation*, Marty Haugen, © 1984, 1985, GIA Publications, Inc.

Mass of the Angels and Saints

80 CHILDREN'S ACCLAMATION 1

Ho - san - na, ho - san - na, ho - san - na in the high - est.

Text: ICEL, © 1975
Music: *Mass of the Angels and Saints*, Steven R. Janco, © 1996, 2010, GIA Publications, Inc.

81 HOLY, HOLY, HOLY

Ho - ly, Ho - ly, Ho - ly Lord God of hosts.

Heav'n and earth are full of your glo - ry. Ho -

san - na, ho - san - na, ho - san - na in the

high - est, ho - san - na, ho - san - na, ho -

san - na in the high - est. Bless - ed is he who comes in the

name of the Lord. Ho - san - na, ho -

san - na, ho - san - na in the high - est, ho -

san - na, ho - san - na, ho - san - na in the high - est.

Text: ICEL, © 2010
Music: *Mass of the Angels and Saints*, Steven R. Janco, © 1996, 2010, GIA Publications, Inc.

CHILDREN'S ACCLAMATION 2 82

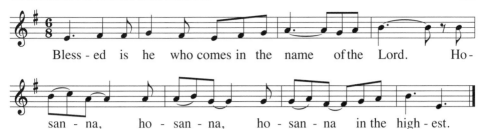

Bless - ed is he who comes in the name of the Lord. Ho -
san - na, ho - san - na, ho - san - na in the high - est.

Text: ICEL, © 1975
Music: *Mass of the Angels and Saints*, Steven R. Janco, © 1996, 2010, GIA Publications, Inc.

In Eucharistic Prayer 1, this acclamation precedes the Holy, Holy, Holy.

MEMORIAL ACCLAMATION A 83

We pro - claim your Death, O Lord, and pro -
fess your Res - ur - rec - tion un - til you come a - gain.

Text: ICEL, © 2010
Music: *Mass of the Angels and Saints*, Steven R. Janco, © 1996, 2010, GIA Publications, Inc.

MEMORIAL ACCLAMATION B 84

When we eat this Bread and drink this Cup,
we pro - claim your Death, O Lord, un - til you come a - gain.

Text: ICEL, © 2010
Music: *Mass of the Angels and Saints*, Steven R. Janco, © 1996, 2010, GIA Publications, Inc.

MEMORIAL ACCLAMATION C 85

Save us, Sav - ior of the world, for by your
Cross and Res - ur - rec - tion you have set us free.

Text: ICEL, © 2010
Music: *Mass of the Angels and Saints*, Steven R. Janco, © 2010, GIA Publications, Inc.

86 CHILDREN'S ACCLAMATION 3

Cantor: Je-sus has giv-en his life for us. *All:* Je-sus has giv-en his life for us.

Text: ICEL, © 1975
Music: *Mass of the Angels and Saints*, Steve R. Janco, © 2000, GIA Publications, Inc.

87 CHILDREN'S ACCLAMATION 4

Cantor: We praise you, we bless you, we thank you.

All: We praise you, we bless you, we thank you.

Text: ICEL, © 1975
Music: *Mass of the Angels and Saints*, Steve R. Janco, © 2000, GIA Publications, Inc.

88 AMEN

A - men, a - men, a - men.

A - men, a - men, a - men.

Music: *Mass of the Angels and Saints*, Steven R. Janco, © 1996, GIA Publications, Inc.

Mass of Christ, Our Hope

89 CHILDREN'S ACCLAMATION 1

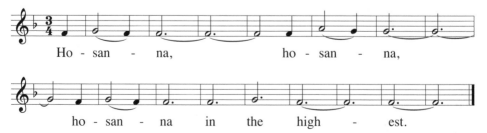

Ho - san - na, ho - san - na,

ho - san - na in the high - est.

Text: ICEL, © 1975
Music: *Mass of Christ, Our Hope*, David Haas, © 2014, GIA Publications, Inc.

HOLY, HOLY, HOLY 90

Ho - ly, Ho - ly, Ho - ly Lord God of hosts.

Heav-en and earth are full of your glo - ry.

Ho - san - na, ho - san - na,

ho - san - na in the high - est.

Bless - ed, bless-ed is he who comes in the name of the

Lord. Ho - san - na, ho - san - na,

ho - san - na in the high - est.

Text: ICEL, © 2010
Music: *Mass of Christ, Our Hope,* David Haas, © 2014, GIA Publications, Inc.

CHILDREN'S ACCLAMATION 2 91

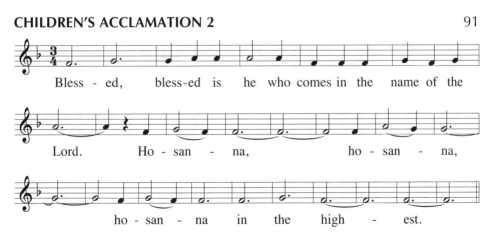

Bless - ed, bless-ed is he who comes in the name of the

Lord. Ho - san - na, ho - san - na,

ho - san - na in the high - est.

Text: ICEL, © 1975
Music: *Mass of Christ, Our Hope,* David Haas, © 2014, GIA Publications, Inc.

In Eucharistic Prayer 1, this acclamation precedes the Holy, Holy, Holy.

92 MEMORIAL ACCLAMATION A

We pro - claim your Death, O Lord,
and pro - fess your Res - ur - rec - tion
un - til you come, un - til you come,
un - til you come a - gain.

Text: ICEL, © 2010
Music: *Mass of Christ, Our Hope,* David Haas, © 2014, GIA Publications, Inc.

93 MEMORIAL ACCLAMATION B

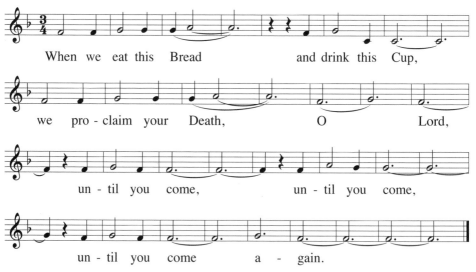

When we eat this Bread and drink this Cup,
we pro - claim your Death, O Lord,
un - til you come, un - til you come,
un - til you come a - gain.

Text: ICEL, © 2010
Music: *Mass of Christ, Our Hope,* David Haas, © 2014, GIA Publications, Inc.

MEMORIAL ACCLAMATION C 94

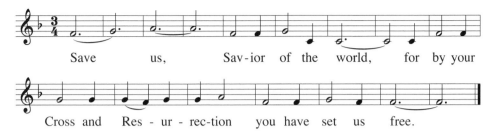

Save us, Sav-ior of the world, for by your

Cross and Res - ur - rec-tion you have set us free.

Text: ICEL, © 2010
Music: *Mass of Christ, Our Hope,* David Haas, © 2014, GIA Publications, Inc.

CHILDREN'S ACCLAMATION 3 95

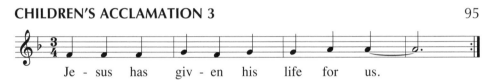

Je - sus has giv - en his life for us.

Text: ICEL, © 1975
Music: *Mass of Christ, Our Hope,* David Haas, © 2014, GIA Publications, Inc.

CHILDREN'S ACCLAMATION 4 96

We praise you, we bless you, we thank you.

Text: ICEL, © 1975
Music: *Mass of Christ, Our Hope,* David Haas, © 2014, GIA Publications, Inc.

AMEN 97

A - men, a - men.

A - men, a - men.

Music: *Mass of Christ, Our Hope,* David Haas, © 2014, GIA Publications, Inc.

Mass of Plenty

98 HOLY, HOLY, HOLY

Ho - ly, Ho - ly, Ho - ly Lord God of hosts. Heav-en and earth, heav-en and earth are full of your glo - ry. Ho - san - na in the high - est, ho - san - na in the high - est. Bless-ed is he, bless-ed is he who comes in the name of the Lord. Ho - san - na in the high - est, ho - san - na in the high - est. Ho - san - na in the high - est, ho - san - na in the high - est.

Text: ICEL, © 2010
Music: *Mass of Plenty*, Rob Glover, © 2000, 2010, GIA Publications, Inc.

MEMORIAL ACCLAMATION A 99

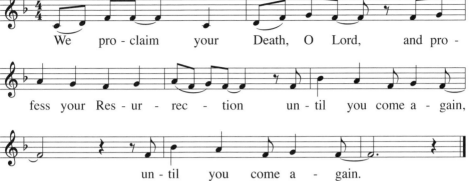

We pro - claim your Death, O Lord, and pro -
fess your Res - ur - rec - tion un - til you come a - gain,
un - til you come a - gain.

Text: ICEL, © 2010
Music: *Mass of Plenty,* Rob Glover, © 2010, GIA Publications, Inc.

AMEN 100

A - men, a - men, a -
men, a - men, a - men, a -
men, a - men, a - men.

Music: *Mass of Plenty,* Rob Glover, © 2000, GIA Publications, Inc.

101 SANCTUS (HOLY, HOLY, HOLY)

San-ctus, San-ctus, San-ctus Dó-mi-nus De-us Sá-ba-oth.

Ple-ni sunt cae-li et ter-ra gló-ri-a tu-a. Ho-sán-na

in ex-cél-sis. Be-ne-dí-ctus qui ve-nit in nó-mi-ne

Dó-mi-ni. Ho-sán-na in ex-cél-sis.

Music: *Sanctus XVIII, Vatican Edition;* acc. by Gerard Farrell, OSB, © 1986, GIA Publications, Inc.

102 AGNUS DEI (LAMB OF GOD)

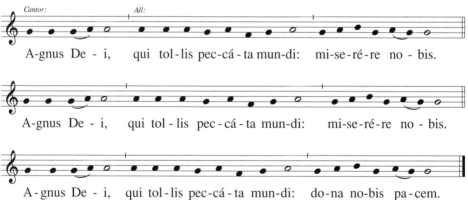

Cantor: *All:*

A-gnus De-i, qui tol-lis pec-cá-ta mun-di: mi-se-ré-re no-bis.

A-gnus De-i, qui tol-lis pec-cá-ta mun-di: mi-se-ré-re no-bis.

A-gnus De-i, qui tol-lis pec-cá-ta mun-di: do-na no-bis pa-cem.

Music: Vatican Edition XVIII; acc. by Robert J. Batastini, © 1993, GIA Publications, Inc.

LAMB OF GOD

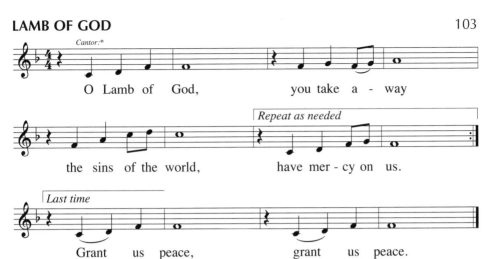

O Lamb of God, you take a - way the sins of the world, have mer - cy on us.

Repeat as needed

Last time

Grant us peace, grant us peace.

*The assembly echoes each phrase of the cantor at the interval of one measure.

Music: Ralph R. Stewart, © 1999, GIA Publications, Inc.; acc. by Robert J. Batastini, © 2003, GIA Publications, Inc.

LAMB OF GOD

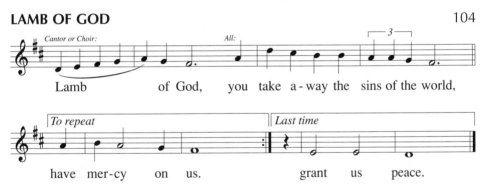

Lamb of God, you take a - way the sins of the world,

To repeat

Last time

have mer - cy on us. grant us peace.

Music: *Holy Cross Mass,* David Clark Isele, © 1979, GIA Publications, Inc.

105 LAMB OF GOD

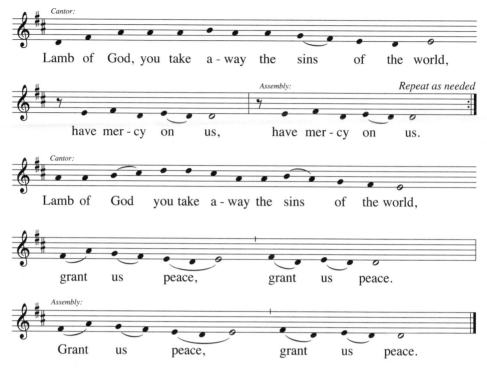

Cantor:

Lamb of God, you take a - way the sins of the world,

Assembly: *Repeat as needed*

have mer - cy on us, have mer - cy on us.

Cantor:

Lamb of God you take a - way the sins of the world,

grant us peace, grant us peace.

Assembly:

Grant us peace, grant us peace.

Music: *Corpus Christi Mass, Adoro te devote,* setting by Richard Proulx, © 1992, 2002, GIA Publications, Inc.

106 LAMB OF GOD

Cantor: *All:*   *Repeat ad lib.*

Have mer - cy on us. Have mer - cy on us.

Cantor: *All:*

Grant us peace. Grant us peace.

Music: *Mass of the Angels and Saints,* Steven R. Janco, © 1996, GIA Publications, Inc.

LAMB OF GOD — CORDERO DE DIOS 107

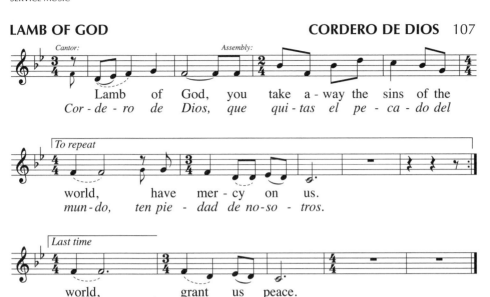

Lamb of God, you take a-way the sins of the
Cor - de - ro de Dios, que qui - tas el pe - ca - do del

world, have mer - cy on us.
mun - do, ten pie - dad de no - so - tros.

world, grant us peace.
mun - do, da - nos la paz.

Music: *Mass of Creation,* Marty Haugen; adapt. by Tony E. Alonso, © 1984, 1985, 2013, GIA Publications, Inc.

LAMB OF GOD 108

Lamb of God, you take a - way the sins of the

world, have mer-cy on us. world, grant us peace.

Music: *Mass of Christ, Our Hope,* David Haas, © 2014, GIA Publications, Inc.

109 O Come, O Come, Emmanuel

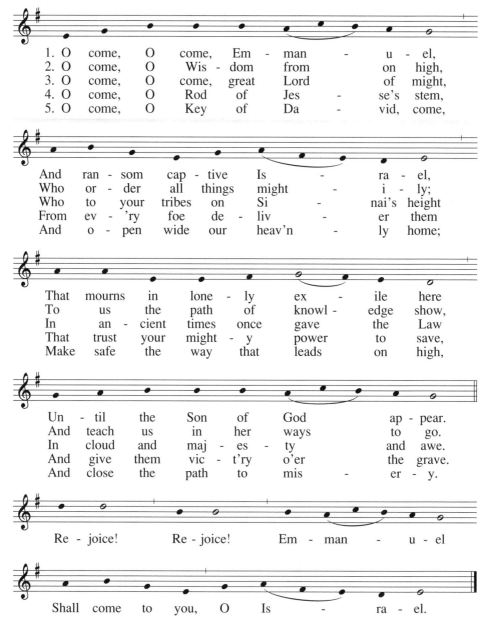

1. O come, O come, Em - man - u - el,
2. O come, O Wis - dom from on high,
3. O come, O come, great Lord of might,
4. O come, O Rod of Jes - se's stem,
5. O come, O Key of Da - vid, come,

And ran - som cap - tive Is - ra - el,
Who or - der all things might - i - ly;
Who to your tribes on Si - nai's height
From ev - 'ry foe de - liv - er them
And o - pen wide our heav'n - ly home;

That mourns in lone - ly ex - ile here
To us the path of knowl - edge show,
In an - cient times once gave the Law
That trust your might - y power to save,
Make safe the way that leads on high,

Un - til the Son of God ap - pear.
And teach us in her ways to go.
In cloud and maj - es - ty and awe.
And give them vic - t'ry o'er the grave.
And close the path to mis - er - y.

Re - joice! Re - joice! Em - man - u - el

Shall come to you, O Is - ra - el.

6. O come, O Dayspring from on high,
And cheer us by your drawing nigh;
Disperse the gloomy clouds of night,
And death's dark shadow put to flight.

7. O come, Desire of nations, bind
In one the hearts of humankind;
O bid our sad divisions cease,
And be for us our King of Peace.

Text: *Veni, veni Emmanuel*; Latin 9th C.; tr. by John M. Neale, 1818–1866, alt.
Tune: VENI EMMANUEL, LM with refrain; Mode I; adapt. by Thomas Helmore, 1811–1890; acc. by Richard Proulx, 1937–2010, © 1975, GIA Publications, Inc.

Come, Emmanuel   110

Verse 1
Cantor:
Awake now, friends, the time is near! *Verse Response*
Soon the Lord of Life will appear. *Verse Response*
Stay awake, prepare God's way: *Verse Response*
This is what the Scriptures say! *Refrain*

Verse Response

Come, O come, Em - man - u - el!

Refrain

Re - joice!   Re - joice!   Em - man - u - el   shall

come   to   you,   O   Is - ra - el.

Verse 2
Cantor:
Let us see your living face, *Verse Response*
sons and daughters of one living race. *Verse Response*
Show us mercy, show us love. *Verse Response*
Send salvation from above. *Refrain*

Verse 3
Cantor:
God's glory now shall be revealed. *Verse Response*
The blind will see, the sick be healed. *Verse Response*
All will sing together in peace. *Verse Response*
All will sit together at the feast. *Refrain*

Text: Tony E. Alonso, b.1980
Tune: Based on VENI EMMANUEL; Tony E. Alonso, b.1980
© 2001, GIA Publications, Inc.

111 My Soul in Stillness Waits

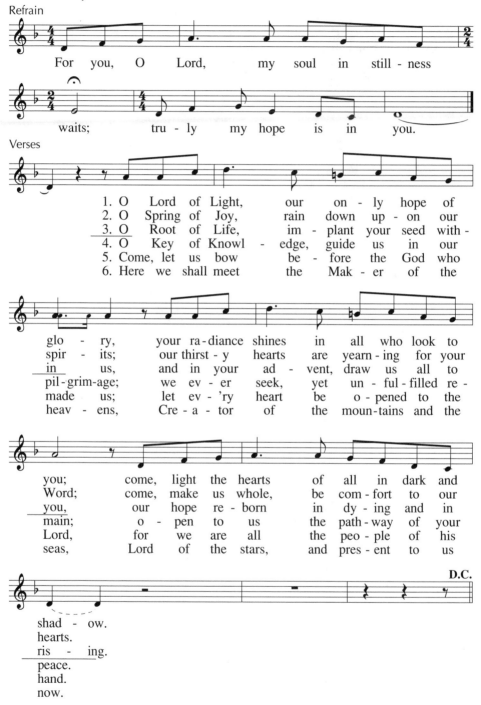

Refrain

For you, O Lord, my soul in still-ness waits; tru-ly my hope is in you.

Verses

1. O Lord of Light, our on-ly hope of
2. O Spring of Joy, rain down up-on our
3. O Root of Life, im-plant your seed with-
4. O Key of Knowl - edge, guide us in our
5. Come, let us bow be-fore the God who
6. Here we shall meet the Mak-er of the

glo - ry, your ra-diance shines in all who look to
spir - its; our thirst-y hearts are yearn-ing for your
in us, and in your ad - vent, draw us all to
pil-grim-age; we ev-er seek, yet un-ful-filled re-
made us; let ev-'ry heart be o-pened to the
heav - ens, Cre-a-tor of the moun-tains and the

you; come, light the hearts of all in dark and
Word; come, make us whole, be com-fort to our
you, our hope re-born in dy-ing and in
main; o - pen to us the path-way of your
Lord, for we are all the peo-ple of his
seas, Lord of the stars, and pres-ent to us

D.C.

shad - ow.
hearts.
ris - ing.
peace.
hand.
now.

Text: Psalm 95 and "O" Antiphons; Marty Haugen, b.1950
Tune: Marty Haugen, b.1950
© 1982, GIA Publications, Inc.

Watch for Messiah 112

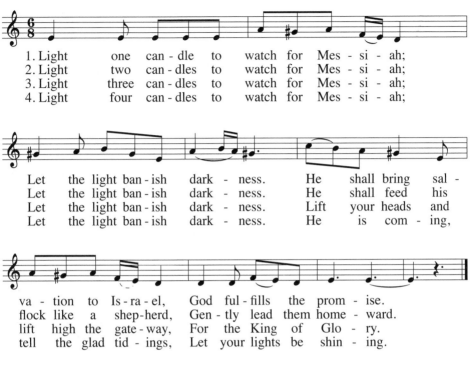

1. Light one can-dle to watch for Mes - si - ah;
2. Light two can-dles to watch for Mes - si - ah;
3. Light three can-dles to watch for Mes - si - ah;
4. Light four can-dles to watch for Mes - si - ah;

Let the light ban-ish dark - ness. He shall bring sal -
Let the light ban-ish dark - ness. He shall feed his
Let the light ban-ish dark - ness. Lift your heads and
Let the light ban-ish dark - ness. He is com - ing,

va - tion to Is-ra - el, God ful-fills the prom - ise.
flock like a shep-herd, Gen - tly lead them home - ward.
lift high the gate - way, For the King of Glo - ry.
tell the glad tid - ings, Let your lights be shin - ing.

Text: Wayne L. Wold
Tune: TIF IN VELDELE, 10 7 10 6; Yiddish traditional; arr. by Wayne L. Wold
© 1984, Augsburg Fortress

Wait for the Lord / Contemplaré 113

Ostinato Refrain

Wait for the Lord, whose day is near.
Con - tem - pla - ré tu vi - da en mí.

Wait for the Lord: be strong, take heart!
Con - tem - pla - ré, Se - ñor, tu a - mor.

Text: Isaiah 40, Philippians 4, Matthew 6–7; Taizé Community, 1984
Tune: Jacques Berthier, 1923–1994
© 1984, Les Presses de Taizé, GIA Publications, Inc., agent

114 People, Look East

1. Peo - ple, look East. The time is near
2. Fur - rows, be glad. Though earth is bare,
3. Birds, though you long have ceased to build,
4. Stars, keep the watch. When night is dim,
5. An - gels an - nounce with shouts of mirth

Of the crown - ing of the year.
One more seed is plant - ed there.
Guard the nest that must be filled.
One more light the bowl shall brim,
Him who brings new life to earth.

Make your house fair as you are a - ble,
Give up your strength the seed to nour - ish,
E - ven the hour when wings are fro - zen
Shin - ing be - yond the frost - y weath - er,
Set ev - 'ry peak and val - ley hum - ming

Trim the hearth and set the ta - ble.
That in course the flow'r may flour - ish.
God for fledg - ing - time has cho - sen.
Bright as sun and moon to - geth - er.
With the word, the Lord is com - ing.

Peo - ple, look East and sing to - day—

Love, the Guest, is on the way.
Love, the Rose, is on the way.
Love, the Bird, is on the way.
Love, the Star, is on the way.
Love, the Lord, is on the way.

Text: Eleanor Farjeon, 1881–1965, © David Higham Assoc. Ltd.
Tune: BESANÇON, 87 98 87; French carol; harm. by Martin Shaw, 1875–1958, © Oxford University Press

Stay Awake, Be Ready 115

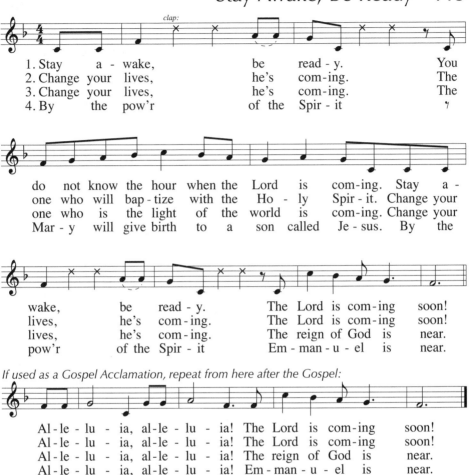

1. Stay a - wake, be read - y. You do not know the hour when the Lord is com - ing. Stay a - wake, be read - y. The Lord is com - ing soon!
2. Change your lives, he's com - ing. The one who will bap - tize with the Ho - ly Spir - it. Change your lives, he's com - ing. The Lord is com - ing soon!
3. Change your lives, he's com - ing. The one who is the light of the world is com - ing. Change your lives, he's com - ing. The reign of God is near.
4. By the pow'r of the Spir - it Mar - y will give birth to a son called Je - sus. By the pow'r of the Spir - it Em - man - u - el is near.

If used as a Gospel Acclamation, repeat from here after the Gospel:

Al - le - lu - ia, al - le - lu - ia! The Lord is com - ing soon!
Al - le - lu - ia, al - le - lu - ia! The Lord is com - ing soon!
Al - le - lu - ia, al - le - lu - ia! The reign of God is near.
Al - le - lu - ia, al - le - lu - ia! Em - man - u - el is near.

Text: Christopher Walker, b.1947
Tune: Christopher Walker, b.1947
© 1988, 1989, 1990, Christopher Walker. Published by OCP.

Prepare the Way of the Lord 116

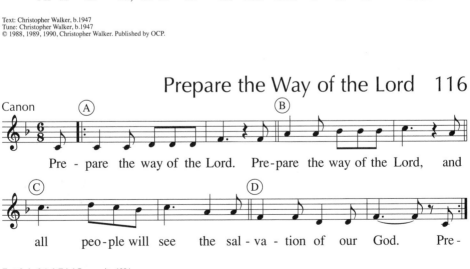

Canon

Pre - pare the way of the Lord. Pre - pare the way of the Lord, and all peo - ple will see the sal - va - tion of our God. Pre -

Text: Luke 3:4, 6; Taizé Community, 1984
Tune: Jacques Berthier, 1923–1994
© 1984, Les Presses de Taizé, GIA Publications, Inc., agent

117 Awake to the Day

Refrain

A - wake to the day of the com-ing of the Lord. Sing

out! Re-joice in this land. Make straight the way for the

Last time to Coda

To verses

King-dom of God is at hand.

Verse 1

Cantor: *All:*

1. Signs in the sun and the moon and the stars, We pre-pare for you,

Cantor:

Lord. Then all shall sing of the pow - er of God.

All:

We pre-pare for you, Lord. As long as the sun shall re -

D.S.

main so the name of the Lord God will reign. A -

Verse 2

Cantor: *All:*

2. Wrapped in the cloak of jus-tice from God, We pre-pare for you,

Lord. Gath-ered at the word of the Ho - ly One,

We pre-pare for you, Lord. Ev-'ry moun-tain and hill be made

low that the glo - ry of God we may know. A -

A - wake to the day of the com-ing of the Lord. Sing

out! Re-joice in this land. Make straight the way for the

King-dom of God is at hand. Make the way!

Text: Ed Bolduc, b.1969, and John Barker
Tune: Ed Bolduc, b.1969, and John Barker
© 2003, World Library Publications

118 Come Now, O Prince of Peace

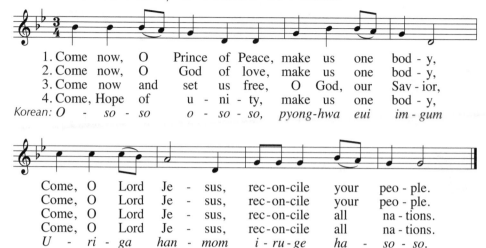

1. Come now, O Prince of Peace, make us one bod - y,
2. Come now, O God of love, make us one bod - y,
3. Come now and set us free, O God, our Sav - ior,
4. Come, Hope of u - ni - ty, make us one bod - y,
Korean: O - so - so o - so - so, pyong-hwa eui im - gum

Come, O Lord Je - sus, rec-on-cile your peo - ple.
Come, O Lord Je - sus, rec-on-cile your peo - ple.
Come, O Lord Je - sus, rec-on-cile all na - tions.
Come, O Lord Je - sus, rec-on-cile all na - tions.
U - ri - ga han - mom i - ru - ge ha - so - so.

Text: *O-so-sô*, Geonyong Lee, b.1947; para. by Marion Pope, alt.
Tune: OSOSO, 11 11; Geonyong Lee, b.1947
© 1991, GIA Publications, Inc.

119 Creator of the Stars of Night

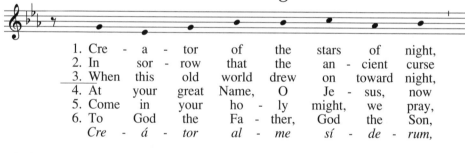

1. Cre - a - tor of the stars of night,
2. In sor - row that the an - cient curse
3. When this old world drew on toward night,
4. At your great Name, O Je - sus, now
5. Come in your ho - ly might, we pray,
6. To God the Fa - ther, God the Son,
Cre - á - tor al - me sí - de - rum,

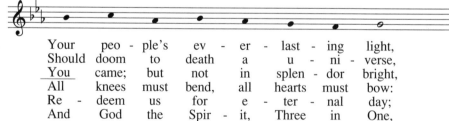

Your peo - ple's ev - er - last - ing light,
Should doom to death a u - ni - verse,
You came; but not in splen - dor bright,
All knees must bend, all hearts must bow:
Re - deem us for e - ter - nal day;
And God the Spir - it, Three in One,
Ae - tér - na lux cre - dén - ti - um,

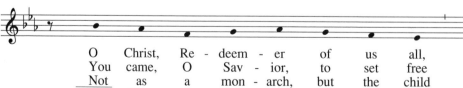

O Christ, Re - deem - er of us all,
You came, O Sav - ior, to set free
Not as a mon - arch, but the child
All things on earth with one ac - cord,
De - fend us while we dwell be - low
Praise, hon - or, might, and glo - ry be
Je - su, Re - démp - tor ó - mni - um,

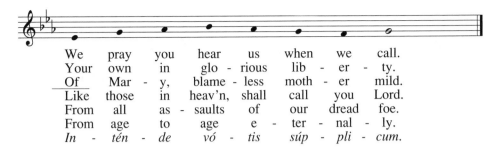

We pray you hear us when we call.
Your own in glo - rious lib - er - ty.
Of Mar - y, blame - less moth - er mild.
Like those in heav'n, shall call you Lord.
From all as - saults of our dread foe.
From age to age e - ter - nal - ly.
In - tén - de vó - tis súp - pli - cum.

Text: *Creator alme siderum*, Latin 9th. C., revised 1632; tr. *The Hymnal 1982*, alt., © 1985, The Church Pension Fund
Tune: CONDITOR ALME SIDERUM, LM; Mode IV, Sarum, 9th C.; acc. by Gerard Farrell, OSB, 1919–2009, © 1986, GIA Publications, Inc.

Away in a Manger 120

1. A - way in a man - ger, no crib for a bed,
2. The cat - tle are low - ing; the ba - by a - wakes,
3. Be near me, Lord Je - sus; I ask you to stay

The lit - tle Lord Je - sus laid down his sweet head.
But lit - tle Lord Je - sus, no cry - ing he makes.
Close by me for - ev - er, and love me, I pray.

The stars in the bright sky looked down where he lay,
I love you, Lord Je - sus! Look down from the sky
Bless all the dear chil - dren in your ten - der care,

The lit - tle Lord Je - sus, a - sleep on the hay.
And stay by my cra - dle till morn - ing is nigh.
And fit us for heav - en, to live with you there.

Text: Sts. 1, 2, anonymous; st. 3, John T. McFarland, 1851–1913
Tune: MUELLER, 11 11 11 11; James R. Murray, 1841–1905; harm. by Robert J. Batastini, b.1942, © 1994, GIA Publications, Inc.

121 Angels We Have Heard on High

1. An - gels we have heard on high Sweet - ly sing - ing
2. Shep - herds, why this ju - bi - lee? Why your joy - ous
3. Come to Beth - le - hem and see Him whose birth the
4. See him in a man - ger laid Whom the choirs of

o'er the plains, And the moun - tains in re - ply
strains pro - long? Say what may the tid - ings be
an - gels sing; Come, a - dore on bend - ed knee
an - gels praise; Mar - y, Jo - seph, lend your aid,

Ech - o back their joy - ous strains.
Which in - spire your heav'n - ly song.
Christ the Lord, the new - born King.
While our hearts in love we raise.

Gló - - - ri - a
in ex - cél - sis De - o. Gló - -
- - ri - a in ex - cél - sis De - o.

Text: *Les anges dans nos campagnes;* French carol, c. 18th C.; tr. from *Crown of Jesus Music,* London, 1862
Tune: GLORIA, 7 7 7 7 with refrain; French carol

Joy to the World 122

1. Joy to the world, the Lord is come! Let
2. Joy to the earth, the Sav - ior reigns! Let
3. No more let sin and sor - row grow, Nor
4. He rules the world with truth and grace, And

[⌢]

earth re - ceive her king; Let ev - 'ry
us our songs em - ploy; While fields and
thorns in - fest the ground; He comes to
makes the na - tions prove The glo - ries

heart pre - pare him room And heav'n and na - ture
floods, rocks, hills and plains Re - peat the sound - ing
make his bless - ings flow Far as the curse is
of his right - eous - ness, And won - ders of his

sing, And heav'n and na - ture sing, And
joy, Re - peat the sound - ing joy, Re -
found, Far as the curse is found, Far
love, And won - ders of his love, And

heav'n, and heav'n and na - ture sing.
peat, re - peat the sound - ing joy.
as, far as the curse is found.
won - ders, won - ders of his love.

Text: Psalm 98; Isaac Watts, 1674–1748
Tune: ANTIOCH, CM; arr. from George F. Handel, 1685–1759, in T. Hawkes' *Collection of Tunes*, 1833

123 Silent Night, Holy Night / Noche de Paz

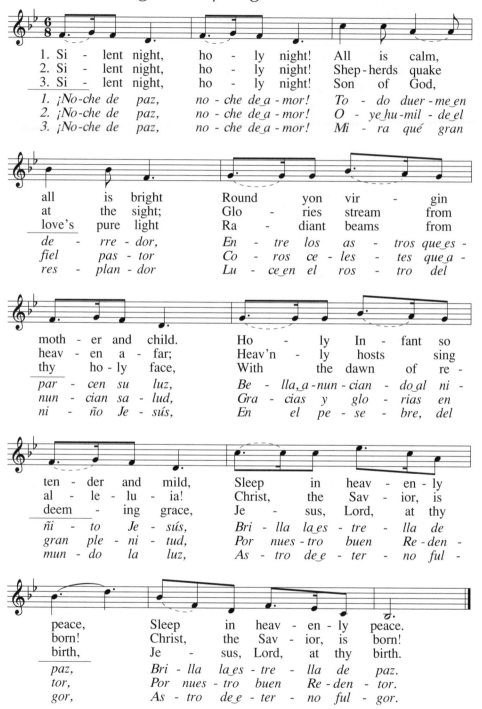

1. Si - lent night, ho - ly night! All is calm,
2. Si - lent night, ho - ly night! Shep-herds quake
3. Si - lent night, ho - ly night! Son of God,

1. ¡No-che de paz, no - che de a - mor! To - do duer - me en
2. ¡No-che de paz, no - che de a - mor! O - ye hu-mil - de el
3. ¡No-che de paz, no - che de a - mor! Mi - ra qué gran

all is bright Round yon vir - gin
at the sight; Glo - ries stream from
love's pure light Ra - diant beams from

de - rre - dor, En - tre los as - tros que es -
fiel pas - tor Co - ros ce - les - tes que a -
res - plan - dor Lu - ce en el ros - tro del

moth - er and child. Ho - ly In - fant so
heav - en a - far; Heav'n - ly hosts sing
thy ho - ly face, With the dawn of re -

par - cen su luz, Be - lla, a-nun-cian - do al ni -
nun - cian sa - lud, Gra - cias y glo - rias en
ni - ño Je - sús, En el pe - se - bre, del

ten - der and mild, Sleep in heav - en - ly
al - le - lu - ia! Christ, the Sav - ior, is
deem - ing grace, Je - sus, Lord, at thy

ñi - to Je - sús, Bri - lla la es - tre - lla de
gran ple - ni - tud, Por nues-tro buen Re - den -
mun - do la luz, As - tro de e - ter - no ful -

peace, Sleep in heav - en - ly peace.
born! Christ, the Sav - ior, is born!
birth, Je - sus, Lord, at thy birth.

paz, Bri - lla la es - tre - lla de paz.
tor, Por nues - tro buen Re - den - tor.
gor, As - tro de e - ter - no ful - gor.

Text: *Stille Nacht, heilige Nacht;* Joseph Mohr, 1792–1848; English tr. by John F. Young, 1820–1885; Spanish tr. by Federico Fliedner, 1845–1901
Tune: STILLE NACHT, 66 89 66; Franz X. Gruber, 1787–1863

Night of Silence 124

1. Cold are the peo - ple, win - ter of life, We
2. Voice in the dis - tance, call in the night, On
3. Spir - it a - mong us, shine like the star, Your

trem - ble in shad - ows this cold end - less night.
wind you en - fold us, you speak of the light.
light that guides shep - herds and kings from a - far.

Fro - zen in the snow lie ros - es sleep-ing,
Gen - tle on the ear you whis-per, soft - ly,
Shim-mer in the sky so emp-ty, lone - ly,

Flow - ers that will ech - o the sun - rise.
Ru - mors of a dawn so em - brac - ing.
Ris - ing in the warmth of the Son's love.

Fire of hope is our on - ly warmth;
Breath-less love a - waits dark - ened souls.
Star un - know - ing of night and day,

Wea - ry, its flame will be dy - ing soon.
Soon will we know of the morn - ing.
Spir - it, we wait for the lov - ing Son.

Text: Daniel Kantor, b.1960
Tune: Daniel Kantor, b.1960

125 Gloria, Gloria

Canon

Gló - ri - a, gló - ri - a, in ex - cél - sis De - o!

Gló - ri - a, gló - ri - a, al - le - lú - ia, al - le - lú - ia!

Tune: Jacques Berthier, 1923–1994, © 1979, 1988, Les Presses de Taizé, GIA Publications, Inc., agent

126 Go Tell It on the Mountain

Refrain

Go tell it on the moun-tain, O-ver the hills and ev - 'ry-where;

Go tell it on the moun - tain That Je - sus Christ is born!

Verses

1. While shep - herds kept their watch - ing O'er
2. The shep - herds feared and trem - bled When,
3. Down in a low - ly man - ger The

si - lent flocks by night, Be - hold, through - out the
lo, a - bove the earth Rang out the an - gel
hum - ble Christ was born, And God sent us sal -

D.C.

heav - ens There shone a ho - ly light.
cho - rus That hailed our Sav - ior's birth.
va - tion That bless - ed Christ - mas morn.

Text: African American spiritual; verses by John W. Work, Jr., 1872–1925
Tune: GO TELL IT ON THE MOUNTAIN, 7 6 7 6 with refrain; African American spiritual; harm. by Robert J. Batastini, b.1942, © 1995, GIA
   Publications, Inc.

He Came Down 127

He came down that we may have *love; He

came down that we may have love; He came down that we may

Cantor: Why did he come?

have love, Hal-le - lu - jah for ev-er-more.

Substitute peace, joy, hope, life, etc.

Text: Cameroon traditional
Tune: Cameroon traditional; transcribed and arr. by John L. Bell, b.1949, © 1990, Iona Community, GIA Publications, Inc., agent

Jesus Our Brother, Kind and Good 128

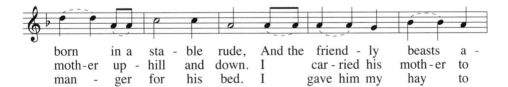

1. Je - sus our broth - er, kind and good, Was hum - bly
2. "I," said the don - key, shag-gy and brown, "I car-ried his
3. "I," said the cow, all white and red, "I gave him my

born in a sta - ble rude, And the friend - ly beasts a -
moth-er up - hill and down. I car-ried his moth-er to
man - ger for his bed. I gave him my hay to

round him stood, Je - sus our broth - er, kind and good.
Beth-le-hem town. I," said the don - key shag-gy and brown.
pil - low his head. I," said the cow all white and red.

Text: Traditional English carol
Tune: ORIENTIS PARTIBUS, 8 9 9 8; Pierre de Corbiel, d.1222; harm. by Margaret Mealy, b.1922, © 1961, General Convention of the Episcopal
Church, USA

129 The Virgin Mary Had a Baby Boy

1. The vir-gin Mar-y had a ba-by boy, the vir-gin
2. The an-gels sang when the ba-by born, the an-gels
3. The wise men saw where the ba-by born, the wise men

Mar-y had a ba-by boy, the vir-gin Mar-y had a
sang when the ba-by born, the an-gels sang when the
saw where the ba-by born, the wise men went where the

ba - by boy, and they say that his name was Je-sus.
ba - by born, and they say that his name was Je-sus.
ba - by born, and they say that his name was Je-sus.

He come from the glo - ry, he come from the

Oh, Oh,

glo-rious king-dom. Oh, yes! be-liev-er! Oh,

yes! be-liev - er! He come from the glo - ry,

he come from the glo-rious king-dom.

Text: West Indian carol, © 1945, Boosey and Co., Ltd.
Tune: West Indian carol, © 1945, Boosey and Co., Ltd.; acc. by Robert J. Batastini, b.1942, © 1993, GIA Publications, Inc.

Hark! The Herald Angels Sing 130

1. Hark! The her - ald an - gels sing, "Glo - ry to the new - born King!
2. Christ, by high - est heav'n a - dored; Christ, the ev - er - last - ing Lord!
3. Hail the heav'n - born Prince of Peace! Hail the Sun of Right-eous-ness!

Peace on earth and mer - cy mild, God and sin - ners rec - on - ciled!"
Late in time be - hold him come, Off - spring of the Vir - gin's womb.
Light and life to all he brings, Ris'n with heal - ing in his wings.

Joy - ful, all you na - tions, rise; Join the tri - umph of the skies;
Veiled in flesh the God - head see; Hail the in - car - nate De - i - ty,
Mild he lays his glo - ry by, Born that we no more may die,

With the an - gel - ic host pro-claim, "Christ is born in Beth - le-hem!"
Pleased as man with us to dwell, Je - sus, our Em-man - u - el.
Born to raise each child of earth, Born to give us sec - ond birth.

Hark! The her-ald an-gels sing, "Glo-ry to the new-born King!"

Text: Charles Wesley, 1707–1788, alt.
Tune: MENDELSSOHN, 77 77 D with refrain; Felix Mendelssohn, 1809–1847

131 O Come, All Ye Faithful / Venid, Fieles Todos / Adeste Fideles

1. O come, all ye faith-ful, joy-ful and tri - um - phant, O
2. God of God, Light of Light,
1. Ve - nid, fie - les to - dos, a Be - lén mar - che - mos De
2. El que_es Hi - jo_e - ter - no del e - ter - no Pa - dre, Y
1. Ad - é - ste fi - dé - les, laé - ti, tri - um - phán - tes, Ve -
2. De - um de De - o, Lu - men de Lú - mi-ne

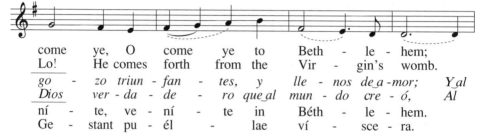

come ye, O come ye to Beth - le - hem;
Lo! He comes forth from the Vir - gin's womb.
go - zo triun - fan - tes, y lle - nos de_a -mor; Y_al
Dios ver - da - de - ro que_al mun - do cre - ó, Al
ní - te, ve - ní - te in Béth - le - hem.
Ge - stant pu - él - lae ví - sce - ra.

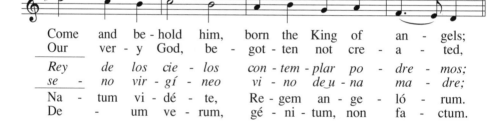

Come and be - hold him, born the King of an - gels;
Our ver - y God, be - got - ten not cre - a - ted,
Rey de los cie - los con - tem - plar po - dre - mos;
se - no vir - gí - neo vi - no de_u - na ma - dre;
Na - tum vi - dé - te, Re - gem an - ge - ló - rum.
De - um ve - rum, gé - ni - tum, non fa - ctum.

O come, let us a - dore him, O come, let us a - dore
Ve - nid, a - do - re - mos, ve - nid, a - do - re -
Ve - ní - te a - do - ré - mus, ve - ní - te a - do - ré -

him, O come, let us a - dore him, Christ, the Lord!
mos, ve - nid, a - do - re - mos a Cris - to_el Se - ñor.
mus, ve - ní - te a - do - ré - mus Dó - mi-num.

3. Sing, choirs of angels,
sing in exultation,
Sing, all ye citizens of heav'n above!
Glory to God, all
glory in the highest;

4. Yea, Lord, we greet thee,
born this happy morning,
Jesus, to thee be all glory giv'n;
Word of the Father,
now in flesh appearing;

3. *Cantad jubilosas,*
   célicas criaturas:
   Resuenen los cielos con vuestra canción;
   ¡Al Dios bondadoso,
   gloria en las alturas;

4. *Jesús, celebramos*
   tu bendito nombre
   Con himnos solemnes de grato loor;
   Por siglos eternos
   todo ser te adore;

3. Cantet nunc io,
   chorus angelórum,
   Cantet nunc aula caeléstium.
   Glória, glória in excélsis Deo.

4. Ergo qui natus
   Die hodiérna,
   Jesu tibi sit glória.
   Patris aetérnae verbum caro factum.

Text: *Adeste fideles;* John F. Wade, c.1711–1786; English tr. by Frederick Oakeley, 1802–1880, alt.; Spanish tr. by Juan Bautista Cabrera, 1837–1916
Tune: ADESTE FIDELES, Irregular with refrain; John F. Wade, c.1711–1786

What Child Is This   132

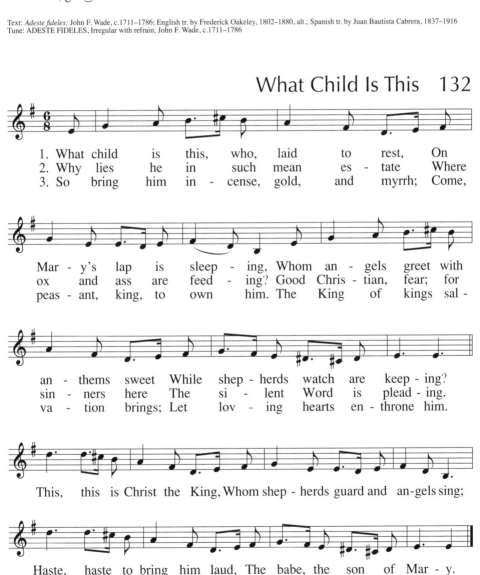

1. What child is this, who, laid to rest, On
2. Why lies he in such mean es - tate Where
3. So bring him in - cense, gold, and myrrh; Come,

Mar - y's lap is sleep - ing, Whom an - gels greet with
ox and ass are feed - ing? Good Chris - tian, fear; for
peas - ant, king, to own him. The King of kings sal -

an - thems sweet While shep - herds watch are keep - ing?
sin - ners here The si - lent Word is plead - ing.
va - tion brings; Let lov - ing hearts en - throne him.

This, this is Christ the King, Whom shep - herds guard and an-gels sing;

Haste, haste to bring him laud, The babe, the son of Mar - y.

Text: William C. Dix, 1837–1898
Tune: GREENSLEEVES, 8 7 8 7 with refrain; English melody, 16th C.; harm. by John Stainer, 1840–1901

133 The First Nowell

1. The first No - well the an - gel did say Was to
2. They look - ed up and saw a star Shin - ing
3. And by the light of that same star Three
4. This star drew nigh to the north - west, O'er
5. Then en - tered in those wise men three, Full
6. Then let us all with one ac - cord Sing

cer - tain poor shep - herds in fields as they lay; In
in the east be - yond them far; And
wise men came from coun - try far; To
Beth - le - hem it took its rest; And
rev - 'rent - ly up - on their knee, And
prais - es to our heav - 'nly Lord, Who

fields where they lay keep - ing their sheep, On a
to the earth it gave great light, And
seek for a king was their in - tent, And to
there it did both stop and stay Right
of - fered there in his pres - ence Their
made the heav'ns and earth of naught, And

cold win - ter's night that was so deep.
so it con - tin - ued both day and night.
fol - low the star where - ev - er it went.
o - ver the place where Je - sus lay.
gold and myrrh and frank - in - cense.
with his blood our life has bought.

No - well, No - well, No - well, No - well!

Born is the King of Is - ra - el.

Text: English carol, 17th C.
Tune: THE FIRST NOWELL, Irregular with refrain; English carol; harm. from *Christmas Carols New and Old*, 1871

We Three Kings of Orient Are 134

1. We three kings of O - ri - ent are; Bear - ing
2. Born a King on Beth - le - hem's plain, Gold I
3. Frank - in - cense to of - fer have I; In - cense
4. Myrrh is mine: its bit - ter per - fume Breathes a
5. Glo - rious now be - hold him a - rise, King and

gifts, we trav - erse a - far Field and foun - tain,
bring to crown him a - gain; King for - ev - er,
owns a De - i - ty nigh; Prayer and prais - ing,
life of gath - er - ing gloom; Sor - rowing, sigh - ing,
God and Sac - ri - fice; "Al - le - lu - ia,

Moor and moun - tain, Fol - low - ing yon - der star.
Ceas - ing nev - er, O - ver us all to reign.
Glad - ly rais - ing, Wor - ship - ing God on high.
Bleed - ing, dy - ing, Sealed in the stone - cold tomb.
Al - le - lu - ia!" Sounds through the earth and skies.

O star of won - der, star of night, Star with

roy - al beau - ty bright, West - ward lead - ing,

still pro - ceed - ing, Guide us to the per - fect Light.

Text: Matthew 2:1–11; John H. Hopkins, Jr., 1820–1891, alt.
Tune: KINGS OF ORIENT, 88 44 6 with refrain; John H. Hopkins, Jr., 1820–1891

135 O Sun of Justice

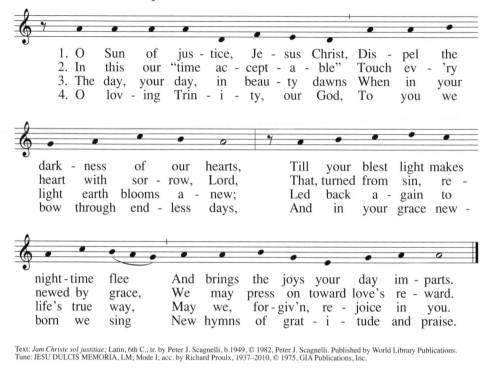

1. O Sun of jus - tice, Je - sus Christ, Dis - pel the
2. In this our "time ac - cept - a - ble" Touch ev - 'ry
3. The day, your day, in beau - ty dawns When in your
4. O lov - ing Trin - i - ty, our God, To you we

dark - ness of our hearts, Till your blest light makes
heart with sor - row, Lord, That, turned from sin, re -
light earth blooms a - new; Led back a - gain to
bow through end - less days, And in your grace new -

night - time flee And brings the joys your day im - parts.
newed by grace, We may press on toward love's re - ward.
life's true way, May we, for - giv'n, re - joice in you.
born we sing New hymns of grat - i - tude and praise.

Text: *Jam Christe sol justitiae;* Latin, 6th C.; tr. by Peter J. Scagnelli, b.1949, © 1982, Peter J. Scagnelli. Published by World Library Publications.
Tune: JESU DULCIS MEMORIA, LM; Mode I; acc. by Richard Proulx, 1937–2010, © 1975, GIA Publications, Inc.

136 Return to God / Volvamos Hoy a Nuestro Dios

Refrain

Re - turn to God with all your heart, the source of grace and
Vol - va - mos hoy a nues - tro Dios, Se - ñor de to - da

mer - cy; come seek the ten - der faith - ful - ness of God.
gra - cia, bus - can - do su per - dón y le - al - tad.

Verses

1. Now the time of grace has come,
   the day of salvation;
   come and learn now the way of our God.

1. Día de la salvación,
   y tiempo favorable;
   caminemos por las sendas de Dios.

2. I will take your heart of stone
   and place a heart within you,
   a heart of compassion and love.

2. Quitaré tu corazón de piedra;
   te daré un corazón
   de amor y compasión.

3. If you break the chains of oppression,
   if you set the pris'ner free;
   if you share your bread with the hungry,
   give protection to the lost;
   give a shelter to the homeless,
   clothe the naked in your midst,
   then your light shall break forth
      like the dawn.

3. *Si tú rompes vínculos injustos,*
   y a los presos das libertad;
   ofreciendo pan al hambriento,
   protección al extraviado;
   dando abrigo a quien está
      sin techo,
   y vestido al desnudo;
   surgirá tu luz como la aurora.

Text: Marty Haugen, b.1950; tr. by Ronald F. Krisman, b.1946
Tune: Marty Haugen, b.1950
© 1990, 1991, tr. 2005, GIA Publications, Inc.

Again We Keep This Solemn Fast 137

1. A - gain we keep this sol - emn fast,
   A gift of faith from a - ges past,
   This Lent which binds us lov - ing - ly
   To faith and hope and char - i - ty.

2. The law and proph - ets from of old
   In fig - ured ways this Lent fore - told,
   Which Christ, all a - ges' Lord and Guide,
   In these last days has sanc - ti - fied.

3. More spar - ing, there - fore, let us make
   The words we speak, the food we take,
   Our sleep, our laugh - ter, ev - 'ry sense;
   Learn peace through ho - ly pen - i - tence.

4. Let us a - void each harm - ful way
   That lures the care - less mind a - stray;
   By watch - ful prayer our spir - its free
   From schem - ing of the En - e - my.

5. We pray, O bless - ed Three in One,
   Our God while end - less a - ges run,
   That this, our Lent of for - ty days,
   May bring us growth and give you praise.

Text: *Ex more docti mystico;* ascr. to Gregory the Great, c.540–604; tr. by Peter J. Scagnelli, b.1949, © 1975, 2011, Peter J. Scagnelli.
   Published by World Library Publications.
Tune: OLD HUNDREDTH, LM; Louis Bourgeois, c.1510–1561

138 Somebody's Knockin' at Your Door

Some-bod - y's knock-in' at your door. Some-bod - y's knock-in' at your door. O sin - ner, why don't you an - swer? Some-bod - y's knock-in' at your door.

Solo:
All:

1. Knocks like Je - sus,
2. Can't you hear him?
3. Je - sus calls you,
4. Can't you trust him?

Some-bod - y's knock-in' at your door.

Solo:
All:

Knocks like Je - sus,
Can't you hear him?
Je - sus calls you,
Can't you trust him?

Some-bod - y's knock-in' at your door.

O sin - ner, why don't you an - swer?

Some-bod - y's knock-in' at your door.

Text: African American spiritual
Tune: SOMEBODY'S KNOCKIN', Irregular; African American spiritual; harm. by Richard Proulx, 1937–2010, © 1986, GIA Publications, Inc.

Remember You Are Dust   139

Refrain

Turn a-way from sin and be faith-ful to the Gos-pel. Re-mem-ber you are dust, and to dust you will re - turn.

Verses

Cantor: 1.–4. Re - pent, the king-dom is at hand. Re-pent, the king-dom is at hand.

*Cantor:

1. Rend your
2. Blow the
3. For -
4. Now, the

1. hearts, not your gar-ments.
2. trum - pet in Zi - on.
3. give one an-oth - er.
4. day of sal - va - tion.

Now, the ac-cept-a - ble

All: time.   Now, the ac-cept-a - ble time.

D.C.

Additional verses for the season of Lent:

Seek the God of compassion…
Live in kindness and mercy…
Trust in God and be faithful…
Praise the God of salvation…
Let us bow down in worship…

Text: Joel 2:12–18, 2 Corinthians 5:20—6:2; Paul A. Tate, b.1968, © 2003, GIA Publications, Inc.; refrain from the *Sacramentary*, © 1973, ICEL
Tune: Paul A. Tate, b.1968, © 2003, GIA Publications, Inc.

140 Mercy, O God

Refrain

Mer-cy, O God, have mer-cy on us. Send down your
mer-cy to set us free. Mer-cy, O God, have mer-cy on us.
Send down your mer-cy to set us free.

Verses

1. Gath - er the peo - ple, the chil - dren, the eld - ers;
2. Now is the hour, the day of sal - va - tion;
3. Long is the jour - ney and steep are the moun - tains,
4. Wash us a - new in your life - giv - ing wa - ter;
5. Once lost in dark-ness you did not for - sake us, but
6. Wake, O sleep - er, a - wake from your slum - ber;

come now and gath - er be - fore the Lord.
now is the time to re - turn to God.
come now and guide us, O gra - cious God.
come quench the thirst of our yearn - ing hearts.
called us your chil - dren and gave us light.
rise from the chains of the dark, cold tomb.

O - pen your hearts to com - pas - sion and mer - cy;
O - pen your lives to for - give-ness and mer - cy;
Show us your face, give us hope for the jour - ney;
Break through the si - lence, the fear and the long-ing; em -
O - pen our eyes, come re - move all our blind - ness.
Walk in the light of com - pas - sion and mer - cy;

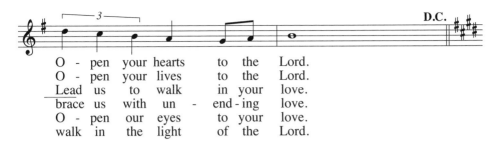

O - pen your hearts to the Lord.
O - pen your lives to the Lord.
Lead us to walk in your love.
brace us with un - end - ing love.
O - pen our eyes to your love.
walk in the light of the Lord.

Text: Francis Patrick O'Brien, b.1958
Tune: Francis Patrick O'Brien, b.1958
© 2001, GIA Publications, Inc.

Deep Within 141

Refrain

Deep with - in   I will plant my law,

not on stone,   but in your heart.

Fol - low me,   I will bring you back,   you will

be my own, and I will be your God.

Verses

1. I will give you a new heart,   a new spir - it with -
2.   Seek my face,   and see your
3. Re - turn to me,   with all your

in you,   for I will be your strength.
God,   for I will be your hope.
heart,   and I will bring you back.

Text: Jeremiah 31:33, Ezekiel 36:26, Joel 2:12; David Haas, b.1957
Tune: David Haas, b.1957; acc. by Jeanne Cotter, b.1964
© 1987, GIA Publications, Inc.

142 Stations of the Cross

INTRODUCTION

All make the sign of the cross.

Leader: Lord Jesus,
We seek to follow you in all we do.
As we walk these stations of the cross,
make us aware of your great love for us.
Set us out on a path of loving service
as we journey through life
to the kingdom of your Easter glory.

All: **Amen.**

PROCESSION

The introductory stanza and stanza one (below) are sung during the procession to the first station. The leader is accompanied by a cross bearer and candle bearers. All who are gathered, or a small group, may join in the procession.

When the procession arrives at each station, it is announced, followed by:

Leader: We adore you, O Christ, and we praise you.
All genuflect and say: **Because by your holy cross you have redeemed the world.**

A brief reflection may be read or silence may be observed. During the procession to the next station, the corresponding stanza is sung.

143 Stations Hymn

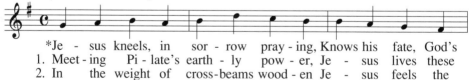

*Je - sus kneels, in sor - row pray - ing, Knows his fate, God's
1. Meet - ing Pi - late's earth - ly pow - er, Je - sus lives these
2. In the weight of cross-beams wood - en Je - sus feels the
3. Stum-bling un - der weight so crush - ing, Jeer - ing crowds up -

will o - bey - ing: "Let your will, not mine, be done."
fi - nal ho - urs Con - fi - dent in heav - en's might.
heav - y bur - den Of our frail hu - man - i - ty.
on him rush - ing, Je - sus falls, re - turns to dust.

*Introductory stanza

1. Jesus is condemned

2. Jesus carries his cross

3. Jesus falls the first time

4. Jesus meets his mother
She who knew her heart in sorrow
Would be pierced, here bravely follows
In her Son's distress and pain.

5. Simon helps Jesus carry his cross
Simon, one with Jesus bearing,
Shows the way of our own sharing,
Taking up our daily cross.

6. Veronica wipes the face of Jesus
Boldly facing disapproval
She, in cleansing, seeks removal
Of the stains of agony.

7. Jesus falls a second time
Falling once again, Lord Jesus
Shows the suffering that frees us
As we struggle on our way.

8. Jesus meets the women of Jerusalem
Israel's own daughters, weeping
Come to Jesus, comfort seeking
In the time of their distress.

9. Jesus falls the third time
Jesus weakened, bruised and feeble,
Falls again, appears unable
To complete his painful road.

10. Jesus is stripped of his garments
Naked, stark, in desolation,
Jesus knows humiliation,
Robbed of his last dignity.

11. Jesus is nailed to the cross
Hands which heal and bless and feed us,
Feet which to the kingdom lead us,
Now are pierced with brutal steel.

12. Jesus dies on the cross
There between the earth and heaven
Death appears, in triumph, proven:
Jesus draws his dying breath.

13. Jesus is taken down from the cross
Oh, what sorrow, pain and anguish
Comes to those who saw him perish
As they take his body down.

14. Jesus is laid in the tomb
Some believe the awful journey
Finishes all bleak and stony,
Yet a new life will arise.

Concluding stanza
Let us walk with Christ while praying
As he did, God's will obeying,
"Let your will, not mine, be done."

The following refrain may be used instead of the previous hymn. Other suitable songs include the refrain of Now We Remain, *no. 319, or* Jesus, Remember Me / Jesús, Recuérdame, *no. 147.*

In the Cross of Christ   144

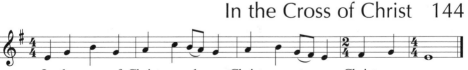

In the cross of Christ, our glo-ry, Christ, our sto-ry, Christ, our song.

145 Tree of Life

1. Tree of Life and awe-some mys-t'ry, In your
2. Seed that dies to rise in glo-ry, May we
3. We re-mem-ber truth once spo-ken, Love passed
4. Gen-tle Je-sus, might-y Spir-it, Come in-
5. Christ, you lead and we shall fol-low, Stum-bling

death we are re-born, Though you die in all of
see our-selves in you, If we learn to live your
on through act and word, Ev-'ry per-son lost and
flame our hearts a-new, We may all your joy in-
though our steps may be, One with you in joy and

his-t'ry, Still you rise with ev-'ry morn, Still you
sto-ry We may die to rise a-new, We may
bro-ken Wears the bod-y of our Lord, Wears the
her-it If we bear the cross with you, If we
sor-row, We the riv-er, you the sea, We the

rise with ev-'ry morn.
die to rise a-new.
bod-y of our Lord.
bear the cross with you.
riv-er, you the sea.

Lenten Verses

General: Light of life beyond conceiving, Mighty Spirit of our Lord;
Give new strength to our believing, Give us faith to live your word.

1st Sunday: From the dawning of creation, You have loved us as your own;
Stay with us through all temptation, Make us turn to you alone.

2nd Sunday: In our call to be a blessing, May we be a blessing true;
May we live and die confessing Christ as Lord of all we do.

3rd Sunday: Living Water of salvation, Be the fountain of each soul;
Springing up in new creation, Flow in us and make us whole.

4th Sunday: Give us eyes to see you clearly, Make us children of your light;
Give us hearts to live more nearly As your gospel shining bright.

5th Sunday: God of all our fear and sorrow, God who lives beyond our death;
Hold us close through each tomorrow, Love as near as every breath.

Text: Marty Haugen, b.1950
Tune: THOMAS, 8 7 8 77; Marty Haugen, b.1950
© 1984, GIA Publications, Inc.

What Wondrous Love Is This   146

1. What won-drous love is this, O my soul, O my soul!
2. To God and to the Lamb I will sing, I will sing;
3. And when from death I'm free, I'll sing on, I'll sing on;

What won-drous love is this, O my soul!
To God and to the Lamb I will sing.
And when from death I'm free, I'll sing on.

What won-drous love is this that caused the Lord of bliss
To God and to the Lamb, who is the great I AM,
And when from death I'm free, I'll sing and joy-ful be,

To bear the dread-ful curse for my soul, for my soul;
While mil-lions join the theme, I will sing, I will sing;
And through e - ter - ni - ty I'll sing on, I'll sing on;

To bear the dread - ful curse for my soul!
While mil - lions join the theme, I will sing.
And through e - ter - ni - ty I'll sing on.

Text: Alexander Means, 1801–1883
Tune: WONDROUS LOVE, 12 9 12 12 9; *Southern Harmony,* 1835; harm. from *Cantate Domino, 1980,* © 1980, World Council of Churches

147 Jesus, Remember Me / Jesús, Recuérdame

Ostinato Refrain

Je-sus,   re-mem-ber me   when you come in-to your   King-dom.
Je-sús,   re-cuér-da-me   cuan-do   en-tres en   tu   Rei - no.

Je-sus,   re-mem-ber me   when you come in-to your King-dom.
Je-sús,   re-cuér-da-me   cuan-do   en-tres en   tu   Rei - no.

Text: Luke 23:42; Taizé Community, 1981
Tune: Jacques Berthier, 1923–1994
© 1981, Les Presses de Taizé, GIA Publications, Inc., agent

148 Stay Here and Keep Watch

Ostinato Refrain

Stay here   and keep watch with me.   The   hour   has come.

Stay here   and keep watch with me.   Watch   and pray.

Text: from Matthew 26; Taizé Community
Tune: Jacques Berthier, 1923–1994
© 1984, Les Presses de Taizé, GIA Publications, Inc., agent

O How Good Is Christ the Lord! / 149
¡Oh, Qué Bueno Es Jesús!

O how good is Christ the Lord! On the cross he
¡Oh, qué bue - no es Je - sús! Que por mí mu -

died for me. In three days he rose a - gain.
rió_en la cruz. Y_en tres días re - su - ci - tó.

Glo - ry be to Je - sus! Glo - ry be to
¡Y_a su nom - bre glo - ria! ¡Y_a su nom - bre

Je - sus! Glo - ry be to Je - sus! In three days he
glo - ria! ¡Y_a su nom - bre glo - ria! Y_en tres días re -

rose a - gain. Glo - ry be to Je - sus!
su - ci - tó. ¡Y_a su nom - bre glo - ria!

Text: Puerto Rican traditional
Tune: OH QUÉ BUENO ES JESÚS, 7 7 7 6 6 6 7 6; Puerto Rican traditional; acc. by Robert J. Batastini, b.1942, © 2000, GIA Publications, Inc.

150   Were You There

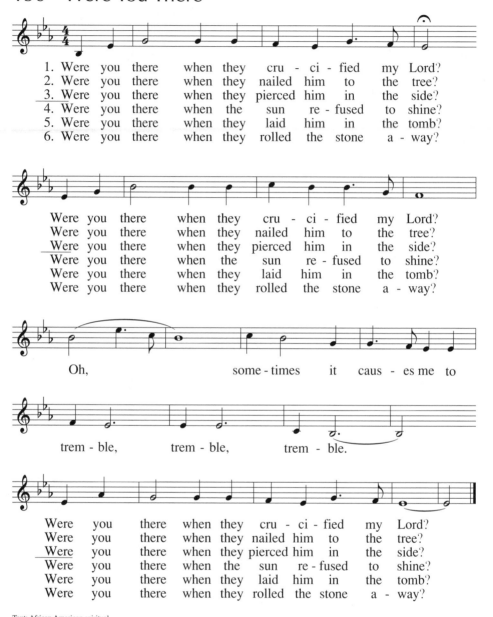

1. Were you there when they cru - ci - fied my Lord?
2. Were you there when they nailed him to the tree?
3. Were you there when they pierced him in the side?
4. Were you there when the sun re - fused to shine?
5. Were you there when they laid him in the tomb?
6. Were you there when they rolled the stone a - way?

Were you there when they cru - ci - fied my Lord?
Were you there when they nailed him to the tree?
Were you there when they pierced him in the side?
Were you there when the sun re - fused to shine?
Were you there when they laid him in the tomb?
Were you there when they rolled the stone a - way?

Oh,   some - times   it   caus - es me to

trem - ble,   trem - ble,   trem - ble.

Were   you   there   when they   cru - ci - fied   my   Lord?
Were   you   there   when they   nailed him   to   the   tree?
Were   you   there   when they   pierced him   in   the   side?
Were   you   there   when the   sun   re - fused   to   shine?
Were   you   there   when they   laid   him   in   the   tomb?
Were   you   there   when they   rolled   the   stone   a - way?

Text: African American spiritual
Tune: WERE YOU THERE, 10 10 with refrain; African American spiritual; harm. by Robert J. Batastini, b.1942, © 1987, GIA Publications, Inc.

Alleluia! Sing to Jesus 151

1. Al - le - lu - ia! Sing to Je - sus! His the
2. Al - le - lu - ia! Not as or - phans Are we
3. Al - le - lu - ia! Bread of an - gels, Here on
4. Al - le - lu - ia! King e - ter - nal, You the

scep - ter, his the throne. Al - le - lu - ia! His the
left in sor - row now; Al - le - lu - ia! He is
earth our food, our stay! Al - le - lu - ia! Here the
Lord of lords we own; Al - le - lu - ia! Born of

tri - umph, His the vic - to - ry a - lone.
near us; Faith be - lieves, nor ques - tions how.
sin - ful Flee to you from day to day.
Mar - y, Earth your foot - stool, heav'n your throne.

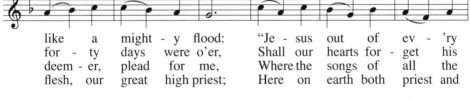

Hark! The songs of peace - ful Zi - on Thun - der
Though the cloud from sight re - ceived him When the
In - ter - ces - sor, friend of sin - ners, Earth's re -
You with - in the veil have en - tered, Robed in

like a might - y flood: "Je - sus out of ev - 'ry
for - ty days were o'er, Shall our hearts for - get his
deem - er, plead for me, Where the songs of all the
flesh, our great high priest; Here on earth both priest and

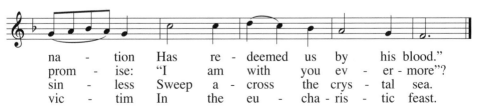

na - tion Has re - deemed us by his blood."
prom - ise: "I am with you ev - er - more"?
sin - less Sweep a - cross the crys - tal sea.
vic - tim In the eu - cha - ris - tic feast.

Text: Revelation 5:9; William C. Dix, 1837–1898
Tune: HYFRYDOL, 8 7 8 7 D; Rowland H. Prichard, 1811–1887

152 Sing a New Song

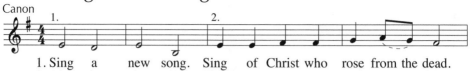

Canon

1. Sing a new song. Sing of Christ who rose from the dead.
2. Al - le - lu - ia! Sing and dance a song of joy!
3. All God's chil - dren, Hearts and souls we lift in joy!

Al - le - lu - ia! Al - le - lu - ia! Sing a new song.
Christ now lives a - mong us. Al - le - lu - ia!
Give thanks to the Lord as Chil - dren of God.

Text: Robert W. Piercy, Jr., 1958–2011, © 2001, GIA Publications, Inc.
Tune: Thomas Ravenscroft, c.1582–1635; acc. by Robert N. Roth, © 2000, GIA Publications, Inc.

153 Alleluia, Alleluia, Give Thanks

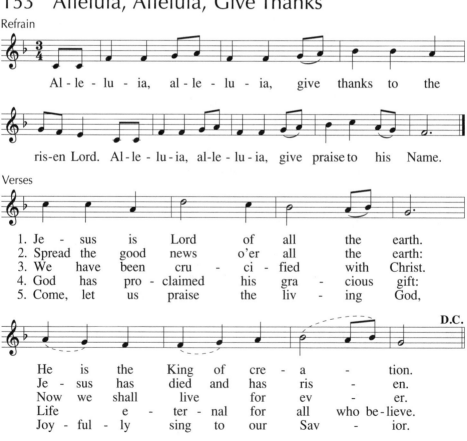

Refrain

Al - le - lu - ia, al - le - lu - ia, give thanks to the

ris-en Lord. Al - le - lu - ia, al-le - lu - ia, give praise to his Name.

Verses

1. Je - sus is Lord of all the earth.
2. Spread the good news o'er all the earth:
3. We have been cru - ci - fied with Christ.
4. God has pro - claimed his gra - cious gift:
5. Come, let us praise the liv - ing God,

D.C.

He is the King of cre - a - tion.
Je - sus has died and has ris - en.
Now we shall live for ev - er.
Life e - ter - nal for all who be - lieve.
Joy - ful - ly sing to our Sav - ior.

Text: Donald Fishel, b.1950
Tune: ALLELUIA NO. 1, 8 8 with refrain; Donald Fishel, b.1950
© 1973, International Liturgy Publications

Christ the Lord Is Risen Today / 154
Hail the Day That Sees Him Rise

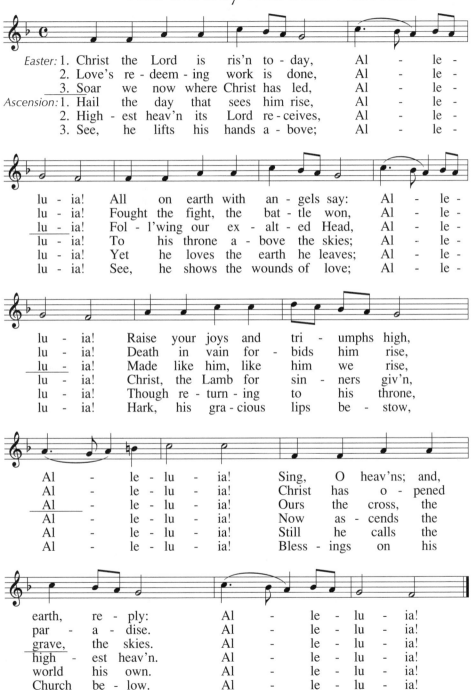

Easter: 1. Christ the Lord is ris'n to-day, Al - le -
2. Love's re-deem-ing work is done, Al - le -
3. Soar we now where Christ has led, Al - le -
Ascension: 1. Hail the day that sees him rise, Al - le -
2. High-est heav'n its Lord re-ceives, Al - le -
3. See, he lifts his hands a-bove; Al - le -

lu - ia! All on earth with an-gels say: Al - le -
lu - ia! Fought the fight, the bat-tle won, Al - le -
lu - ia! Fol-l'wing our ex-alt-ed Head, Al - le -
lu - ia! To his throne a-bove the skies; Al - le -
lu - ia! Yet he loves the earth he leaves; Al - le -
lu - ia! See, he shows the wounds of love; Al - le -

lu - ia! Raise your joys and tri - umphs high,
lu - ia! Death in vain for - bids him rise,
lu - ia! Made like him, like him we rise,
lu - ia! Christ, the Lamb for sin - ners giv'n,
lu - ia! Though re - turn - ing to his throne,
lu - ia! Hark, his gra-cious lips be - stow,

Al - le - lu - ia! Sing, O heav'ns; and,
Al - le - lu - ia! Christ has o - pened
Al - le - lu - ia! Ours the cross, the
Al - le - lu - ia! Now as - cends the
Al - le - lu - ia! Still he calls the
Al - le - lu - ia! Bless - ings on his

earth, re - ply: Al - le - lu - ia!
par - a - dise. Al - le - lu - ia!
grave, the skies. Al - le - lu - ia!
high - est heav'n. Al - le - lu - ia!
world his own. Al - le - lu - ia!
Church be - low. Al - le - lu - ia!

Text: Charles Wesley, 1707–1788
Tune: LLANFAIR, 77 77 with alleluias; Robert Williams, 1781–1821

155 We Walk His Way / Ewe, Thina

his way.
thi - na.
Un-armed, he
He breaks the
The tree of
Si - zo - wa

We walk his way.
E - we, thi - na.
We walk his way.
E - we, thi - na.

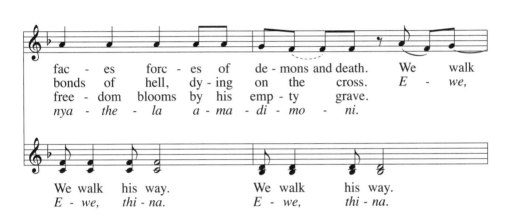

fac - es forc - es of de - mons and death. We walk
bonds of hell, dy - ing on the cross. *E - we,*
free - dom blooms by his emp - ty grave.
nya - the - la a - ma - di - mo - ni.

We walk his way.
E - we, thi - na.
We walk his way.
E - we, thi - na.

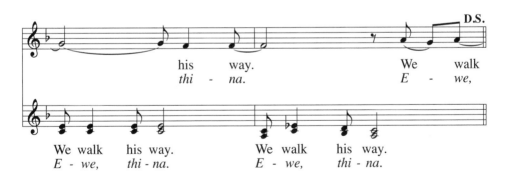

D.S.

his way.
thi - na.
We walk
E - we,

We walk his way.
E - we, thi - na.
We walk his way.
E - we, thi - na.

Text: South African (Xhosa); tr. by Anders Nyberg, b.1955, and Sven-Bernhard Fast
Tune: South African melody; arr. by Anders Nyberg, b.1955

156 Christ the Lord Is Risen!

1. Christ the Lord is ris'n! Christ the Lord is ris'n!
2. He has con-quered death. He has con-quered death.
3. Sin has done its worst. Sin has done its worst.
4. He is King of kings. He is King of kings.
5. He is Lord of lords. He is Lord of lords.
6. All the world is his. All the world is his.
7. Come and wor-ship him. Come and wor-ship him.
8. Christ our Lord is ris'n! Christ our Lord is ris'n!
9. Hal-le-lu-jah! Hal-le-lu-jah!

Je-su. Christ the Lord is ris'n!
Je-su. He has con-quered death.
Je-su. Sin has done its worst.
Je-su. He is King of kings.
Je-su. He is Lord of lords.
Je-su. All the world is his.
Je-su. Come and wor-ship him.
Je-su. Christ our Lord is ris'n!
Je-su. Hal-le-lu-jah!

Christ the Lord is ris'n! Je-su.
He has con-quered death. Je-su.
Sin has done its worst. Je-su.
He is King of kings. Je-su.
He is Lord of lords. Je-su.
All the world is his. Je-su.
Come and wor-ship him. Je-su.
Christ our Lord is ris'n! Je-su.
Hal-le-lu-jah! Je-su.

Text: Tom Colvin, 1925–2000
Tune: GARU, 55 2 55 2, Ghanian folk song, adapt. by Tom Colvin, 1925–2000, arr. by Kevin R. Hackett, b.1956
© 1969, Hope Publishing Company

Jesus Christ Is Risen Today   157

1. Je - sus Christ is ris'n to - day, Al - le - lu - ia!
2. Hymns of praise then let us sing, Al - le - lu - ia!
3. But the pains which he en - dured, Al - le - lu - ia!
4. Sing we to our God a - bove, Al - le - lu - ia!

Our tri - um-phant ho - ly day, Al - le - lu - ia!
Un - to Christ, our heav'n-ly King, Al - le - lu - ia!
Our sal - va - tion have pro - cured; Al - le - lu - ia!
Praise e - ter - nal, as his love; Al - le - lu - ia!

Who did once up - on the cross, Al - le - lu - ia!
Who en - dured the cross and grave, Al - le - lu - ia!
Now a - bove the sky he's King, Al - le - lu - ia!
Praise him, now his might con - fess, Al - le - lu - ia!

Suf - fer to re - deem our loss. Al - le - lu - ia!
Sin - ners to re - deem and save. Al - le - lu - ia!
Where the an - gels ev - er sing. Al - le - lu - ia!
Fa - ther, Son, and Spir - it blest. Al - le - lu - ia!

Text: St. 1, *Surrexit Christus hodie,* Latin, 14th C.; para. in *Lyra Davidica,* 1708, alt.; st. 2, 3, *The Compleat Psalmodist,* c.1750, alt.; st. 4, Charles Wesley, 1707–1788, alt.
Tune: EASTER HYMN, 77 77 with alleluias; *Lyra Davidica,* 1708

158 Be Not Afraid

Ostinato Refrain

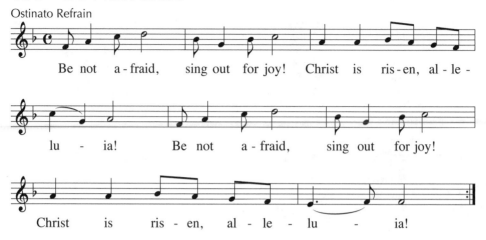

Be not a-fraid, sing out for joy! Christ is ris-en, al-le-lu-ia! Be not a-fraid, sing out for joy! Christ is ris-en, al-le-lu-ia!

Text: Taizé Community
Tune: Taizé Community
© 2007, Les Presses de Taizé, GIA Publications, Inc., agent

159 That Easter Day with Joy Was Bright

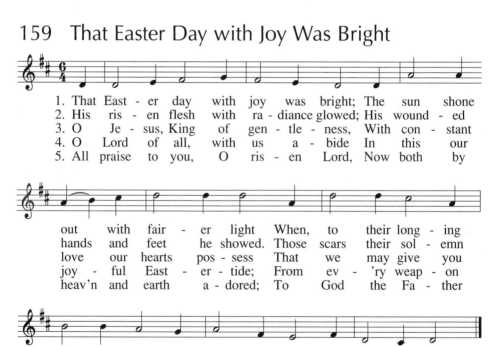

1. That East-er day with joy was bright; The sun shone out with fair-er light When, to their long-ing eyes re-stored, The a-pos-tles saw their ris-en Lord!
2. His ris-en flesh with ra-diance glowed; His wound-ed hands and feet he showed. Those scars their sol-emn wit-ness gave That Christ was ris-en from the grave.
3. O Je-sus, King of gen-tle-ness, With con-stant love our hearts pos-sess That we may give you all our days The trib-ute of our grate-ful praise.
4. O Lord of all, with us a-bide In this our joy-ful East-er-tide; From ev-'ry weap-on death can wield Your own re-deemed for-ev-er shield.
5. All praise to you, O ris-en Lord, Now both by heav'n and earth a-dored; To God the Fa-ther e-qual praise, And God the Spir-it, now we raise!

Text: *Claro paschali gaudio*; Latin 5th C.; tr. by John M. Neale, 1818–1866, alt.
Tune: PUER NOBIS, LM; adapt. by Michael Praetorius, 1571–1621

This Day Was Made by the Lord 160

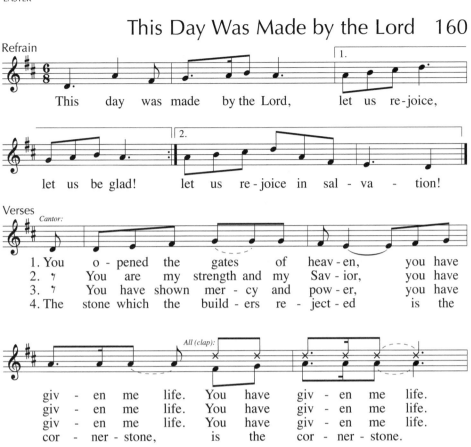

Refrain

This day was made by the Lord, let us re-joice,

let us be glad! let us re-joice in sal - va - tion!

Verses

Cantor:

1. You o - pened the gates of heav - en, you have
2. You are my strength and my Sav - ior, you have
3. You have shown mer - cy and pow - er, you have
4. The stone which the build - ers re - ject - ed is the

All (clap):

giv - en me life. You have giv - en me life.
giv - en me life. You have giv - en me life.
giv - en me life. You have giv - en me life.
cor - ner - stone, is the cor - ner - stone.

D.C.

I will pro - claim the won - ders you do!

161 Easter Alleluia

Refrain

Al-le-lu-ia, al-le-lu-ia, al-le-lu - ia!

Verses

1. Glo - ry   to   God who does   won - drous things, Let   all   the
2. See   how sal - va - tion for   all has been   won,   Up from the
3. Now   in   our   pres - ence the   Lord will ap - pear, Shine in   the
4. Call   us, Good Shep - herd, we   lis - ten for   you, Want-ing to
5. Lord, we   are   o - pen   to   all that you   say, Read - y   to
6. If   we have love, then   we   dwell in   the   Lord, God will pro -

peo - ple God's prais - es now sing,   All of   cre - a - tion in
grave our new   life has   be - gun, Life now per - fect - ed in
fac - es   of   all   of   us   here, Fill   us with joy and cast
see   you in   all that we   do,   We would the gate of   sal -
lis - ten and fol - low your way,   You are   the pot - ter and
tect us from fire   and sword,   Fill   us with love and the

D.C.

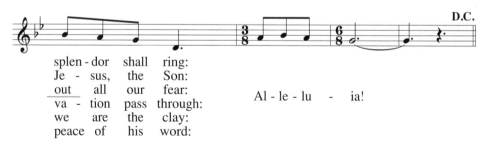

splen - dor shall ring:
Je - sus,   the   Son:
out   all   our   fear: Al - le - lu - ia!
va - tion pass through:
we   are   the   clay:
peace of   his   word:

Text: Marty Haugen, b.1950
Tune: O FILII ET FILIAE, 10 10 10 with alleluias; adapt. by Marty Haugen, b.1950
© 1986, GIA Publications, Inc.

Goodness Is Stronger than Evil 162

Good-ness is strong-er than e - vil; love is strong-er than hate; light is strong-er than dark - ness; life is strong-er than death. Vic-t'ry is ours, vic-t'ry is

Oh, vic-t'ry is ours,

1. 2.
ours through him who loved us. us.

vic-t'ry is ours through him who loved us. us.

Text: Desmond Tutu, b.1931, ©; adapt. by John L. Bell, b.1949
Tune: GOODNESS IS STRONGER, Irregular; John L. Bell, b.1949, © 1996, Iona Community, GIA Publications, Inc., agent

Surrexit Christus / The Lord Is Risen 163

Ostinato Refrain

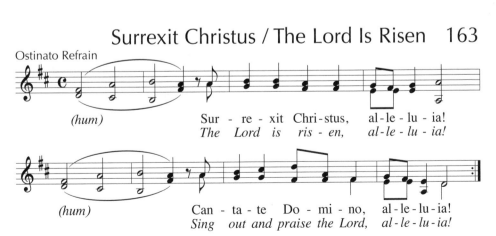

(hum) Sur - re - xit Chri - stus, al-le-lu - ia!
The Lord is ris - en, al-le-lu - ia!

(hum) Can - ta - te Do - mi - no, al-le-lu - ia!
Sing out and praise the Lord, al-le-lu - ia!

Text: *Christ is risen, sing to the Lord;* Daniel 3; Taizé Community, 1984
Tune: Jacques Berthier, 1923–1994
© 1984, Les Presses de Taizé, GIA Publications, Inc., agent

164 Resucitó

Refrain

Re - su - ci - tó,   re - su - ci - tó,   re - su - ci -
A - le - lu - ya,   a - le - lu - ya,   a - le - lu -

To verses | *Final ending*

tó,   a - le - lu - ya.   A - le - lu - ya.
ya,   re - su - ci - tó.

Verses

1.   La muer - te   ¿dón - de es - tá la
2.   Gra - cias se - an   da - das al
3.   A - le - grí - a,   a - le - grí-a her -
4.   Si con él mo - ri - mos,   ʎ con él vi -
1.   *And death now,*   *van - ished is the*
2.   *The king - dom,*   *praise to God, the*
3.   *Our glad - ness,*   *bliss - ful in our*
4.   *With him then,*   *die and live with*

muer - te?   ¿Dón - de es - tá mi
Pa - dre   que nos pa - só a su
ma - nos,   que si hoy nos que -
vi - mos,   ʎ con él can -
fear now,   *ban - ished are my*
king - dom!   *Raised up to the*
glad - ness,   *this will be our*
him then,   *rise and sing our*

D.C.

muer - te?   ¿Dón - de su vic - to - ria?
rei - no   dón - de se vi - ve de a - mor.
re - mos   es que re - su - ci - tó.
ta - mos.   ʎ ¡A - le - lu - ya!
tears now,   *death has passed a - way.*
king - dom,   *we shall live in love.*
glad - ness,   *that he is a - live.*
hymn then,   *sing al - le - lu - ia.*

Text: Spanish, Kiko Argüello, © 1973, Kiko Argüello; tr. by Robert C. Trupia, © 1988, OCP
Tune: Kiko Argüello, © 1973, Kiko Argüello; acc. by Diana Kodner, b.1957
Published by OCP.

Sing with All the Saints in Glory 165

1. Sing with all the saints in glo - ry, Sing the res - ur -
2. O what glo - ry, far ex - ceed - ing All that eye has
3. Life e - ter - nal! heav'n re - joic - es: Je - sus lives who
4. Life e - ter - nal! O what won - ders Crowd on faith; what

rec - tion song! Death and sor - row, earth's dark sto - ry,
yet per - ceived! Ho - liest hearts, for a - ges plead - ing,
once was dead. Shout with joy, O death - less voic - es!
joy un - known, When, a - mid earth's clos - ing thun - ders,

To the for - mer days be - long. All a - round the
Nev - er that full joy con - ceived. God has prom - ised,
Child of God, lift up your head! Pa - tri - archs from
Saints shall stand be - fore the throne! Oh, to en - ter

clouds are break - ing, Soon the storms of time shall cease;
Christ pre - pares it, There on high our wel - come waits.
dis - tant a - ges, Saints all long - ing for their heav'n,
that bright por - tal, See that glow - ing fir - ma - ment,

In God's like - ness we a - wak - en,
Ev - 'ry hum - ble spir - it shares it;
Proph - ets, psalm - ists, seers, and sag - es,
Know, with you, O God im - mor - tal,

Know - ing ev - er - last - ing peace.
Christ has passed the e - ter - nal gates.
All a - wait the glo - ry giv'n.
Je - sus Christ whom you have sent!

Text: 1 Corinthians 15:20; William J. Irons, 1812–1883, alt.
Tune: HYMN TO JOY, 8 7 8 7 D; arr. from Ludwig van Beethoven, 1770–1827, by Edward Hodges, 1796–1867

166 This Is a Day of New Beginnings

Refrain

Christ is a-live, and goes be-fore us to show and share what love can do. This is a day of new be-gin-nings; our God is mak-ing all things new, our God is mak - ing all things new.

Verses

1. This is a day of new be-gin-nings, time to re-mem - ber,
2. For by the life and death of Je - sus, love's might-y Spir - it,
3. Then let us, with the Spir - it's dar - ing, step from the past, and

and move on, time to be-lieve what love is bring-ing,
now as then, can make for us a world of dif - f'rence
leave be - hind our dis - a - point - ment, guilt, and griev-ing,

D.C.

lay - ing to rest the pain that's gone.
as faith and hope are born a - gain.
seek-ing new paths, and sure to find.

Text: Brian Wren, b.1936, © 1983, 1987, Hope Publishing Company
Tune: Lori True, b.1961, © 2003, GIA Publications, Inc.

Send Us Your Spirit 167

Refrain

*1.   2.

Come Lord Je-sus, send us your Spir-it, re-
new the face of the earth. Come Lord
Je-sus, send us your Spir-it, re-new the face of the
earth.

Verses

1. Come to us, Spir-it of God, breathe in us
2. Fill us with the fire of your love, burn in us
3. Send us the wings of new birth, fill all the

now, we sing to-geth-er. Spir-it of
now, bring us to-geth-er. Come to us,
earth with the love you have taught us. Let all cre-

hope and of light, fill our lives,
dwell in us, change our lives, O Lord,
a-tion now be shak-en with love,

D.C.

come to us, Spir-it of God.
come to us, Spir-it of God.
come to us, Spir-it of God.

*May be sung in canon.

Text: David Haas, b.1957
Tune: David Haas, b.1957; acc. by Jeanne Cotter, b.1964
© 1981, 1982, 1987, GIA Publications, Inc.

168 Envía Tu Espíritu

Refrain

En - ví - a tu Es - pí - ri - tu, en - ví - a tu Es - pí - ri - tu,

en - ví - a tu Es - pí - ri - tu, se - a re - no - va-

da la faz de la tie - rra. Se - a re - no - va-

da la faz de la tie - rra.

Verses

1. Spir - it of the liv - ing God,
2. Wind of prom - ise, wind of change,
3. Breath of life and ho - li - ness,

burn in our hearts, and make us a peo-
friend of the poor, em - pow - er your peo-
heal ev - 'ry wound, and lead us be - yond

D.C.

ple of hope and com - pas - sion.
ple to make peace and jus - tice.
ev - 'ry sin that di - vides us.

Text: *Send out your spirit and renew the face of the earth;* Psalm 104:30; the Sequence of Pentecost; Bob Hurd, b.1950
Tune: Bob Hurd, b.1950; acc. by Craig Kingsbury, b.1952, © 1988, Bob Hurd
Published by OCP.

O Holy Spirit, by Whose Breath   169

1. O Ho - ly Spir - it, by whose breath Life
2. You are the seek - er's sure re - source, Of
3. In you God's en - er - gy is shown, To
4. Flood our dull sens - es with your light; In
5. From in - ner strife grant us re - lease; Turn
6. Praise to the Fa - ther, Christ the Word, And

ris - es vi - brant out of death: Al - le - lu - ia,
burn - ing love the liv - ing source, Al - le - lu - ia,
us your var - ied gifts make known. Al - le - lu - ia,
mu - tual love our hearts u - nite. Al - le - lu - ia,
na - tions to the ways of peace. Al - le - lu - ia,
to the Spir - it: God the Lord, Al - le - lu - ia,

al - le - lu - ia; Come to cre - ate, re - new, in - spire;
al - le - lu - ia; Pro - tec - tor in the midst of strife,
al - le - lu - ia; Teach us to speak, teach us to hear;
al - le - lu - ia; Your pow'r the whole cre - a - tion fills;
al - le - lu - ia; To full - er life your peo - ple bring
al - le - lu - ia; To whom all hon - or, glo - ry be

Come, kin - dle in our hearts your fire.
The giv - er and the Lord of life.
Yours is the tongue and yours the ear.
Con - firm our weak, un - cer - tain wills.
That as one bod - y we may sing:
Both now and for e - ter - ni - ty.

Al - le - lu - ia, al - le - lu - ia; Al - le - lu - ia,

al - le - lu - ia, al - le - lu - ia.

Text: *Veni Creator Spiritus;* attr. to Rabanus Maurus, 776–865; tr. by John W. Grant, 1919–2006, © 1971
Tune: LASST UNS ERFREUEN, LM with alleluias; *Geistliche Kirchengesänge*, 1623; harm. by Ralph Vaughan Williams, 1872–1958

170 Send Down the Fire

Refrain

Send down the fire of your jus-tice,

Send down the rains of your love; Come,

send down the Spir-it, breathe life in your peo-ple, and

we shall be peo-ple of God.

Verses

1. Call us to be your com - pas - sion,
2. Call us to learn of your mer - cy,
3. Call us to an - swer op - pres - sion,
4. Call us to wit - ness your King - dom,

Teach us the song of your love; Give us
Teach us the way of your peace; Give us
Teach us the fire of your truth; Give us
Give us the pres - ence of Christ; May your

hearts that sing, Give us deeds that ring, Make us
hearts that feel, Give us hands that heal, Make us
right - eous souls, 'Til your jus - tice rolls, Make us
ho - ly light Keep us shin - ing bright, Ev - er

D.C.

ring with the song of your love.
walk in the way of your peace.
burn with the fire of your truth.
shine with the pres - ence of Christ.

Text: Marty Haugen, b.1950
Tune: Marty Haugen, b.1950
© 1989, GIA Publications, Inc.

Every Time I Feel the Spirit   171

Refrain

Ev - 'ry time I feel the Spir - it mov - ing in my heart, I will pray. Ev - 'ry time I feel the Spir - it mov - ing in my heart, I will pray.

Verses

1. Up - on the moun - tain when my God spoke,
   All a - round me, it looked so shine,
2. 'Ol Jor - dan Riv - er, chill - y and cold,
   There ain't but one train that's on this track,

D.C.

Out of God's mouth came fire and smoke.
I asked my Lord if all was mine.
It chills the bod - y, but not the soul.
It runs to heav - en and runs right back.

Text: African American spiritual
Tune: FEEL THE SPIRIT, 98 98 with refrain; African American spiritual; arr. by Nolan Williams, Jr., b.1969, © 2000, GIA Publications, Inc.

Holy Spirit, Come to Us / Ven, Espíritu   172

Ostinato Refrain

Ho - ly Spir - it, come to us, kin - dle in us the fire of your love.
Ven, Es - pí - ri - tu de Dios, y de tu a-mor en - cien - de la lla - ma.
Ve - ni San - cte Spí - ri - tus, tu - i a - mó - ris i - gnem ac - cén - de.

Ho - ly Spir - it, come to us, Ho - ly Spir - it, come to us.
Ven, Es - pí - ri - tu de a-mor, ven, Es - pí - ri - tu de a-mor.
Ve - ni San - cte Spí - ri - tus, ve - ni San - cte Spí - ri - tus.

Text: John 13:35, 15:12–13, 1 John 3:16, 4:10, 16
Tune: Jacques Berthier, 1923–1994
© 1998, Les Presses de Taizé, GIA Publications, Inc., agent

173 Spirit of God

Refrain

Spir - it of God, who dwells in me, O - pen my
eyes that I may see. Come fill my heart
and make me whole. Spir - it of God, I am yours.

Verses

1. This is the Spir-it of the liv-ing God,
2. Come, Ho - ly Spir-it, and set me free

Who hears your ev - 'ry sin-gle prayer. O
To do the best I can. O

this is the Spir - it of the liv - ing God,
come, Ho - ly Spir - it, and set me free

D.C.

Who is al - ways right there.
To be all that I am.

Text: James E. Moore, Jr., b.1951
Tune: James E. Moore, Jr., b.1951

O Breathe on Me, O Breath of God 174

1. O breathe on me, O Breath of God, Fill me with life a - new, That I may love the things you love And do what you would do.
2. O breathe on me, O Breath of God, Un - til my heart is pure; Un - til my will is one with yours, To do and to en - dure.
3. O breathe on me, O Breath of God, My will to yours in - cline, Un - til this self - ish part of me Glows with your fire di - vine.
4. O breathe on me, O Breath of God, So shall I nev - er die, But live with you the per - fect life Of your e - ter - ni - ty.

Text: Edwin Hatch, 1835–1889
Tune: ST. COLUMBA, CM; Irish melody; harm. by A. Gregory Murray, OSB, 1905–1992, © Downside Abbey

Father, I Adore You 175

1. Fa - ther, I a - dore you, Lay my life be - fore you, How I love you.
2. Je - sus, I a - dore you, Lay my life be - fore you, How I love you.
3. Spir - it, I a - dore you, Lay my life be - fore you, How I love you.

*May be sung as a 3-part round.

Text: Terrye Coelho-Strom, b.1952
Tune: MARANATHA, 6 6 4; Terrye Coelho-Strom, b.1952
© 1972, CCCM Music/Universal Music–Brentwood Benson Publishing (admin. CapitolCMGPublishing.com)

176 Let There Be Light

Final Refrain

Ho - ly and bless - ed Three, glo - ri - ous Trin - i -

ty: Wis - dom, Love, and Might! Let there be light! Let there be

light! Oh, let there be light!

Text: John Marriott, 1780–1825; adapt. by Paul Melley, b.1973
Tune: Paul Melley, b.1973
© 2008, GIA Publications, Inc.

Sing Praise to Our Creator 177

1. Sing praise to our Cre - a - tor, Re -
2. To Je - sus Christ give glo - ry, God's
3. Now praise the Ho - ly Spir - it Poured

deemed of A - dam's race; God's chil - dren by a -
co - e - ter - nal Son; As mem - bers of his
forth up - on the earth, Who sanc - ti - fies and

dop - tion, Bap - tized in liv - ing grace.
bod - y We are in Christ made one.
guides us, Con - firmed in our re - birth.

O most ho - ly Trin - i - ty, Un - di - vid - ed u - ni - ty;

Ho - ly God, might-y God, God im - mor - tal, be a - dored!

Text: Omer Westendorf, 1916–1997; © 1962, World Library Publications
Tune: GOTT VATER SEI GEPRIESEN, 76 76 with refrain; *Limburg Gesangbuch*, 1838; harm. by Healey Willan, 1880–1968, © 1958,
     Ralph Jusko Publications, Inc.

178 The King of Glory

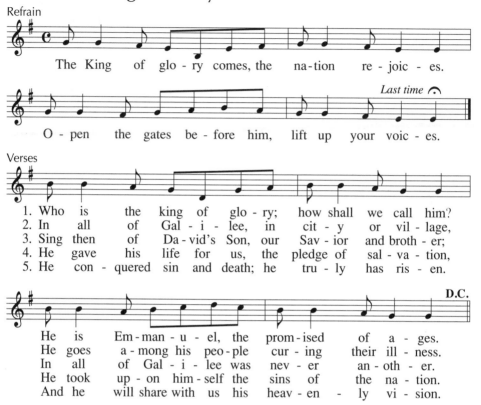

Refrain

The King of glo-ry comes, the na-tion re-joic-es.

Last time

O - pen the gates be - fore him, lift up your voic - es.

Verses

1. Who is the king of glo - ry; how shall we call him?
2. In all of Gal - i - lee, in cit - y or vil - lage,
3. Sing then of Da - vid's Son, our Sav - ior and broth - er;
4. He gave his life for us, the pledge of sal - va - tion,
5. He con - quered sin and death; he tru - ly has ris - en.

D.C.

He is Em - man - u - el, the prom - ised of a - ges.
He goes a - mong his peo - ple cur - ing their ill - ness.
In all of Gal - i - lee was nev - er an - oth - er.
He took up - on him - self the sins of the na - tion.
And he will share with us his heav - en - ly vi - sion.

Text: Willard F. Jabusch, b.1930, © 1966, 1982, Rev. Willard F. Jabusch. Published by OCP.
Tune: KING OF GLORY, 12 12 with refrain; Israeli; harm. by Richard Proulx, 1937–2010, © 1986, GIA Publications, Inc.

179 Jesus Christ, Yesterday, Today, and Forever / Jesucristo Ayer

Ostinato Refrain

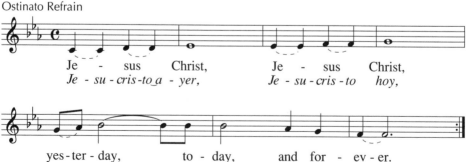

Je - sus Christ, Je - sus Christ,
Je - su - cris - to a - yer, Je - su - cris - to hoy,

yes - ter - day, to - day, and for - ev - er.
siem - pre se - rá el Se - ñor.

Text: Suzanne Toolan, RSM, b.1927; Spanish tr. by Ronald F. Krisman, b.1946
Tune: Suzanne Toolan, RSM, b.1927
© 1988, 2004, GIA Publications, Inc.

Praise to You, O Christ, Our Savior   180

Refrain

Praise to you, O Christ, our Sav-ior, Word of the Fa-ther, call-ing us to life;

Son of God who leads us to free-dom: glo-ry to you, Lord Je-sus Christ!

Verses

1. You are the Word who calls us out of dark - ness;
2. You are the one whom proph - ets hoped and longed for;
3. You are the Word who calls us to be ser - vants;
4. You are the Word who binds us and u - nites us;

you are the Word who leads us in - to light;
you are the one who speaks to us to - day;
you are the Word whose on - ly law is love;
you are the Word who calls us to be one;

you are the Word who brings us through the des - ert:
you are the one who leads us to our fu - ture:
you are the Word - made - flesh who lives a - mong us:
you are the Word who teach - es us for - give - ness:

D.C.

glo - ry to you, Lord Je - sus Christ!
glo - ry to you, Lord Je - sus Christ!
glo - ry to you, Lord Je - sus Christ!
glo - ry to you, Lord Je - sus Christ!

Text: Bernadette Farrell, b.1957
Tune: Bernadette Farrell, b.1957
© 1986, Bernadette Farrell. Published by OCP.

181 Jesus in the Morning

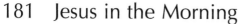

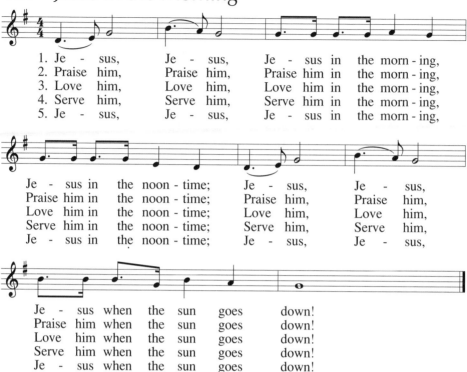

1. Je - sus, Je - sus, Je - sus in the morn - ing,
2. Praise him, Praise him, Praise him in the morn - ing,
3. Love him, Love him, Love him in the morn - ing,
4. Serve him, Serve him, Serve him in the morn - ing,
5. Je - sus, Je - sus, Je - sus in the morn - ing,

Je - sus in the noon - time; Je - sus, Je - sus,
Praise him in the noon - time; Praise him, Praise him,
Love him in the noon - time; Love him, Love him,
Serve him in the noon - time; Serve him, Serve him,
Je - sus in the noon - time; Je - sus, Je - sus,

Je - sus when the sun goes down!
Praise him when the sun goes down!
Love him when the sun goes down!
Serve him when the sun goes down!
Je - sus when the sun goes down!

Text: African American folk song
Tune: African American folk song

182 Behold, I Make All Things New

Be - hold, be - hold, I make all things new, be -

gin - ning with you and start - ing from to - day. Be -

hold, be - hold, I make all things new, my

prom-ise is true, for I am Christ, the way.

Text: John L. Bell, b.1949
Tune: John L. Bell, b.1949
© 1994, Iona Community, GIA Publications, Inc., agent

Joyful, Joyful, We Adore You   183

1. Joy - ful, joy - ful, we a - dore you, God of glo - ry,
2. All your works with joy sur - round you, Earth and heav'n re -
3. You are giv - ing and for - giv - ing, Ev - er bless - ing,
4. Mor - tals, join the might - y cho - rus, Which the morn - ing

Lord of love; Hearts un - fold like flow'rs be - fore you,
flect your rays, Stars and an - gels sing a - round you,
ev - er blest, Well - spring of the joy of liv - ing,
stars be - gan; God's own love is reign - ing o'er us,

O - p'ning to the sun a - bove. Melt the clouds of
Cen - ter of un - bro - ken praise. Field and for - est,
O - cean - depth of hap - py rest! God our Fa - ther,
Join - ing peo - ple hand in hand. Ev - er sing - ing,

sin and sad - ness; Drive the dark of doubt a - way;
vale and moun - tain, Flow - 'ry mead - ow, flash - ing sea,
Christ our broth - er, Let your light up - on us shine;
march we on - ward, Vic - tors in the midst of strife;

Giv - er of im - mor - tal glad - ness, Fill us with the light of day!
Chant - ing bird, and flow - ing foun - tain Sound their praise e - ter - nal - ly!
Teach us how to love each oth - er, Lift us to the joy di - vine.
Joy - ful mu - sic leads us sun - ward In the tri - umph-song of life.

Text: Henry van Dyke, 1852–1933, alt.
Tune: HYMN TO JOY, 8 7 8 7 D; arr. from Ludwig van Beethoven, 1770–1827, by Edward Hodges, 1796–1867

184 Alabaré

Refrain

A - la - ba - ré,   a - la - ba - ré,   we
A - la - ba - ré,   a - la - ba - ré,   a -

sing the prais-es of our God.   A-la-ba - ré,   a-la-ba -
la - ba - ré a mi Se - ñor.   A-la-ba - ré,   a-la-ba -

ré,   we   sing   the prais-es   of our   God.
ré,   a - la - ba - ré a   mi Se - ñor.

Verses

1. John had a vis - ion of those re-deemed by Je - sus, And
2. One in our prais - ing, with joy - ful hearts and voic - es, We
3. We are your chil - dren, O God, e - ter - nal Fa - ther. You
1. *Juan vio el nú - me - ro de los re - di - mi-dos, Y*
2. *To - dos u - ni - dos, a - le - gres can - ta - mos*
3. *So - mos tus hi - jos, Dios Pa - dre e - ter - no,*

all were prais - ing God with one ac - cord.
glo - ri - fy the Lord who reigns a - bove:
guide us and pro - tect us all our days.
to - dos a - la - ba - ban al Se - ñor.
Glo - ria y a - la - ban - zas al Se - ñor.
Tú nos has cre - a - do por a - mor.

Thou-sands were pray-ing,   thou-sands   were sing - ing,   But
Praise to the Fa - ther,   praise to   Christ Je - sus,   And
With all cre - a - tion,   in ju - bi - la - tion,   We
U - nos o - ra - ban,   o - tros   can - ta - ban,   Y
¡Glo - ria al Pa - dre!   ¡Glo - ria   al Hi - jo!   Y
Te a - do - ra - mos,   te ben - de - ci - mos,   Y

D.S.

all were joined in prais - es to the Lord.
praise to God the Spir - it, bond of love. A-la-ba-
hon - or you with songs of end - less praise.
to - dos a - la - ba - ban al Se - ñor.
¡Glo - ria al Es - pí - ri - tu de a - mor! A-la-ba-
to - dos can - ta - mos en tu ho - nor.

Text: Manuel José Alonso, José Pagán; tr. by Ronald F. Krisman, b.1946
Tune: Manuel José Alonso, José Pagán; acc. by Ronald F. Krisman, b.1946
© 1979, 2011, Manuel José Alonso and José Pagán. Published by OCP.

Halleluya! We Sing Your Praises   185

Refrain

Hal - le - lu - ya! We sing your prais - es, all our

Claps:

hearts are filled with glad - ness. Hal - le - lu - ya! We sing your

prais - es, all our hearts are filled with glad - ness.

Verses

1. Christ the Lord to us said: I am
2. Now he sends us all out, strong in

wine, I am bread, I am wine, I am
faith, free of doubt, strong in faith, free of

bread, give to all who thirst and hun - ger.
doubt, to pro - claim the joy - ful Gos - pel.

Text: South African
Tune: South African
© 1984, Peace of Music Publishing AB, admin. by Walton Music Corp., a division of GIA Publications, Inc.

186 Holy God, We Praise Thy Name

1. Ho - ly God, we praise thy name;
2. Hark! the loud ce - les - tial hymn
3. Lo, the ap - os - tol - ic train
4. Ho - ly Fa - ther, Ho - ly Son,

Lord of all, we bow be - fore thee!
An - gel choirs a - bove are rais - ing;
Joins, the sa - cred name to hal - low;
Ho - ly Spir - it, Three we name thee;

All on earth thy scep - ter claim,
Cher - u - bim and Ser - a - phim,
Proph - ets swell the loud re - frain,
While in es - sence on - ly One,

All in heav'n a - bove a - dore thee;
In un - ceas - ing cho - rus prais - ing,
And the white - robed mar - tyrs fol - low;
Un - di - vid - ed God we claim thee;

In - fi - nite thy vast do - main,
Fill the heav'ns with sweet ac - cord:
And from morn to set - ting sun,
And a - dor - ing bend the knee,

Repeat ad lib.

Ev - er - last - ing is thy reign.
"Ho - ly, ho - ly, ho - ly Lord!"
Through the Church the song goes on.
While we own the mys - ter - y.

Text: *Grosser Gott, wir loben dich;* ascr. to Ignaz Franz, 1719–1790; tr. by Clarence Walworth, 1820–1900, alt.
Tune: GROSSER GOTT, 7 8 7 8 77; *Katholisches Gesangbuch*, Vienna, c.1774

In the Lord I'll Be Ever Thankful / 187
El Señor Es Mi Fortaleza

Ostinato Refrain

In the Lord I'll be ev-er thank-ful, in the Lord I will re-
El Se-ñor es mi for-ta - le - za, el Se-ñor es mi can-

joice! Look to God, do not be a-fraid; lift up your
ción. Él nos da la sal - va-ción. En él con-

voic-es, the Lord is near; lift up your voic-es, the Lord is near.
fí - o, no te - me - ré. En él con - fí - o, no te - me - ré.

Text: Taizé Community
Tune: Jacques Berthier, 1923–1994
© 1986, 1991, 2011, Les Presses de Taizé, GIA Publications, Inc., agent

Praise and Thanksgiving 188

Canon

1. Praise and thanks - giv - ing let ev - 'ry - one bring
2. All peo - ple, join us and sing out God's praise.
3. May we go out from here God's love to share.

Un - to our God for ev - 'ry good thing.
For ev - 'ry bless - ing your hap - py songs raise.
Sing - ing out God's love to all ev - 'ry - where.

All to - geth - er joy - ful - ly sing!

Text: St. 1, Alsatian traditional; tr. Edith Lovell Thomas, alt.; sts. 2, 3, Marie Post, © 1987, CRC Publications, alt.
Tune: LOBET UND PREISET, 10 9 8; Alsatian traditional; acc. by Robert J. Batastini, b.1942, © 2000, GIA Publications, Inc.

189 Jubilate, Servite / Raise a Song of Gladness

Canon

Ju - bi - lá - te De - o o - mnis ter - ra.
Raise a song of glad-ness, peo - ples of the earth.
Al Se - ñor a - cla - ma, tie - rra en - te - ra.

Sér - vi - te Dó - mi - no in lae - tí - ti - a.
Christ has come, bring - ing peace, joy to ev - 'ry heart.
Sír - ve - lo, dán - do - le gra - cias por su a - mor.

Al - le - lú - ia, al - le - lú - ia, in lae - tí - ti - a!
Al - le - lu - ia, al - le - lu - ia, joy to ev - 'ry heart!
¡A - le - lu - ya, a - le - lu - ya, gra - cias por su a - mor!

Al - le - lú - ia, al - le - lú - ia, in lae - tí - ti - a!
Al - le - lu - ia, al - le - lu - ia, joy to ev - 'ry heart!
¡A - le - lu - ya, a - le - lu - ya, gra - cias por su a - mor!

Text: Psalm 100, *Rejoice in God, all the earth, Serve the Lord with gladness*; Taizé Community, 1978
Tune: Jacques Berthier, 1923–1994
© 1979, 2011, Les Presses de Taizé, GIA Publications, Inc., agent

190 Rejoice in the Lord Always

Canon

Re - joice in the Lord al - ways, a - gain I say, re - joice! Re -

joice in the Lord al - ways, a - gain I say, re - joice! Re - joice! Re - joice! A -

Last time

gain I say, re - joice! Re - joice! Re - joice! A - gain I say, re - joice!

Text: Traditional
Tune: Traditional; acc. by Robert J. Batastini, b.1942, © 2000, GIA Publications, Inc.

Sing, Sing, Praise and Sing! 191

Refrain

Sing, sing, praise and sing! Hon - or God for ev - 'ry-thing.

Sing to God and let it ring. Sing and praise and sing!

Verses
D.C.

1. Clap your hands, lift your voice, Praise our God and re - joice!
2. Full of joy, full of rest, Through our God, we are blessed.
3. Cym - bal, harp, vi - o - lin, Tam - bou - rine, all join in!

Text: Elizabeth Syré, South Africa, alt.
Tune: SING, SING, PRAISE AND SING, 66 with refrain; South African traditional; adapt. by Elizabeth Syré; acc. by Robert N. Roth,
© 2000, GIA Publications, Inc.

I Just Came to Praise the Lord 192

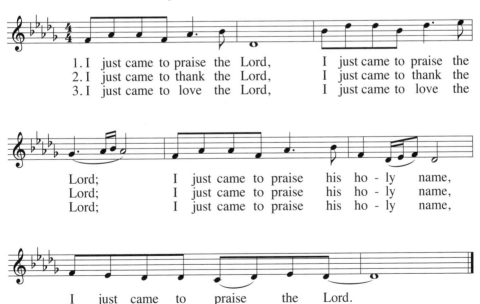

1. I just came to praise the Lord, I just came to praise the
2. I just came to thank the Lord, I just came to thank the
3. I just came to love the Lord, I just came to love the

Lord; I just came to praise his ho - ly name,
Lord; I just came to praise his ho - ly name,
Lord; I just came to praise his ho - ly name,

I just came to praise the Lord.
I just came to thank the Lord.
I just came to love the Lord.

Text: Wayne Romero, b.1950
Tune: Wayne Romero, b.1950
© 1975, New Spring Publishing, Inc. (admin. CapitolCMGPublishing.com)

193 Now Thank We All Our God

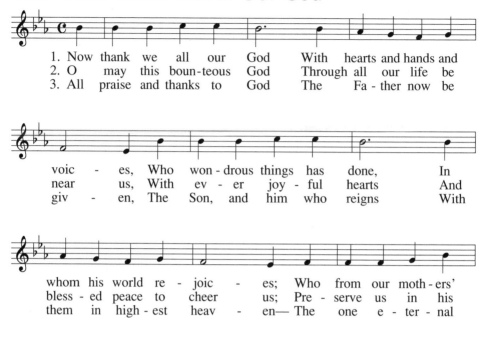

1. Now thank we all our God With hearts and hands and
2. O may this boun-teous God Through all our life be
3. All praise and thanks to God The Fa - ther now be

voic - es, Who won - drous things has done, In
near us, With ev - er joy - ful hearts And
giv - en, The Son, and him who reigns With

whom his world re - joic - es; Who from our moth-ers'
bless - ed peace to cheer us; Pre - serve us in his
them in high - est heav - en— The one e - ter - nal

arms Has blessed us on our way With
grace, And guide us in dis - tress, And
God, Whom earth and heav'n a - dore— For

count-less gifts of love, And still is ours to - day.
free us from all harm Till heav - en we pos - sess.
thus it was, is now, And shall be ev - er - more.

Text: *Nun danket alle Gott;* Martin Rinkhart, 1586–1649; tr. by Catherine Winkworth, 1827–1878, alt.
Tune: NUN DANKET, 6 7 6 7 6 6 6 6; Johann Crüger, 1598–1662; harm. by A. Gregory Murray, OSB, 1905–1992

Over My Head 194

Refrain

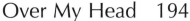

O-ver my head, I hear mu-sic in the air; o-ver my

head, I hear mu-sic in the air; o-ver my head, I hear

mu-sic in the air; there must be a God some-where.

Verses

1. Oh, when the world is si - lent,
2. And when I'm feel-ing lone-ly, I hear mu-sic in the air.
3. Now when I think on Je - sus,

oh, when the world is si - lent,
and when I'm feel-ing lone-ly, I hear mu-sic in the air.
now when I think on Je - sus,

oh, when the world is si - lent,
and when I'm feel-ing lone-ly, I hear mu-sic in the air.
now when I think on Je - sus,

D.C.

There must be a God some - where.

Text: African American spiritual
Tune: African American spiritual; arr. by John L. Bell, b.1949, © 1998, Iona Community, GIA Publications, Inc., agent

195 Shout for Joy

1. Shout for joy, loud and long, God be praised
2. By God's word all was made, Heav'n and earth,
3. Yet our pride makes us fall! So Christ came
4. Now has Christ tru - ly ris'n And his spir -
5. Rich and poor, we will sing, Hear - ing words
6. So we stand with our song! We will work

with a song! To the Lord we be - long— Chil - dren
light and shade, Na - ture's won - ders dis - played, We to
for us all— Not the right - eous to call— By his
it is giv'n To all those un - der heav'n Who will
that will ring, Bread and wine we will bring Here be -
all as one For the king - dom we long; We will

of our mak - er, God the great life - giv - er!
rule cre - a - tion From its first foun - da - tion.
cross and pas - sion, Bring - ing us sal - va - tion!
walk be - side him, Though they once de - nied him!
fore this ta - ble, With the weak and a - ble!
sing to - geth - er, With our God for - ev - er!

Shout for joy, joy, joy! Shout for joy, joy, joy!

God is love, God is light, God is ev - er - last - ing!

Text: Sts. 1–4, David Mowbray, b.1938, alt., © 1982, The Jubilate Group (admin. by Hope Publishing Company); sts. 5, 6, David Haas, b.1957, © 1993, GIA Publications, Inc.
Tune: PERSONENT HODIE, 666 66 with refrain; *Piae Cantiones*, Griefswald, 1582; harm. by Diana Kodner, b.1957, © 1992, GIA Publications, Inc.

Sing a New Song to the Lord 196

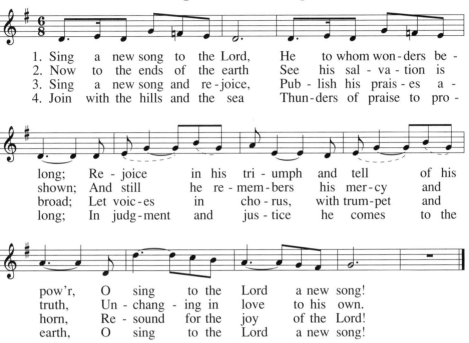

1. Sing a new song to the Lord, He to whom won-ders be -
2. Now to the ends of the earth See his sal - va - tion is
3. Sing a new song and re -joice, Pub - lish his prais - es a -
4. Join with the hills and the sea Thun-ders of praise to pro -

long; Re - joice in his tri - umph and tell of his
shown; And still he re - mem - bers his mer-cy and
broad; Let voic - es in cho - rus, with trum-pet and
long; In judg-ment and jus - tice he comes to the

pow'r, O sing to the Lord a new song!
truth, Un - chang - ing in love to his own.
horn, Re - sound for the joy of the Lord!
earth, O sing to the Lord a new song!

Text: Psalm 98; Timothy Dudley-Smith, b.1926, © 1973, Hope Publishing Company
Tune: CANTATE DOMINO (ONSLOW SQUARE), Irregular; David G. Wilson, b.1940, © 1973, The Jubilate Group
    (admin. by Hope Publishing Company)

Amen Siakudumisa / 197
Amen, We Praise Your Name

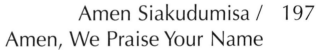

A - men si - a - ku - du - mi - sa. A - men si -
A - men, we praise your name, O God. A-men, we

a - ku - du - mi - sa. A - men ba - wo,
praise your name, O God. A - men, sing praise,

A - men ba - wo, A - men si - a - ku - du - mi - sa.
A - men, sing praise, A - men, we praise your name, O God.

Text: Amen. Praise the name of the Lord. South African traditional; English text, Hymnal Version
Tune: Attributed to S.C. Molefe as taught by George Mxadana; arr. by John L. Bell, b.1949, © 1990, Iona Community, GIA Publications, Inc., agent

198 Cantad al Señor / Sing Praise to the Lord

1. Can - tad al Se - ñor un cán - ti - co nue - vo.
2. Él es Cre - a - dor y due - ño de to - do.
3. Can - tad a Je - sús, por - que él es dig - no.
1. *Sing praise to the Lord, O sing out a new song.*
2. *Cre - a - tor of all, God rules with com - pas - sion.*
3. *Ac - claim Je - sus Christ as wor - thy of hon - or.*

Can - tad al Se - ñor un cán - ti - co nue - vo.
Él es Cre - a - dor y due - ño de to - do.
Can - tad a Je - sús, por - que él es dig - no.
Sing praise to the Lord, O sing out a new song.
Cre - a - tor of all, God rules with com - pas - sion.
Ac - claim Je - sus Christ as wor - thy of hon - or.

Can - tad al Se - ñor un cán - ti - co nue - vo.
Él es Cre - a - dor y due - ño de to - do.
Can - tad a Je - sús, por - que él es dig - no.
Sing praise to the Lord, O sing out a new song.
Cre - a - tor of all, God rules with com - pas - sion.
Ac - claim Je - sus Christ as wor - thy of hon - or.

¡Can - tad al Se - ñor, can - tad al Se - ñor!
Sing praise to the Lord, sing praise to our God.

4. Es él quien nos da su Espíritu Santo. . .
   ¡Cantad al Señor, cantad al Señor!

5. Cantad al Señor: "¡Amén, aleluya!". . .
   ¡Cantad al Señor, cantad al Señor!

4. Give thanks to the Lord,
   who sends us the Spirit. . .
Sing praise to the Lord,
   sing praise to our God.

5. Sing praise to the Lord,
   "Amen, Alleluia!". . .
Sing praise to the Lord,
   sing praise to our God.

Text: Traditional Brazilian; Spanish tr., anonymous, alt.; English tr. by Ronald F. Krisman, b.1946, © 2005, GIA Publications, Inc.
Tune: CANTAI AO SENHOR, 11 11 11 10; traditional Brazilian; harm. by Ronald F. Krisman, b.1946, © 2005, GIA Publications, Inc.

Lord, I Lift Your Name on High   199

Lord, I lift your name on high. Lord, I love to sing your prais-es. I'm so glad you're in my life. I'm so glad you came to save us. save us. You came from heav-en to earth to show the way. From the earth to the cross, my debt to pay. From the cross to the grave, from the grave to the sky; Lord, I lift your name on high. high. Lord, I lift your name on high. Lord, I lift your name on high. Lord, I lift your name on high.

Text: Rick Founds, b.1954
Tune: Rick Founds, b.1954; arr. by Ed Bolduc, b.1969

200   Canticle of the Turning

Verses

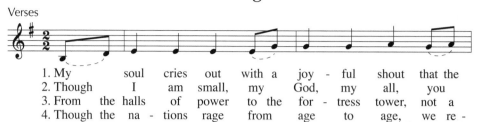

1. My   soul   cries   out   with a   joy - ful   shout   that the
2. Though   I   am   small,   my   God,   my   all,   you
3. From   the halls   of   power   to the   for - tress   tower,   not a
4. Though the   na - tions   rage   from   age   to   age,   we re -

God   of my heart   is   great,   And my   spir - it   sings   of the
work   great   things   in   me,   And your   mer - cy will last   from the
stone   will be   left   on   stone.   Let   the   king   be - ware   for your
mem - ber who holds   us   fast: God's   mer - cy   must   de -

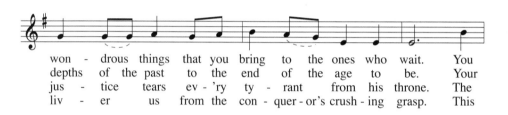

won - drous   things   that you   bring   to   the ones   who   wait.   You
depths   of the past   to the   end   of   the   age   to   be.   Your
jus - tice   tears   ev - 'ry   ty - rant   from   his   throne.   The
liv - er   us   from the   con - quer - or's crush - ing   grasp.   This

fixed   your   sight   on your   ser - vant's   plight,   and my
ver - y   name   puts the   proud   to   shame,   and to
hun - gry   poor   shall   weep   no   more,   for the
sav - ing   word   that our   fore - bears   heard   is   the

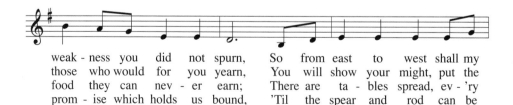

weak - ness you   did   not spurn,   So   from east   to   west shall my
those   who would   for   you yearn,   You   will show   your   might, put the
food   they can   nev - er   earn;   There are   ta - bles   spread, ev - 'ry
prom - ise which holds   us bound,   'Til   the spear   and   rod   can be

name   be   blest. Could the world   be a - bout   to   turn?
strong   to   flight,   for the world   is a - bout   to   turn.
mouth   be   fed,   for the world   is a - bout   to   turn.
crushed by   God,   who is turn - ing the world a -   round.

Refrain

My   heart   shall   sing   of the   day   you   bring.   Let   the

fires   of your jus - tice   burn.   Wipe a - way   all   tears,   for the

dawn   draws   near,   And the world   is a - bout   to   turn!

Text: Luke 1:46–58; Rory Cooney, b.1952
Tune: STAR OF THE COUNTY DOWN, Irregular with refrain; Irish melody; arr. by Rory Cooney, b.1952
© 1990, GIA Publications, Inc.

201 Sing Alleluia to the Lord

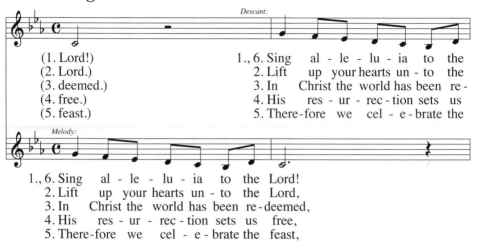

Descant:

(1. Lord!)
(2. Lord.)
(3. deemed.)
(4. free.)
(5. feast.)

1., 6. Sing   al - le - lu - ia   to   the
2. Lift   up your hearts un - to   the
3. In   Christ the world has been   re -
4. His   res - ur - rec - tion sets   us
5. There-fore   we   cel - e - brate the

Melody:

1., 6. Sing   al - le - lu - ia   to   the   Lord!
2. Lift   up   your hearts un - to   the   Lord,
3. In   Christ the   world has been   re - deemed,
4. His   res - ur - rec - tion sets   us   free,
5. There-fore   we   cel - e - brate the   feast,

Lord!
Lord.
deemed.
free.
feast.

Sing   al - le - lu - ia,

Sing   al - le - lu - ia   to   the   Lord!
lift   up   your hearts un - to   the   Lord.
in   Christ the world has   been   re - deemed.
his   res - ur - rec - tion   sets   us   free.
there - fore   we   cel - e - brate   the   feast.

al - le - lu - ia!

Sing al - le - lu - ia,   sing   al - le - lu - ia!

Sing   al - le -
Lift   up your
In   Christ the
His   res - ur -
There - fore   we

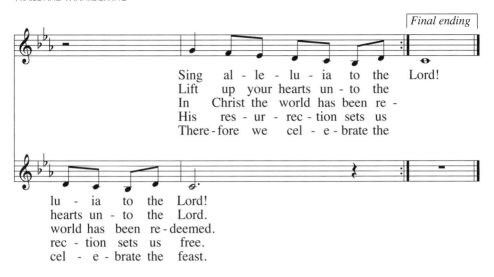

Final ending

Sing   al - le - lu - ia   to the   Lord!
Lift   up   your hearts un - to the
In   Christ the   world has been re -
His   res - ur - rec - tion sets us
There - fore we   cel - e - brate the

lu - ia   to the   Lord!
hearts un - to   the   Lord.
world has   been re - deemed.
rec - tion sets   us   free.
cel - e - brate the   feast.

Text: Sts. 1, 6 by Linda Stassen; sts. 2–5 from early Christian liturgy
Tune: Linda Stassen; acc. by Dale Grotenhuis
© 1974, Linda Stassen and New Song Creations

Know That God Is Good / Mungu ni Mwema   202

Know   that   God is   good.   Know that
Hal - le,   hal - le - lu - jah.   Hal - le,
Mun - gu   ni   mwe - ma.   Mun - gu

God is   good.   Know that   God is   good,
hal - le - lu - jah.   Hal - le,   hal - le - lu - jah,
ni   mwe - ma.   Mun - gu   ni   mwe - ma,

God   is   good,   God is   good.
hal - le - lu - jah,   hal - le - lu - jah.
ni   mwe - ma,   ni   mwe - ma.

Text: Anonymous
Tune: Anonymous; arr. by John L. Bell, b.1949, Iona Community, GIA Publications, Inc., agent

203 Ten Thousand Reasons

Refrain

Bless the Lord, O my soul, O my soul;
wor-ship your ho - ly name. Sing like nev-er be-fore,

Last time to Coda ⊕

O my soul; I'll wor-ship your ho - ly name.

Verses

1. The sun comes up, it's a new day dawn - ing;
2. You're rich in love, and you're slow to an - ger. Your
3. And on that day when my strength is fail - ing, the

it's time to sing your song a - gain. What - ev - er may
name is great and your heart is kind. For all your
end draws near, and my time has come; still, my

pass, and what - ev-er lies be - fore me, let me be
good-ness, I will keep on sing-ing— ten thou-sand
soul will sing your praise un - end-ing— ten thou-sand

D.C.

sing - ing when the eve - ning comes.
rea - sons for my heart to find.
years and then for - ev - er - more!

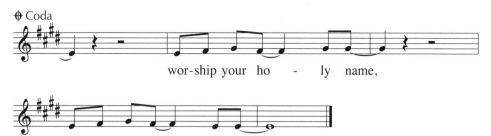

✠ Coda

wor-ship your ho - ly name,

wor-ship your ho - ly name.

Text: Jonas Myrin and Matt Redman
Tune: Jonas Myrin and Matt Redman
© 2011, Worshiptogether.com Songs/Sixsteps Music/Said and Done Music/Shout! Music Publishing/Thankyou Music
(admin. CapitolCMGPublishing.com)

Sing Our God Together 204

Refrain

Sing, O peo - ple, sing our God to - geth - er,

raise your voic - es: sing al - le - lu - ia!

Verses

Solo: All:

1. Sing with one an - oth - er: Sing the love that gave us breath!
2. Dance the steps of beau - ty: Dance the love that gave us breath!
3. Serve all those who suf - fer: Serve the love that gave us breath!
4. Teach the way of Je - sus: Teach the love that gave us breath!
5. Seek the chil - dren's wis-dom: Seek the love that gave us breath!

Solo: All: D.C.

Sing, each sis - ter, broth - er: Sing the God be - yond all death!
Dance, de - light and du - ty: Dance the God be - yond all death!
Serve, that love might con - quer: Serve the God be - yond all death!
Teach the way that frees us: Teach the God be - yond all death!
Seek God's way of free-dom: Seek the God be - yond all death!

Text: David Haas, b.1957, and Marty Haugen, b.1950
Tune: David Haas, b.1957, and Marty Haugen, b.1950
© 1993, GIA Publications, Inc.

205 Center of My Life

Refrain

O Lord,   you   are the   cen-ter   of my life:

I will al-ways praise   you,   I will al-ways serve   you,

I will   al - ways keep you   in   my   sight.

Verses 1–3

1. Keep me safe, O God,   I take ref-uge in you.   I
2. I   will bless the Lord who gives me   coun - sel,   who
3. And   so   my heart re - joic - es, my   soul is   glad;

say   to   the Lord, "You are   my   God.   My
e - ven at night di - rects my   heart.   I
e - ven in safe - ty shall my   bod-y rest.   For

hap - pi - ness   lies in you a - lone;   my
keep   the Lord   ev - er in my sight: since
you   will not leave   my   soul a - mong the dead,   nor

D.C.

hap - pi - ness   lies in   you a - lone."
he   is at my right   hand,   I shall stand   firm.
let   your be - lov - ed know de - cay.

Verse 4

4. You will show me the path of life, the
full - ness of joy in your pres - ence, at your right hand,

D.C.

at your right hand hap - pi - ness for ev - er.

Text: Psalm 16; verses trans. © 1963, The Grail, GIA Publications, Inc., agent; refrain, Paul Inwood, b.1947, © 1985, Paul Inwood
Tune: Paul Inwood, b.1947, © 1985, Paul Inwood
Published by OCP.

Jubilate Deo / In the Lord Rejoicing!   206

Canon

Ju - bi - la - te De - o, ju - bi - la - te
In   the   Lord re - joic - ing! Christ   is   ris - en

De - o, al - le - lu - ia!
from   the   dead!   Al - le - lu - ia!

Text: Psalm 100:1; tr. Taizé Community, 1990, © 1978, 1990, Les Presses de Taizé, GIA Publications, Inc., agent
Tune: Michael Praetorius, 1571–1621; acc. by Jacques Berthier, 1923–1994, © 1978, 1990, Les Presses de Taizé, GIA Publications, Inc., agent

207 Here I Am to Worship

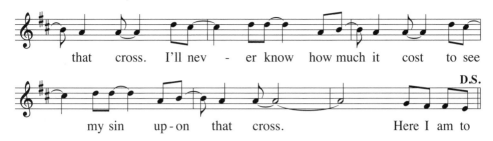

that cross. I'll nev - er know how much it cost to see

D.S.

my sin up - on that cross. Here I am to

Text: Tim Hughes
Tune: Tim Hughes
© 2001, Thankyou Music (admin. CapitolCMGPublishing.com)

When in Our Music God Is Glorified 208

1. When in our mu - sic God is glo - ri - fied,
2. How of - ten, mak - ing mu - sic, we have found
3. So has the Church, in lit - ur - gy and song,
4. And did not Je - sus sing a psalm that night
5. Let ev - 'ry in - stru - ment be tuned for praise!

And ad - o - ra - tion leaves no room for pride,
A new di - men - sion in the world of sound,
In faith and love, through cen - tu - ries of wrong,
When ut - most e - vil strove a - gainst the Light?
Let all re - joice who have a voice to raise!

It is as though the whole cre - a - tion cried:
As wor - ship moved us to a more pro - found
Borne wit - ness to the truth in ev - 'ry tongue: Al - le - lu -
Then let us sing, for whom he won the fight:
And may God give us faith to sing al - ways:

ia! Al - le - lu - ia! Al - le - lu - ia!

Text: Fred Pratt Green, 1903–2000, © 1972, Hope Publishing Company
Tune: MAYFLOWER, 10 10 10 with alleluias; Marty Haugen, b.1950, © 1989, GIA Publications, Inc.

209 Sing Out, Earth and Skies

Verses

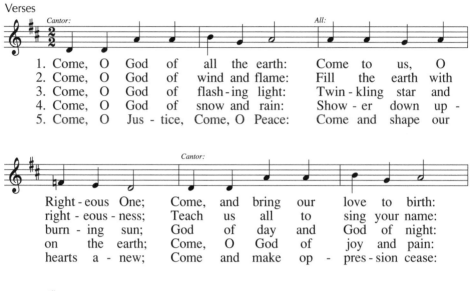

1. Come, O God of all the earth: Come to us, O
2. Come, O God of wind and flame: Fill the earth with
3. Come, O God of flash-ing light: Twin-kling star and
4. Come, O God of snow and rain: Show-er down up-
5. Come, O Jus-tice, Come, O Peace: Come and shape our

Right-eous One; Come, and bring our love to birth:
right-eous-ness; Teach us all to sing your name:
burn-ing sun; God of day and God of night:
on the earth; Come, O God of joy and pain:
hearts a-new; Come and make op - pres-sion cease:

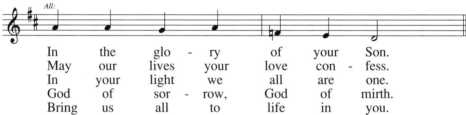

In the glo - ry of your Son.
May our lives your love con - fess.
In your light we all are one.
God of sor - row, God of mirth.
Bring us all to life in you.

Refrain

Sing out, earth and skies! Sing of the God who loves you!

Raise your joy-ful cries! Dance to the life a - round you!

Text: Marty Haugen, b.1950
Tune: SING OUT, 7 7 7 7 with refrain; Marty Haugen, b.1950
© 1985, GIA Publications, Inc.

All Creatures of Our God and King   210

1. All creatures of our God and King,
   Lift up your voice and with us sing:
   Al-le-lu-ia! Al-le-lu-ia!
   O burn-ing sun with gold-en beam
   And sil-ver moon with soft-er gleam:
   Al-le-lu-ia! Al-le-lu-ia!
   Al-le-lu-ia, al-le-lu-ia, al-le-lu-ia!

2. O rush-ing wind and breez-es soft,
   O clouds that ride the winds a-loft:
   Al-le-lu-ia! Al-le-lu-ia!
   O ris-ing morn, in praise re-joice,
   O lights of eve-ning, find a voice.
   Al-le-lu-ia! Al-le-lu-ia!
   Al-le-lu-ia, al-le-lu-ia, al-le-lu-ia!

3. O flow-ing wa-ters, pure and clear,
   Make mu-sic for your Lord to hear.
   Al-le-lu-ia! Al-le-lu-ia!
   O fire so mas-ter-ful and bright,
   Pro-vid-ing us with warmth and light,
   Al-le-lu-ia! Al-le-lu-ia!
   Al-le-lu-ia, al-le-lu-ia, al-le-lu-ia!

4. Dear moth-er earth, who day by day
   Un-folds rich bless-ings on our way,
   Al-le-lu-ia! Al-le-lu-ia!
   The fruits and flow'rs that ver-dant grow,
   Let them God's glo-ry al-so show.
   Al-le-lu-ia! Al-le-lu-ia!
   Al-le-lu-ia, al-le-lu-ia, al-le-lu-ia!

5. O ev-'ry one of ten-der heart,
   For-giv-ing oth-ers, take your part,
   Al-le-lu-ia! Al-le-lu-ia!
   All you who pain and sor-row bear,
   Praise God and cast on God your care.
   Al-le-lu-ia! Al-le-lu-ia!
   Al-le-lu-ia, al-le-lu-ia, al-le-lu-ia!

6. And you, most kind and gentle death,
   Waiting to hush our final breath,
      Alleluia! Alleluia!
   You lead to heav'n the child of God,
   Where Christ our Lord the way has trod.
      Alleluia! Alleluia!
      Alleluia, alleluia, alleluia!

7. Let all things their Creator bless,
   And worship God in humbleness,
      Alleluia! Alleluia!
   Oh praise the Father, praise the Son,
   And praise the Spirit, Three in One!
      Alleluia! Alleluia!
      Alleluia, alleluia, alleluia!

Text: *Laudato si, mi Signor;* Francis of Assisi, 1182-1226; tr. by William H. Draper, 1855-1933, alt.
Tune: LASST UNS ERFREUEN, LM with alleluias; *Geistliche Kirchengesänge,* 1623; harm. by Ralph Vaughan Williams, 1872-1958

211 All Things Bright and Beautiful

Refrain

All things bright and beau - ti - ful, All
crea - tures great and small, All things wise and
won - der - ful: The Lord God made them all.

Verses

1. Each lit - tle flow'r that o - pens, Each
2. The pur - ple - head - ed moun - tains, The
3. The cold wind in the win - ter, The
4. God gave us eyes to see them, And

lit - tle bird that sings, God made their glow - ing
riv - er run - ning by, The sun - set, and the
pleas - ant sum - mer sun, The ripe fruits in the
lips that we might tell How great is God Al -

D.C.

col - ors, God made their ti - ny wings.
morn - ing That bright - ens up the sky.
gar - den: God made them ev - 'ry one.
might - y, Who has made all things well.

Text: Cecil F. Alexander, 1818–1895, alt.
Tune: ROYAL OAK, 7 6 7 6 with refrain; English melody; adapt. by Martin Shaw, 1875–1958

For the Beauty of the Earth   212

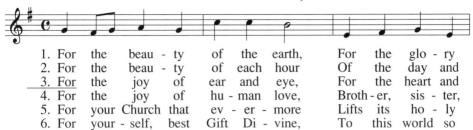

1. For the beau-ty of the earth, For the glo-ry
2. For the beau-ty of each hour Of the day and
3. For the joy of ear and eye, For the heart and
4. For the joy of hu-man love, Broth-er, sis-ter,
5. For your Church that ev-er-more Lifts its ho-ly
6. For your-self, best Gift Di-vine, To this world so

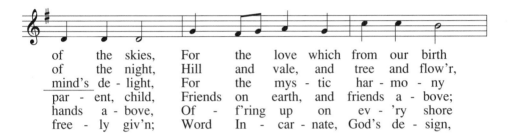

of the skies, For the love which from our birth
of the night, Hill and vale, and tree and flow'r,
mind's de-light, For the mys-tic har-mo-ny
par-ent, child, Friends on earth, and friends a-bove;
hands a-bove, Of-f'ring up on ev-'ry shore
free-ly giv'n; Word In-car-nate, God's de-sign,

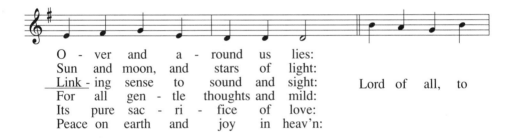

O-ver and a-round us lies:
Sun and moon, and stars of light:
Link-ing sense to sound and sight: Lord of all, to
For all gen-tle thoughts and mild:
Its pure sac-ri-fice of love:
Peace on earth and joy in heav'n:

you we raise This our hymn of grate-ful praise.

Text: Folliot S. Pierpont, 1835–1917, alt.
Tune: DIX, 7 7 7 7 with refrain; arr. from Conrad Kocher, 1786–1872, by William H. Monk, 1823–1889

213 Canticle of the Sun

Refrain

The heav-ens are tell-ing the glo-ry of God,

and all cre-a-tion is shout-ing for joy. Come,

dance in the for-est, come, play in the field, and

sing, sing to the glo-ry of the Lord.

Verses

1. Praise for the sun, the bring-er of day, He car-ries the
2. Praise for the wind that blows through the trees, The seas' might-y
3. Praise for the rain that wa-ters our fields, And bless-es our
4. Praise for the fire who gives us his light, The warmth of the
5. Praise for the earth who makes life to grow, The crea-tures you
6. Praise for our death that makes our life real, The knowl-edge of

light of the Lord in his rays; The moon and the stars who
storms, ˀ the gen-tl-est breeze; They blow where they will, they
crops ˀ so all the earth yields; From death un-to life her
sun ˀ to bright-en our night; He danc-es with joy, his
made ˀ to let your life show; The flow-ers and trees that
loss ˀ that helps us to feel; The gift of your-self, your

D.C.

light up the way Un-to your throne.
blow where they please To please the Lord.
mys-t'ry re-vealed Springs forth in joy.
spir-it so bright, He sings of you.
help us to know The heart of love.
pres-ence re-vealed To lead us home.

Text: *Altissimu, onnipotente bon Signore*; St. Francis of Assisi, 1181–1226; adapt. by Marty Haugen, b.1950
Tune: Marty Haugen, b.1950
© 1980, GIA Publications, Inc.

In the Bulb There Is a Flower   214

1. In the bulb there is a flow - er; In the
2. There's a song in ev - 'ry si - lence, Seek - ing
3. In our end is our be - gin - ning; In our

seed, an ap - ple tree; In co - coons, a hid - den
word and mel - o - dy; There's a dawn in ev - 'ry
time, in - fin - i - ty; In our doubt there is be -

prom - ise: But - ter - flies will soon be free! In the
dark - ness, Bring-ing hope to you and me. From the
liev - ing; In our life, e - ter - ni - ty. In our

cold and snow of win - ter There's a spring that waits to be,
past will come the fu - ture; What it holds, a mys - ter - y,
death, a res - ur - rec - tion; At the last, a vic - to - ry,

Un - re - vealed un - til its sea - son, Some - thing God a - lone can see.

Text: Natalie Sleeth, 1930–1992
Tune: PROMISE, 8 7 8 7 D; Natalie Sleeth, 1930–1992
© 1986, Hope Publishing Company

215 Touch the Earth Lightly

1. Touch the earth light - ly, Use the earth gen - tly,
2. We who en - dan - ger, Who cre - ate hun - ger,
3. Let there be green - ing, Birth from the burn - ing,
4. God of all liv - ing, God of all lov - ing,

Nour - ish the life of the world in our care:
A - gents of death for all crea - tures that live,
Wa - ter that bless - es, and air that is sweet,
God of the seed - ling, the snow, and the sun,

Gift of great won - der, Ours to sur - ren - der,
We who would fos - ter Clouds of dis - as - ter—
Health in God's gar - den, Hope in God's chil - dren,
Teach us, de - flect us, Christ re - con - nect us,

Trust for the chil - dren to - mor - row will bear.
God of our plan - et, fore - stall and for - give!
Re - gen - er - a - tion that peace will com - plete.
Us - ing us gen - tly, and mak - ing us one.

Text: Shirley Erena Murray, b.1931, © 1992, Hope Publishing Company
Tune: Tony E. Alonso, b.1980, © 2007, GIA Publications, Inc.

I Want to Walk as a Child of the Light 216

1. I want to walk as a child of the light.
2. I want to see the bright-ness of God.
3. I'm look - ing for the com - ing of Christ.

I want to fol - low Je - sus.
I want to look at Je - sus.
I want to be with Je - sus.

God set the stars to give light to the world. The
Clear sun of right - eous - ness shine on my path And
When we have run with pa - tience the race, We

star of my life is Je - sus.
show me the way to the Fa - ther.
shall know the joy of Je - sus.

In him there is no dark - ness at all. The

night and the day are both a - like. The

Lamb is the light of the cit - y of God.

Shine in my heart, Lord Je - sus.

Text: Ephesians 5:8–10, Revelation 21:23, John 12:46, 1 John 1:5, Hebrews 12:1; Kathleen Thomerson, b.1934, © 1970, 1975, Celebration
Tune: HOUSTON, 10 7 10 8 9 9 10 7; Kathleen Thomerson, b.1934, © 1970, 1975, Celebration; acc. by Robert J. Batastini, b.1942, © 1987, GIA
Publications, Inc.

217 This Little Light of Mine

1. This lit - tle light of mine   I'm gon-na let it shine,
2. Ev - 'ry - where I go,   I'm gon-na let it shine,
3. Je - sus gave it to me,   I'm gon-na let it shine,

This lit - tle light of mine   I'm gon-na let it shine;
Ev - 'ry - where I go,   I'm gon-na let it shine;
Je - sus gave it to me,   I'm gon-na let it shine;

This lit - tle light of mine   I'm gon - na let it shine,
Ev - 'ry - where I go,   I'm gon - na let it shine,
Je - sus gave it to me,   I'm gon - na let it shine,

Let it shine, let it shine, let it shine.
Let it shine, let it shine, let it shine.
Let it shine, let it shine, let it shine.

Text: Harry Dixon Loes, 1895–1965
Tune: Harry Dixon Loes, 1895–1965; harm by Horace Clarence Boyer, 1935–2009, © 1992

218 We Are Walking in the Light

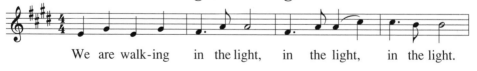

We are walk-ing in the light, in the light, in the light.

We are walk-ing in the light, in the light of God.

Text: Traditional
Tune: James E. Moore, Jr., b.1951, © 1987, GIA Publications, Inc.

Walk, Walk in the Light   219

Walk, walk in the light! we fol - low him as we
Walk, walk in the light! ʾ nev - er to hide it but to
and let our own light
we help each oth - er each and

hear his call.
let it shine.
shine so bright.   Walk, walk in the light!
ev - ʾry day.

Refrain

Walk, walk in the light!   Walk, walk in the light!

Walk, walk in the light;   walk in the light of the Lord!

D.C. 4.   To refrain | Final ending

Lord!   Lord!

Text: Traditional; verses by Carey Landry, © 1996
Tune: Traditional; arr. by Carey Landry and Jeophry Scott; acc. by Carl Rutterson, © 1996, Carey Landry
Published by OCP.

220 We Are Marching / Siyahamba / Marcharemos

We are march - ing* in the light of God,
Si - ya - hamb' e - ku - kha - nyen' kwen - khos',
Mar - cha - re - mos** a la luz de Dios,

1.
we are march - ing in the light of God.
si - ya - hamb' e - ku - kha - nyen' kwen - khos'.
mar - cha - re - mos a la luz de Dios.

2.
God.
khos'.
Dios.

march - ing in the light of, the light of God. We are
hamb' e - ku - kha - nyen' kwen, kha - nyen' kwen - khos'. Si - ya -
re - mos a la luz de, la luz de Dios. Mar - cha -

march - ing, Oo, we are
ham - ba, Oo, si - ya -
re - mos, Oo, mar - cha -

march - ing, march - ing, we are march - ing, march - ing, we are
ham - ba, ham - ba, si - ya - ham - ba, ham - ba, si - ya -
re - mos, jun - tos, mar - cha - re - mos jun - tos, mar - cha -

**Additional texts: dancing, singing, praying*
***Otros textos: bailaremos (a), cantaremos (en), rezaremos (en)*

God.
khos'.
Dios.

march-ing in the light of, the light of God. We are
hamb' e - ku - kha - nyen' kwen, kha - nyen' kwen - khos'. Si - ya -
re - mos a la luz de, la luz de Dios. Mar - cha -

march-ing,   Oo,   we are
ham - ba,   *Oo,*   *si - ya -*
re - mos,   Oo,   mar - cha -

march-ing,   march-ing, we are march-ing,   march-ing, we are
ham - ba,   ham - ba, si - ya - ham - ba,   ham - ba, si - ya -
re - mos   jun - tos, mar-cha - re - mos   jun - tos, mar-cha -

march - ing in the light of God.
hamb' e - ku - kha - nyen' kwen - khos'.
re - mos a la luz de Dios.

Text: South African; tr. hymnal version
Tune: SIYAHAMBA, Irregular; South African

221 We Are Called

1. Come! Live in the light! Shine with the
2. Come! O-pen your heart! Show your
3. Sing! Sing a new song! Sing of that

joy and the love of the Lord! We are called
mer-cy to all those in fear! We are called
great day when all will be one! God will reign,

to be light for the king - dom, to
to be hope for the hope - less so all
and we'll walk with each oth - er as

live in the free-dom of the cit-y of God!
ha-tred and blind-ness will be no more!
sis-ters and broth-ers u - nit-ed in love!

We are called to act with jus-tice, we are called to

love ten-der-ly, we are called to serve one an-oth-er,

to walk hum-bly with God!

Text: Micah 6:8; David Haas, b.1957
Tune: David Haas, b.1957
© 1988, GIA Publications, Inc.

As a Fire Is Meant for Burning   222

1. As a fire is meant for burn - ing With a
2. We are learn - ers; we are teach - ers; We are
3. As a green bud in the spring - time Is a

bright and warm - ing flame, So the Church is meant for
pil - grims on the way. We are seek - ers; we are
sign of life re - newed, So may we be signs of

mis - sion, Giv - ing glo - ry to God's name. As we
giv - ers; We are ves - sels made of clay. By our
one - ness Mid earth's peo - ples, man - y hued. As a

wit - ness to the gos - pel, We would
gen - tle, lov - ing ac - tions, We would
rain - bow lights the heav - ens When a

build a bridge of care, Join - ing hands a - cross the
show that Christ is light. In a hum - ble, lis - t'ning
storm is past and gone, May our lives re - flect the

na - tions, Find - ing neigh - bors ev - 'ry - where.
Spir - it, We would live to God's de - light.
ra - diance Of God's new and glor - ious dawn.

Text: Ruth Duck, b.1947, © 1992, GIA Publications, Inc.
Tune: BEACH SPRING, 8 7 8 7 D; *The Sacred Harp*, 1844; harm. by Marty Haugen, b.1950, © 1985, GIA Publications, Inc.

223 City of God

Verses 1, 2

1. A-wake from your slum-ber! A - rise from your
2. We are sons of the morn-ing; we are daugh-ters of

sleep! A new day is dawn - ing
day. The One who has loved us

for all those who weep. The peo - ple in
has bright-ened our way. The Lord of all

dark - ness have seen a great light. The Lord of our
kind - ness has called us to be a light for his

long - ing has con-quered the night.
peo - ple to set their hearts free.

℅ Refrain

Let us build the cit-y of God. May our tears be

turned in - to danc - ing! For the Lord, our light and our

love, has turned the night in - to day!

Text: Dan Schutte, b.1947.
Tune: Dan Schutte, b.1947; acc. by Robert J. Batastini, b.1942
© 1981, OCP

224 Blest Are They / Benditos los Pobres

Verses 1–3

1. Blest are they, the poor in spir - it;
2. Blest are they, the low - ly ones;
3. Blest are they who show mer - cy;

1. *Ben - di - tos los po - bres en el es - pí - ri - tu,*
2. *Ben - di - tos son los pa - cien - tes,*
3. *Ben - di - tos son los com - pa - si - vos,*

theirs is the king - dom of God.
they shall in - her - it the earth.
mer - cy shall be theirs.

su - yo_es el rei - no de Dios. Di -
he - re - da - rán la tie - rra. Di -
ob - ten - drán pie - dad. Di -

Blest are they, full of sor - row;
Blest are they who hun - ger and thirst;
Blest are they, the pure of heart;

cho - sos son los que llo - ran,
cho - sos los que tie - nen sed y ham - bre,
cho - sos los lim - pios de co - ra - zón,

they shall be con - soled.
they shall have their fill.
they shall see God.

re - ci - bi - rán con - sue - lo.
por - que se - rán sa - cia - dos.
e - llos ve - rán a Dios.

Refrain

Re - joice and be glad! Bless-ed are
¡A - lé - gren-se y con - tén - ten - se! ¡Son los ben -

you, ho-ly are you! Re-joice and be glad!
di - tos de nues-tro Dios! ¡A - lé-gren-se y con -tén-ten-se!

Yours is the king-dom of God!
¡Su - yo_es el rei - no de Dios!

Verses 4, 5

4. ⸰ Blest are they who seek peace;
5. ⸰ Blest are you who suf - fer hate,
4. Ben - di - tos los que por la paz tra - ba-jan,
5. Ben - di - tos son los per - se - gui-dos,

they are the chil - dren of God.
all be - cause of me. Re -
e - llos son hi - jos de Dios. Di -
to - do por cau - sa mí - a. ¡A -

Blest are they who suf - fer in faith; the
joice and be glad, yours is the king - dom;
cho - sos los que por la fe su - fren,
lé - gren - se! Su re - com - pen - sa

To refrain

glo - ry of God is theirs.
shine for all to see.
su - ya_es la glo - ria de Dios.
gran - de_en el cie - lo se - rá.

Text: Matthew 5:3–12; David Haas, b.1957, tr. by Ronald F. Krisman, b.1946
Tune: David Haas, b.1957; vocal arr. by David Haas and Michael Joncas, b.1951

225 Freedom Is Coming

O free - dom, O

(know.) Free - dom is

free - dom, O free - dom,

com - ing, free - dom is com - ing,

free - dom is com - ing, O yes, I

yes, I know, O yes, I know,

know, O yes, I know,

O yes, I know,

O yes, I know, O yes, I

1. O 2.

know, O yes, I yes, I know.

O Jesus, O Jesus,
O Jesus, Jesus is coming,
O yes, I know,

Text: South African
Tune: South African
© 1984, Peace of Music Publishing AB, admin. by Walton Music Corp., a division of GIA Publications, Inc.

God Has Chosen Me 226

Verses

1. God has cho - sen me, God has cho - sen me To
2. God has cho - sen me, God has cho - sen me To
3. God is call - ing me, God is call - ing me In

bring good news to the poor. God has cho - sen me,
set a - light a new fire. God has cho - sen me,
all whose cry is un - heard. God is call - ing me,

God has cho - sen me To bring new sight to those
God has cho - sen me To bring to birth a new
God is call - ing me To raise up the voice with no

search-ing for light: God has cho - sen me, cho - sen me:
king - dom on earth: God has cho - sen me, cho - sen me:
pow - er or choice: God is call - ing me, call - ing me:

Refrain

And to tell the world that God's king-dom is near, To re -

move op - pres-sion and break down fear, Yes, God's time is near,

God's time is near, God's time is near, God's time is near.

Text: Bernadette Farrell, b.1957
Tune: Bernadette Farrell, b.1957
© 1990, Bernadette Farrell. Published by OCP.

227 I Danced in the Morning

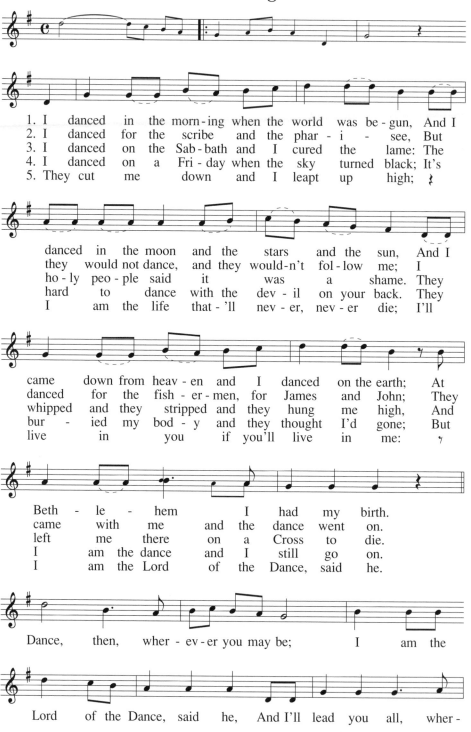

1. I danced in the morn-ing when the world was be-gun, And I
2. I danced for the scribe and the phar - i - see, But
3. I danced on the Sab-bath and I cured the lame: The
4. I danced on a Fri - day when the sky turned black; It's
5. They cut me down and I leapt up high;

danced in the moon and the stars and the sun, And I
they would not dance, and they would-n't fol - low me; I
ho - ly peo - ple said it was a shame. They
hard to dance with the dev - il on your back. They
I am the life that - 'll nev - er, nev - er die; I'll

came down from heav - en and I danced on the earth; At
danced for the fish - er - men, for James and John; They
whipped and they stripped and they hung me high, And
bur - ied my bod - y and they thought I'd gone; But
live in you if you'll live in me:

Beth - le - hem I had my birth.
came with me and the dance went on.
left me there on a Cross to die.
I am the dance and I still go on.
I am the Lord of the Dance, said he.

Dance, then, wher - ev-er you may be; I am the

Lord of the Dance, said he, And I'll lead you all, wher -

ev - er you may be, And I'll lead you all in the Dance, said he.

Text: Sydney Carter, 1915–2004, © 1963, Stainer & Bell, Ltd., London, England. (Admin. by Hope Publishing Company)
Tune: LORD OF THE DANCE, Irregular with refrain; adapted from a traditional Shaker melody by Sydney Carter, 1915–2004, © 1963,
   Stainer & Bell, Ltd., London, England. (Admin. by Hope Publishing Company)

Guide My Feet   228

1. Guide   my   feet   while I run this race.
2. I'm   your   child   while I run this race.
3. Hold   my   hand   while I run this race.
4. Stand   by   me   while I run this race.

Guide   my   feet   while I run this race.
I'm   your   child   while I run this race.
Hold   my   hand   while I run this race.
Stand   by   me   while I run this race.

Guide   my   feet   while I run this race,
I'm   your   child   while I run this race,
Hold   my   hand   while I run this race,   For I
Stand   by   me   while I run this race,

don't want   to   run   this   race   in   vain!

Text: African American spiritual
Tune: African American spiritual; acc. by Robert J. Batastini, b.1942, © 2000, GIA Publications, Inc.

229 I Say "Yes," Lord / Digo "Sí," Señor

Verses

(Invocation)

I say "Yes," my Lord. I say
Di - go "Sí," Se - ñor. Di - go

Refrain

"Yes," my Lord. I say "Yes," my Lord, in
"Sí," Se - ñor. Di - go "Sí," Se - ñor, en

all the good times, through all the bad times, I say
tiem - pos ma - los, en tiem - pos bue - nos, Di - go

"Yes," my Lord, to ev - 'ry word you speak.
"Sí," Se - ñor, a to - do lo que ha - blas.

Text: Donna Peña, b.1955
Tune: Donna Peña, b.1955; arr. by Marty Haugen, b.1950
© 1989, GIA Publications, Inc.

230 The Kingdom of God / El Reino de Dios

Ostinato Refrain

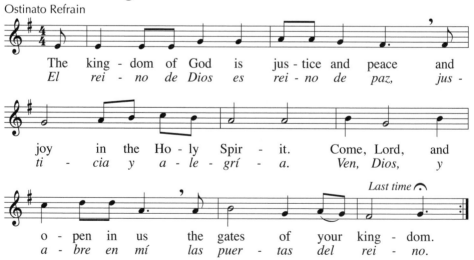

The king - dom of God is jus - tice and peace and
El rei - no de Dios es rei - no de paz, jus -

joy in the Ho - ly Spir - it. Come, Lord, and
ti - cia y a - le - grí - a. Ven, Dios, y

Last time

o - pen in us the gates of your king - dom.
a - bre en mí las puer - tas del rei - no.

Text: Taizé Community
Tune: Taizé Community
© 2001, 2011, Les Presses de Taizé, GIA Publications, Inc., agent

Here I Am, Lord 231

Verses

1. I, the Lord of sea and sky, I have heard my
2. I, the Lord of snow and rain, I have borne my
3. I, the Lord of wind and flame, I will tend the

peo - ple cry. All who dwell in dark and sin
peo - ple's pain. I have wept for love of them.
poor and lame. I will set a feast for them.

My hand will save. I, who made the
They turn a - way. I will break their
My hand will save. Fin-est bread I

stars of night, I will make their dark-ness bright.
hearts of stone, Give them hearts for love a - lone.
will pro - vide Till their hearts be sat - is - fied.

Who will bear my light to them? Whom shall I send?
I will speak my word to them. Whom shall I send?
I will give my life to them. Whom shall I send?

Refrain

Here I am, Lord. Is it I, Lord? I have heard you

call-ing in the night. I will go, Lord, if you

lead me. I will hold your peo - ple in my heart.

Text: Isaiah 6; Dan Schutte, b.1947
Tune: HERE I AM, LORD, 77 7 4 D with refrain; Dan Schutte, b.1947; arr. by Michael Pope, SJ, and John Weissrock
© 1981, OCP

232 Jesu, Jesu / Jesús, Jesús

Refrain

Je - su, Je - su, fill us with your love, show
Je - sús, Je - sús, en - sé - ña - nos tú a_a -

us how to serve the neigh - bors we have from you.
mar y ser - vir al pró - ji - mo ya a - quí.

Verses

1. Kneels at the feet of his friends, Si - lent - ly wash - es their
2. Neigh - bors are wealth-y and poor, Var - ied in col - or and
3. These are the ones we should serve, These are the ones we should
4. Kneel at the feet of our friends, Si - lent - ly wash - ing their

1. *Te_a - rro - di - llas-te_a los pies De tus a - mi - gos, Se -*
2. *Po - bres y ri - cos se - rán, De to - da ra - za_y co -*
3. *Hoy les que - re - mos ser - vir, Hoy les que - re - mos a -*
4. *Nues - tra ro - di - lla do - blar Y_a - sí sus pies la -*

D.C.

feet, Mas - ter who pours out him - self for them.
race, Neigh - bors are near - by and far a - way.
love: All these are neigh - bors to us and you.
feet: This is the way we should live with you.

ñor; Se los la - vas-te_en se - ñal de_a - mor.
lor, De to - do pue - blo_y na - ción tam - bién.
mar; So - mos i - gua - les, Je - sús, en ti.
var, Es el man - da - to que Dios nos da.

Text: Tom Colvin, 1925–2000; tr. by Felicia Fina, alt.
Tune: CHEREPONI, 7 7 9 with refrain; Ghanian folk song; adapt. by Tom Colvin, 1925–2000; acc. by Jane M. Marshall, b.1924
© 1969, arr. and trans. © 1982, Hope Publishing Company

Lord, You Give the Great Commission 233

1. Lord, you give the great com-mis-sion: "Heal the sick and
2. Lord, you call us to your serv-ice: "In my name bap -
3. Lord, you make the com-mon ho - ly: "This my bod - y,
4. Lord, you show us love's true meas-ure: "Fa - ther, what they
5. Lord, you bless with words as - sur - ing: "I am with you

preach the word." Lest the Church ne - glect its mis - sion
tize and teach." That the world may trust your prom - ise,
this my blood." Let us all, for earth's true glo - ry,
do, for - give." Yet we hoard as pri - vate treas - ure
to the end." Faith and hope and love re - stor - ing,

And the Gos - pel go un-heard, Help us wit - ness
Life a - bun - dant meant for each, Give us all new
Dai - ly lift life heav - en - ward, Ask - ing that the
All that you so free - ly give. May your care and
May we serve as you in - tend, And, a - mid the

to your pur - pose With re - newed in - teg - ri - ty;
fer - vor, draw us Clos - er in com - mun - i - ty;
world a - round us Share your chil-dren's lib - er - ty;
mer - cy lead us To a just so - ci - e - ty;
cares that claim us, Hold in mind e - ter - ni - ty;

With the Spir-it's gifts em-pow'r us For the work of min-is-try.

Text: Jeffery Rowthorn, b.1934, © 1978, Hope Publishing Company
Tune: HYMN TO JOY, 8 7 8 7 D; arr. from Ludwig van Beethoven, 1770–1827, by Edward Hodges, 1796–1867

234   When We Are Living / Pues Si Vivimos

1. When we are liv - ing, we are in Christ
2. While we are liv - ing, we have fruit to
3. When sad or hurt - ing, when we feel a -
4. Through-out this wide world man - y peo - ple

1. Pues si vi - vi - mos, pa - ra él vi -
2. En es - ta vi - da fru - tos hay que
3. En la tris - te - za y en el do -
4. En es - te mun - do por do - quier ha -

Je - sus, And when we die,
bear. Good works of serv - ice:
lone, When glimps - ing beau - ty,
mourn, Seek-ing con - so - la - tion

vi - mos; Y si mo - ri - mos,
dar, Y bue - nas o - bras
lor, En la be - lle - za
brá Gen - te que llo - ra

we re - main in him. Both in our
these are ours to share. If we are
and when love is known: Both in our
for their sor - rows borne; And when we

pa - ra él mo - ri - mos. Se - a que vi -
he - mos de o - fren - dar. Se - a ya que
y en el a - mor, Se - a que su -
y sin con - so - lar. Se - a que a - yu -

liv - ing, and in our dy - ing,
giv - ing or are re - ceiv - ing,
suf - f'ring and our re - joic - ing,
help them or when we feed them,

va - mos o que mu - ra - mos,
de - mos o que re - ci - ba - mos,
fra - mos o que go - ce - mos,
de - mos o que a - li - men - te - mos,

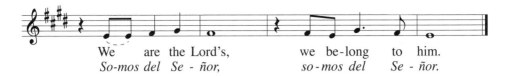

We are the Lord's, we be-long to him.
So-mos del Se - ñor, so-mos del Se - ñor.

Text: Verse 1, Romans 14:8; traditional Mexican; vss. 2–4, Roberto Escamilla, b.1931, © 1983, Abingdon Press; tr. by Ronald F. Krisman, b.1946, © 2004, Abingdon Press
Tune: SOMOS DEL SEÑOR, Irregular; traditional Mexican; arr. by Ronald F. Krisman, b.1946, © 2004, GIA Publications, Inc.

Let Us Talents and Tongues Employ   235

1. Let us tal - ents and tongues em - ploy, Reach-ing out with a
2. Christ is a - ble to make us one, At the ta - ble he
3. Je - sus calls us in, sends us out Bear - ing fruit in a

shout of joy: Bread is bro - ken, the wine is poured,
sets the tone, Teach - ing peo - ple to live to bless,
world of doubt, Gives us love to tell, bread to share:

Christ is spo - ken and seen and heard. Je - sus lives a-gain,
Love in word and in deed ex - press.
God (Im - man - u - el) ev - 'ry - where!

earth can breathe a-gain, pass the Word a-round: loaves a-bound!

Text: Fred Kaan, 1929–2009
Tune: LINSTEAD, LM with refrain; Jamaican folk melody; adapt. by Doreen Potter, 1925–1980
© 1975, Hope Publishing Company

236 'Tis the Gift to Be Simple

'Tis the gift to be sim-ple, 'tis the gift to be free, 'Tis the

gift to come down where we ought to be; And when we find our -

selves in the place just right, 'Twill be in the val - ley of

love and de - light. When true sim - plic - i - ty is gained, To

bow and to bend we shan't be a-shamed; To turn, turn, will

be our de-light, Till by turn - ing, turn - ing we come round right.

Text: Joseph Brackett, Jr., 1797–1882
Tune: SIMPLE GIFTS, 13 11 11 11 with refrain; Joseph Brackett, Jr., 1797–1882; acc. Margaret W. Mealy, b.1922, © 1984

Now I Know 237

Cantor:

1. Now I know, by God's own grace,
2. So with hope, go out in peace,

All:

1. Now I know, by
2. So with hope, go

all of us are the
bring good news to all

God's own grace, all of us
out in peace, bring good news

chil - dren of God.
peo - ple on earth.

are the chil - dren of God.
to all peo - ple on earth.

Text: St. 1, Barnabas Mam, st. 2, Eang Chhun, trans. by I-to Loh, b.1936, and James Minshin
Music: Traditional Cambodian
© 1990, GIA Publications, Inc.

238 The Summons

1. Will you come and fol - low me If I but
2. Will you leave your - self be - hind If I but
3. Will you let the blind - ed see If I but
4. Will you love the "you" you hide If I but
5. Lord, your sum - mons ech - oes true When you but

call your name? Will you go where
call your name? Will you care for
call your name? Will you set the
call your name? Will you quell the
call my name. Let me turn and

you don't know And nev - er be the same?
cruel and kind And nev - er be the same?
pris - 'ners free And nev - er be the same?
fear in - side And nev - er be the same?
fol - low you And nev - er be the same.

Will you let my love be shown, Will you
Will you risk the hos - tile stare Should your
Will you kiss the lep - er clean, And do
Will you use the faith you've found To re -
In your com - pa - ny I'll go Where your

let my name be known, Will you let my
life at - tract or scare? Will you let me
such as this un - seen, And ad - mit to
shape the world a - round, Through my sight and
love and foot - steps show. Thus I'll move and

life be grown In you and you in me?
an - swer prayer In you and you in me?
what I mean In you and you in me?
touch and sound In you and you in me?
live and grow In you and you in me.

Text: John L. Bell, b.1949, © 1987, Iona Community, GIA Publications, Inc., agent
Tune: KELVINGROVE, 7 6 7 6 777 6; Scottish melody; arr. by John L. Bell, b.1949, © 1987, Iona Community, GIA Publications, Inc., agent

Bring Forth the Kingdom 239

Verses

Cantor:

1. You are salt for the earth, O peo - ple:
2. You are a light on the hill, O peo - ple:
3. You are a seed of the Word, O peo - ple:
4. We are a blest and a pil - grim peo - ple:

All: Cantor:

Salt for the King-dom of God! Share the fla - vor of
Light for the Cit - y of God! Shine so ho - ly and
Bring forth the King-dom of God! Seeds of mer - cy and
Bound for the King-dom of God! Love our jour-ney and

All:

life, O peo - ple: Life in the King-dom of God!
bright, O peo - ple: Shine for the King-dom of God!
seeds of jus - tice, Grow in the King-dom of God!
love our home-land: Love is the King-dom of God!

Refrain

Bring forth the King-dom of mer - cy, Bring forth the

King-dom of peace; Bring forth the King-dom of jus - tice,

Bring forth the Cit - y of God!

Text: Marty Haugen, b.1950
Tune: Marty Haugen, b.1950
© 1986, GIA Publications, Inc.

240 Go Make a Difference

Refrain

Go make a dif - f'rence. We can make a dif - f'rence.

Go make a dif - f'rence in the world.

Go make a dif - f'rence. We can make a dif - f'rence.

To verses | *To repeat refrain*

Go make a dif - f'rence in the world.

Verses 1, 2

1. We are the salt of the earth, called to let the peo - ple
2. We are the hands of Christ reach-ing out to those in

see the love of God in you and me.
need, the face of God for all to see.

We are the light of the world, not to be hid - den but be
We are the spir - it of hope; we are the voice of

D.C.

seen. Go make a dif - f'rence in the world.
peace. Go make a dif - f'rence in the world.

Verse 3

3. So let your love shine on, let it shine for all to see.
Go make a dif - f'rence in the world. And the
spir - it of Christ will be with us as we go.

D.C.

Go make a dif -f'rence in the world.

Text: Matthew 5:13–16; Steve Angrisano, b.1965, and Tom Tomaszek, b.1950
Tune: Steve Angrisano, b.1965, and Tom Tomaszek, b.1950; acc. by Rick Modlin, b.1966
© 1997, 1998, Steve Angrisano and Thomas N. Tomaszek. Published by Spirit & Song, a div. of OCP.

We Walk by Faith   241

1., 5. We walk by faith, and not by sight; No
2. We may not touch his hands and side, Nor
3. Help then, O Lord, our un - be - lief; And
4. That, when our life of faith is done, In

gra - cious words we hear   From him who spoke as
fol - low where he trod;   But in his prom - ise
may our faith a - bound   To call on you when
realms of clear - er light   We may be - hold you

none e'er spoke;   But we be - lieve him near.
we re - joice,   And cry, "My Lord and God!"
you are near,   And seek where you are found:
as you are,   With full and end - less sight.

Text: Henry Alford, 1810–1871, alt.
Tune: SHANTI, CM; Marty Haugen, b.1950, © 1984, GIA Publications, Inc.

242 Lead Me, Lord

Verses

1. Bless - ed are the poor in spir - it, long - ing for their
2. Bless - ed are the mer - ci - ful, for mer - cy shall be
3. Blest are they who through their life - times sow the seeds of

Lord, for God's com - ing king - dom shall be
theirs, and the pure in heart shall see their
peace, all will call them chil - dren of the

theirs. Bless - ed are the
God. Blest are they whose
Lord. Blest are you, though

sor - row - ing, for they shall be con - soled,
hun - ger on - ly ho - li - ness can fill,
per - se - cu - ted in your ho - ly life,

and the meek shall come to rule the world.
for I say they shall be sat - is - fied.
for in heav - en, great is your re - ward.

Refrain

Lead me, Lord, lead me, Lord, by the light of

truth to seek and to find the nar - row way.

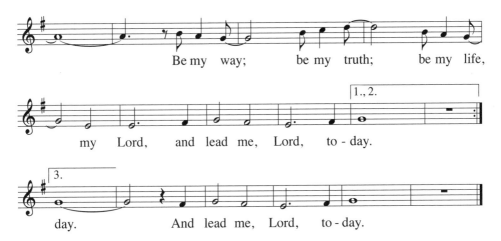

Be my way; be my truth; be my life, my Lord, and lead me, Lord, to-day.

day. And lead me, Lord, to-day.

Text: Matthew 5:3–12, 7:7, 13; John 14:6; adapt. by John D. Becker
Tune: John D. Becker
© 1987, John D. Becker. Published by OCP.

The Servant Song 243

1., 6. Will you let me be your ser-vant, Let me be as
2. We are pil-grims on a jour-ney, We are trav-'lers
3. I will hold the Christ-light for you In the night-time
4. I will weep when you are weep-ing; When you laugh I'll
5. When we sing to God in heav-en We shall find such

Christ to you; Pray that I may have the grace to
on the road; We are here to help each oth-er
of your fear; I will hold my hand out to you,
laugh with you. I will share your joy and sor-row
har-mo-ny, Born of all we've known to-geth-er

Let you be my ser - vant, too.
Walk the mile and bear the load.
Speak the peace you long to hear.
'Til we've seen this jour - ney through.
Of Christ's love and ag - o - ny.

Text: Richard Gillard, b.1953
Tune: Richard Gillard, b.1953; harm. by Betty Pulkingham, b.1929
© 1977, Universal Music—Brentwood Benson Publishing (admin. CapitolCMGPublishing.com)

244 Lord, When You Came / Pescador de Hombres

Verses

1. Lord, when you came to the sea - shore
2. Lord, you knew what my boat car - ried:
3. Lord, have you need of my la - bor,
4. Lord, send me where you would have me,

1. Tú has ve - ni - do_a la_o - ri - lla,
2. Tú sa - bes bien lo que ten - go;
3. Tú ne - ce - si - tas mis ma - nos,
4. Tú, pes - ca - dor de_o - tros la - gos,

You weren't seek - ing the wise or the
Nei - ther mon - ey nor weap - ons for
Hands for serv - ice, a heart made for
To a vil - lage, or heart of the

No_has bus - ca - do ni_a sa - bios, ni_a
En mi bar - ca no_hay o - ro ni_es -
Mi can - san - cio que_a o - tros des -
An - sia_e - ter - na de al - mas que_es-

wealth - y, But on - ly ask - ing
fight - ing, But nets for fish - ing,
lov - ing, My arms for lift - ing
cit - y; I will re - mem - ber

ri - cos; Tan só - lo quie - res
pa - das, Tan só - lo re - des
can - se, A - mor que quie - ra
pe - ran, A - mi - go bue - no,

that I might fol - low.
my dai - ly la - bor.
the poor and bro - ken?
that you are with me.

que yo te si - ga.
y mi tra - ba - jo.
se - guir a - man - do.
que_a - sí me lla - mas.

Refrain

O Lord, in my eyes you were gaz - ing,
Se - ñor, me_has mi - ra - do_a los o - jos,

Kind-ly smil - ing, my name you were
Son - ri - en - do has di - cho mi

say - ing; All I treas - ured,
nom - bre; En la_a - re - na

I have left on the sand there; Close to
he de - ja - do mi bar - ca; Jun - to_a

you, I will find oth - er seas.
ti bus - ca - ré o - tro mar.

Text: *Pescador de Hombres*, Cesáreo Gabaráin, 1936–1991; tr. by Rev. Willard F. Jabusch, b.1930
Tune: PESCADOR DE HOMBRES, 8 10 10 with refrain; Cesáreo Gabaráin, 1936–1991; acc. by Diana Kodner, b.1957
© 1979, 1987, 1989, Cesáreo Gabaráin. Published by OCP.

Ubi Caritas / Where True Charity / 245
Donde Hay Amor

Refrain

U - bi cá - ri - tas et a - mor,
Where true char - i - ty and love a - bide,
Don - de hay a - mor y ca - ri - dad,

u - bi cá - ri - tas De - us i - bi est.
God is dwell-ing there; God is dwell-ing there.
don - de hay a - mor Dios a - llí es - tá.

Text: 1 Corinthians 13:2–8, 13; *Where charity and love are found, God is there;* Taizé Community, 1978
Tune: Jacques Berthier, 1923–1994
© 1979, 2009, 2011, Les Presses de Taizé, GIA Publications, Inc., agent

246 You Are Mine / Contigo Estoy

Verses

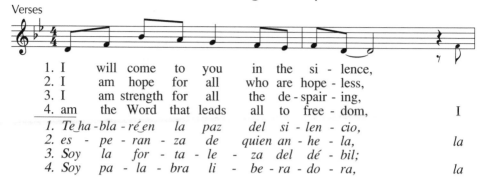

1. I will come to you in the si - lence,
2. I am hope for all who are hope - less,
3. I am strength for all the de - spair - ing,
4. am the Word that leads all to free - dom, I

1. Te_ha - bla - ré_en la paz del si - len - cio,
2. es - pe - ran - za de quien an - he - la, la
3. Soy la for - ta - le - za del dé - bil;
4. Soy pa - la - bra li - be - ra - do - ra, la

I will lift you from all your fear.
I am eyes for all who long to see. In the
heal - ing for the ones who dwell in shame.
am the peace the world can - not give.

y del mie - do te li - bra - ré. Mi
vis - ta de los que no pue - den ver. Los
al a - ver - gon - za - do_e - xal - ta - ré. Tu
paz que_el mun - do no pue - de dar.

You will hear my voice, I claim you as my choice, be
shad - ows of the night, I will be your light,
All the blind will see, the lame will all run free, and
I will call your name, em - brac - ing all your pain. Stand

voz es - cu - cha - rás, y mí - o tú se - rás.
Con in - ten - si - dad bri - lla - ré_en la_os - cu - ri - dad.
cie - gos ve - rán, los li - sia - dos co - rre - rán. Mi
nom - bre lla - ma - ré; tu llan - to to - ma - ré. Le -

still and know I am here. (To verse 2)
come and rest in me. (To refrain)
all will know my name. (To refrain)
up, now walk, and live! (To refrain)

Jun - to a ti es - ta - ré. (A la estrofa 2) 2. Soy
Tu des - can - so quie - ro ser. (Al estribillo)
nom - bre re - ve - la - ré. (Al estribillo)
ván - ta - te a ca - mi - nar. (Al estribillo)

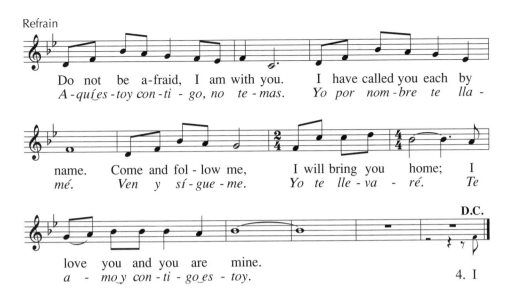

Refrain

Do not be a-fraid, I am with you. I have called you each by
A - quíes - toy con - ti - go, no te - mas. *Yo por nom - bre te lla -*

name. Come and fol - low me, I will bring you home; I
mé. *Ven y sí - gue - me.* *Yo te lle - va - ré.* *Te*

D.C.

love you and you are mine.
a - mo y con - ti - go es - toy. 4. I

Text: David Haas, b.1957; tr. by Santiago Fernández, b.1971
Tune: David Haas, b.1957
© 1991, tr. 2005, GIA Publications, Inc.

Nada Te Turbe / Nothing Can Trouble 247

Ostinato Refrain

1.

Na - da te tur - be, na - da te es - pan - te. Quien a Dios tie - ne
Noth - ing can trou - ble, noth - ing can fright - en. Those who seek God shall

2.

na - da le fal - ta. So - lo Dios bas - ta.
nev - er go want - ing. *God a - lone fills us.*

Text: St. Teresa of Jesus; Taizé Community, 1986, 1991
Tune: Jacques Berthier, 1923–1994
© 1986, 1991, Les Presses de Taizé, GIA Publications, Inc., agent

248 In Every Age

Verse 1

1. Long before the mountains came to be and the land and sea and stars of the night,
   through the endless seasons of all time, you have always been, you will always be.

Refrain

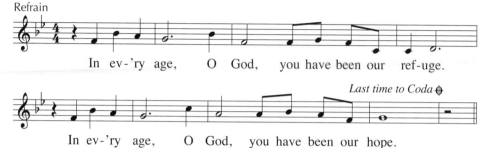

In ev-'ry age, O God, you have been our ref-uge.

Last time to Coda

In ev-'ry age, O God, you have been our hope.

Verses 2, 3

2. Destiny is cast, and at your silent word we return to dust and scatter to the wind.
   A thousand years are like a single moment gone,
   as the light that fades at the end of day.

3. Teach us to make use of the time we have. Teach us to be patient even as we wait.
   Teach us to embrace our ev'ry joy and pain,
   to sleep peacefully, and to rise up strong.

Coda

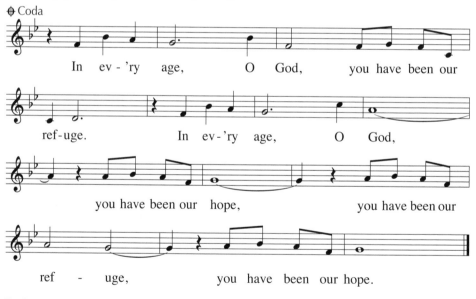

In ev-'ry age, O God, you have been our

ref-uge. In ev-'ry age, O God,

you have been our hope, you have been our

ref - uge, you have been our hope.

Text: Based on Psalm 90:1–4, 12, Janèt Sullivan Whitaker, b.1958
Tune: Janèt Sullivan Whitaker, b.1958
© 1998, 1999, Janèt Sullivan Whitaker. Published by OCP.

With a Shepherd's Care   249

Refrain

With a shep-herd's care   God   leads us.   With   a   fa-ther's

strength   God   guides us.   With   a   moth-er's love   God

nur-tures   us   and   cra-dles us in gen - tle   arms.

Verses

1. When we are lost   and can - not find the way,   God
2. When we are weak,   and cares press all a - round,   God
3. When we are scared   and feel so all a - lone,   God

cares   for   us   and   keeps   us   safe.   For
strength - ens   us   to   face   each   day.   For
loves   us   and   is   by   our   side.   For

God   is   our light   and our faith - ful   guide,   who
God   is   our rock   and our sav - ing   help,   who
God   is   our hope   and our con - stant friend,   who

D.C.

leads   us   with   a   shep - herd's   care.
guides us   with   a   fa - ther's   strength.
nur - tures with   a   moth - er's   love.

Text: James J. Chepponis, b.1956
Tune: SHEPHERD'S CARE, 10 8 10 8 with refrain; James J. Chepponis, b.1956
© 1992, GIA Publications, Inc.

250 Be Not Afraid

Verse 1

1. You shall cross the bar-ren des-ert, but you shall not die of thirst. You shall wan-der far in safe-ty though you do not know the way. You shall speak your words in for-eign lands and all will un-der-stand. You shall see the face of God and live.

℁ Refrain

Be not a-fraid. I go be-fore you al-ways. Come, fol-low me, and I will give you rest.

Verse 2

2. If you pass through rag-ing wa-ters in the sea, you shall not drown. If you walk a-mid the burn-ing flames, you shall not be harmed. If you stand be-fore the

pow'r of hell and death is at your side,

D.S.

know that I am with you through it all.

Verse 3

3. Bless-ed are your poor, for the king-dom shall be

theirs. Blest are you that weep and mourn, for

one day you shall laugh. And if wick-ed tongues in -

sult and hate you all be-cause of me,

D.S.

bless-ed, bless-ed are you!

Text: Isaiah 43:2–3, Luke 6:20ff; Bob Dufford, SJ, b.1943
Tune: Bob Dufford, SJ, b.1943; acc. by Theophane Hytrek, OSF, 1915–1992
© 1975, 1978, Robert J. Dufford, SJ, and OCP

251 On Eagle's Wings

Verse 3

3. You need not fear the ter - ror of the night, nor the ar - row that flies by day; though thou - sands fall a - bout you, near you it shall not come.

D.S.

Verse 4

4. For to his an - gels he's giv - en a com-mand to guard you in all of your ways; up - on their hands they will bear you up, lest you dash your foot a-gainst a stone.

D.S.

Coda

And hold you, hold you in the palm of his hand.

Text: Psalm 91; Michael Joncas, b.1951
Tune: Michael Joncas, b.1951
© 1979, OCP

252 Shepherd Me, O God

Refrain

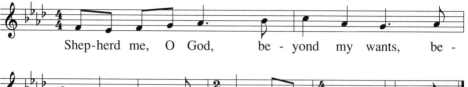

Shep-herd me, O God, be - yond my wants, be -

yond my fears, from death in - to life.

Verses

1. God is my shepherd, so nothing shall I want;
   I rest in the meadows of faithfulness and love;
   I walk by the quiet waters of peace.

2. Gently you raise me and heal my weary soul;
   you lead me by pathways of righteousness and truth;
   my spirit shall sing the music of your name.

3. Though I should wander the valley of death,
   I fear no evil, for you are at my side;
   your rod and your staff, my comfort and my hope.

4. You have set me a banquet of love in the face of hatred,
   crowning me with love beyond my pow'r to hold.

5. Surely your kindness and mercy follow me all the days of my life;
   I will dwell in the house of my God forevermore.

Text: Psalm 23; Marty Haugen, b.1950
Tune: Marty Haugen, b.1950
© 1986, GIA Publications, Inc.

I Heard the Voice of Jesus Say   253

1. I heard the voice of Je - sus say, "Come
2. I heard the voice of Je - sus say, "Be -
3. I heard the voice of Je - sus say, "I

un - to me and rest; Lay down, O wea - ry
hold, I free - ly give The liv - ing wa - ter;
am this dark world's light; Look un - to me, your

one, lay down Your head up - on my breast." I
thirst - y one, Stoop down and drink and live." I
morn shall rise, And all your day be bright." I

came to Je - sus as I was, So
came to Je - sus, and I drank Of
looked to Je - sus, and I found In

wea - ry, worn, and sad; I found in him a
that life - giv - ing stream; My thirst was quenched, my
him my star, my sun; And in that light of

rest - ing place, And he has made me glad.
soul re - vived, And now I live in him.
life I'll walk Till trav - 'ling days are done.

Text: Horatius Bonar, 1808–1889
Tune: KINGSFOLD, CMD; English melody; harm. by Ralph Vaughan Williams, 1872–1958

254   I Love the Lord

Refrain

I love the Lord; he is filled with com - pas-sion. He turned to
me on the day that I called. From the snares of the
dark, O Lord, save my life, be my strength.

Verses

1. Gra - cious is the Lord and just; our
2. How can I re - pay the Lord for
3. I shall live my vows to you be -

God is mer - cy, rest to the wea - ry. Re -
all the good - ness he has shown me? I will
fore your peo - ple. I am your ser - vant. I will

turn, my soul, to the Lord our God, who bids tears a -
raise the cup of sal - va - tion and call on his
of - fer you my sac - ri - fice of praise and of

D.C.

way.
name.   I love the Lord.
prayer.

Text: Based on Psalm 116; Arnel dC. Aquino, SJ, © 2003, Jesuit Communications Foundation, Inc.
Tune: I LOVE THE LORD, Irregular with refrain; Arnel dC. Aquino, SJ, © 2003, Jesuit Communications Foundation, Inc.;
   arr. by Joel Navarro, © 2011, Joel Navarro

Amazing Grace! 255

1. A - maz - ing grace! how sweet the
2. 'Twas grace that taught my heart to
3. The Lord has prom - ised good to
4. Through man - y dan - gers, toils, and
5. When we've been there ten thou - sand

sound, That saved a wretch like me!
fear, And grace my fears re - lieved;
me, His word my hope se - cures;
snares, I have al - read - y come;
years, Bright shin - ing as the sun,

I once was lost, but now am
How pre - cious did that grace ap -
He will my shield and por - tion
'Tis grace has brought me safe thus
We've no less days to sing God's

found; Was blind, but now I see.
pear The hour I first be - lieved!
be As long as life en - dures.
far, And grace will lead me home.
praise Than when we'd first be - gun.

Text: Sts. 1–4, John Newton, 1725–1807; st. 5, attr. to John Rees, fl.1859
Tune: NEW BRITAIN, CM; *Virginia Harmony,* 1831; harm. by Edwin O. Excell, 1851–1921

256   Rain Down

Refrain

Rain down, rain down, rain down your love on your peo - ple. Rain down, rain down, rain down your love, God of life.

Verses

1. Faith - ful and true is the word of our God.
2. We who re - vere and find hope in our God
3. God of cre - a - tion, we long for your truth;

All of God's works are so wor - thy of trust.
live in the kind - ness and joy of God's wing.
you are the wa - ter of life that we thirst.

God's mer - cy falls on the just and the right;
God will pro - tect us from dark - ness and death;
Grant that your love and your peace touch our hearts,

D.C.

full of God's love is the earth.
God will not leave us to starve.
all of our hope lies in you.

Text: Based on Psalm 33; Jaime Cortez, b.1963
Tune: Jaime Cortez, b.1963; acc. by Craig S. Kingsbury, b.1952
© 1991, 1992, Jaime Cortez. Published by OCP.

Give Us Your Peace 257

Text: Michael Mahler, b.1981
Tune: Michael Mahler, b.1981
© 2001, GIA Publications, Inc.

258 Dona Nobis Pacem

Canon

1. Do - na no - bis pa - cem, pa - cem.

Do - na no - bis pa - cem.

2. Do - na no - bis pa - cem.

Do - na no - bis pa - cem.

3. Do - na no - bis pa - cem.

Do - na no - bis pa - cem.

Text: *Grant us peace*
Tune: Traditional; acc. by Diana Kodner, b.1957, © 1994, GIA Publications, Inc.

Make Me a Channel of Your Peace   259

Verses 1, 2, 4

1. Make me a chan-nel of your peace. Where
2. Make me a chan-nel of your peace. Where
4. Make me a chan-nel of your peace. It

there is ha-tred, let me bring your love. Where
there's de-spair in life, let me bring hope. Where
is in par-don-ing that we are par-doned, in

there is in-ju-ry, your par-don, Lord, And
there is dark-ness, on-ly light, And
giv-ing of our-selves that we re-ceive, and in

where there's doubt, true faith in you.
where there's sad-ness, ev-er joy.
dy-ing that we're born to e-ter-nal life.

Verse 3

3. Oh, Mas-ter, grant that I may nev-er seek So much to be con-

soled as to con-sole. To be un-der-stood as to un-der-

stand. To be loved as to love with all my soul.

Text: Prayer of St. Francis; adapt. by Sebastian Temple, 1928–1997
Tune: Sebastian Temple, 1928–1997; acc. by Robert J. Batastini, b.1942
© 1967, OCP
Dedicated to Mrs. Frances Tracy

260 Prayer of Peace

1. Peace be - fore us, peace be - hind us, peace
2. Love be - fore us, love be - hind us, love
3. Light be - fore us, light be - hind us, light
4. Christ be - fore us, Christ be - hind us, Christ
5. Al - le - lu - ia, al - le - lu - ia, al - le -
6. Peace be - fore us, peace be - hind us, peace

un - der our feet. Peace with - in us, peace
un - der our feet. Love with - in us, love
un - der our feet. Light with - in us, light
un - der our feet. Christ with - in us, Christ
lu - ia, Al - le - lu - ia, al - le -
un - der our feet. Peace with - in us, peace

o - ver us, let all a - round us be peace.
o - ver us, let all a - round us be love.
o - ver us, let all a - round us be light.
o - ver us, let all a - round us be Christ.
lu - ia, al - le - lu - ia.
o - ver us, let all a - round us be peace.

Text: Based on a Navajo prayer; David Haas, b.1957
Tune: David Haas, b.1957
© 1987, GIA Publications, Inc.

261 May the Peace of Christ Be with You / Ki Ri Su To No

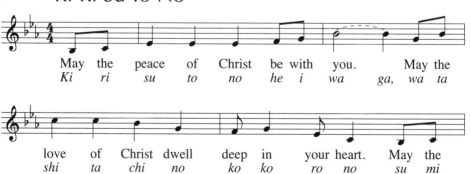

May the peace of Christ be with you. May the
Ki ri su to no he i wa ga, wa ta

love of Christ dwell deep in your heart. May the
shi ta chi no ko ko ro no su mi

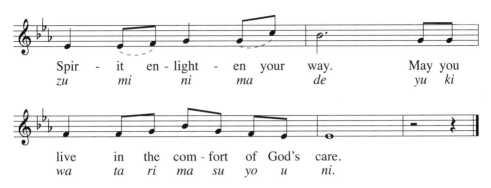

Spir - it en - light - en your way.   May you
zu   mi   ni   ma   de   yu ki

live   in   the   com - fort   of   God's   care.
wa   ta   ri   ma   su   yo   u   ni.

Text: Japanese blessing; additional text by Lori True, b.1961, © 2008, GIA Publications, Inc.
Tune: Japanese folk melody; arr. by Lori True; acc. by Mary Howarth, © 2008, 2010, GIA Publications, Inc.

O God of Love, O King of Peace   262

1. O   God   of   love,   O   King   of   peace,   Make
2. Re - mem - ber,   Lord,   your   works   of   old,   The
3. Whom shall   we   trust   but   you,   O   Lord?   Where
4. Where saints   and   an - gels   dwell   a - bove   All

wars through - out   the   world to   cease; Our greed and   vio - lent
won - ders   that   your   peo - ple   told; Re - mem - ber   not   our
rest   but   on   your   faith - ful   word? None   ev - er   called on
hearts   are   joined   in   ho - ly   love; Oh,   bind   us   in   that

ways   re - strain. Give   peace,   O   God,   give   peace   a - gain.
sins'   deep stain. Give   peace,   O   God,   give   peace   a - gain.
you   in   vain. Give   peace,   O   God,   give   peace   a - gain.
heav'n - ly   chain. Give   peace,   O   God,   give   peace   a - gain.

May be sung as a two- or four-voice canon.

Text: Henry W. Baker, 1821–1877, alt.
Tune: TALLIS' CANON, LM; Thomas Tallis, c.1505–1585

263 We Are Many Parts / Muchos Miembros Hay

Refrain

We are man-y parts,
Mu-chos miem-bros hay
we are all one bod-y,
en un so-lo cuer-po;

and the gifts we have
nues-tros do-nes son
we are giv-en to share.
pa-ra dar y ser-vir.

May the Spir-it of love
Que_el Es-pí-ri-tu de Dios
make us one in-deed;
nos u-na en su_a-mor;

one, the love that we share,
com-par-tien-do_el do-lor,
one, our hope in de-
com-ba-tien-do_el te-

spair,
mor,
one, the cross that we bear.
com-pla-cien-do_al Se-ñor.

Verses

1. God of all, we look to you,
2. So my pain is pain for you,
3. All you seek-ers, great and small,

1. Oh Se-ñor, que-re-mos ser
2. Mi do-lor te due-le_a ti;
3. Quie-nes bus-can de ver-dad

We would be your
In your joy is
Seek the great-est

Ser-vi-do-res
Si te go-zas,
Su ma-yor fe-

D.C.

ser-vants true,
my joy, too;
gift of all;

por do-quier;
soy fe-liz;
li-ci-dad:

Let us be your love to all the world.
All is brought to-geth-er in the Lord.
If you love, then you will know the Lord.

Y_a la_hu-ma-ni-dad lle-var tu_a-mor.
To-do se_u-ne_en tor-no al Se-ñor.
A-men y co-no-ce-rán a Dios.

Text: 1 Corinthians 12, 13; Marty Haugen, b.1950; tr. by Santiago Fernández, b.1971
Tune: Marty Haugen, b.1950
© 1980, 1986, tr. 2005, GIA Publications, Inc.

We Shall Overcome 264

1. We shall o - ver - come, we shall o - ver - come,
2. We'll walk hand in hand, we'll walk hand in hand,
3. We shall live in peace, we shall live in peace,
4. We are not a - fraid, we are not a - fraid,

we shall o - ver - come some - day. Oh,
we'll walk hand in hand some - day. Oh,
we shall live in peace some - day. Oh,
we are not a - fraid to - day. Oh,

deep in my heart I do be - lieve
deep in my heart I do be - lieve
deep in my heart I do be - lieve
deep in my heart I do be - lieve

we shall o - ver - come some - day.
we shall o - ver - come some - day.
we shall o - ver - come some - day.
we shall o - ver - come some - day.

5. We shall stand together...
6. The truth will make us free...
7. The Lord will see us through...
8. We shall be like him...
9. The whole wide world around...

Text: Spiritual
Tune: Spiritual; harm. by J. Jefferson Cleveland, 1937–1986, © 1981, Abingdon Press

265 In Christ There Is No East or West

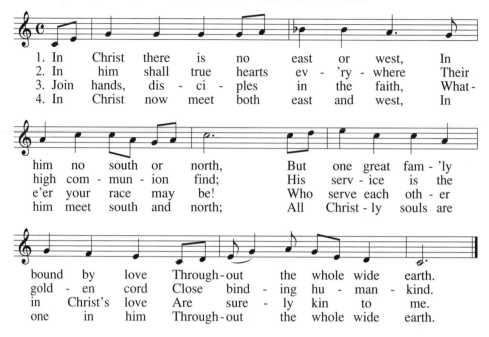

1. In Christ there is no east or west, In
2. In him shall true hearts ev - 'ry - where Their
3. Join hands, dis - ci - ples in the faith, What-
4. In Christ now meet both east and west, In

him no south or north, But one great fam - 'ly
high com - mun - ion find; His serv - ice is the
e'er your race may be! Who serve each oth - er
him meet south and north; All Christ - ly souls are

bound by love Through-out the whole wide earth.
gold - en cord Close bind - ing hu - man - kind.
in Christ's love Are sure - ly kin to me.
one in him Through-out the whole wide earth.

Text: Galatians 3:23; William A. Dunkerley, 1852–1941, alt.
Tune: McKEE, CM; African American; adapt. by Harry T. Burleigh, 1866–1949

266 Bless the Lord / Tengo Sed de Ti

Ostinato Refrain

Bless the Lord, my soul, and bless God's ho - ly name.
Ten - go sed de ti, oh fuen - te del a - mor.

Bless the Lord, my soul, who leads me in - to life.
Ten - go sed de ti: tu a - mor es li - ber - tad.

Text: Psalm 103
Tune: Jacques Berthier, 1923–1994
© 1998, Les Presses de Taizé, GIA Publications, Inc., agent

If You Believe and I Believe 267

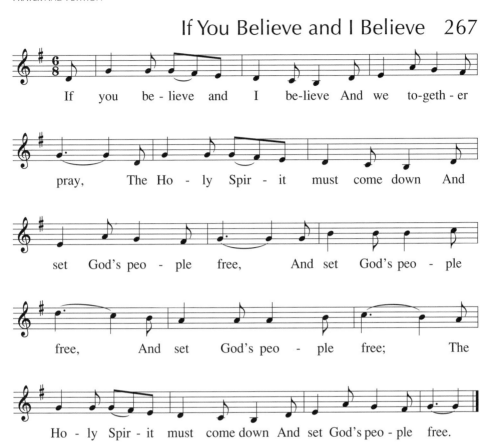

If you be-lieve and I be-lieve And we to-geth-er pray, The Ho - ly Spir - it must come down And set God's peo - ple free, And set God's peo - ple free, And set God's peo - ple free; The Ho - ly Spir - it must come down And set God's peo - ple free.

Text: Zimbabwean traditional
Tune: Zimbabwean traditional; adapt. of English traditional; as taught by Tarasai; arr. by John L. Bell, b.1949, © 1991, Iona Community,
    GIA Publications, Inc., agent

O God, Keep Me Safe 268

Ostinato Refrain

O God, keep me safe, for I trust in you. The path - way to life you teach me. With you is peace and joy in all full-ness.

Text: Taizé Community
Tune: Taizé Community
© 2007, Les Presses de Taizé, GIA Publications, Inc., agent

269 Lead Me, Guide Me

Refrain

Lead me, guide me, a - long the way, For if you
lead me, I can - not stray. Lord, let me walk each
day with thee. Lead me, O Lord, lead me.

Verses

1. I am weak and I need thy strength and pow'r To
2. Help me tread in the paths of right - eous - ness. Be my
3. I am lost if you take your hand from me, I am

help me o - ver my weak - est hour. Help me through the
aid when Sa - tan and sin op - press. I am put - ting
blind with - out thy Light to see. Lord, just al - ways

D.C.

dark-ness thy face to see. Lead me, O Lord, lead me.
all my trust in thee. Lead me, O Lord, lead me.
let me thy ser - vant be. Lead me, O Lord, lead me.

Text: Doris M. Akers, 1922–1995
Tune: LEAD ME, Irregular with refrain; Doris M. Akers, 1922–1995; harm. by Richard Smallwood, b.1948
© 1953, (renewed), arr. © 2011, Doris M. Akers, admin. by Chappell & Co., Inc.

Seek Ye First 270

1. Seek ye first the king - dom of God
2. Ask, and it shall be giv - en un - to you,
3. You do not live by bread a - lone,
4. Where two or three are gath - ered in my name,

and his right - eous - ness,
seek, and you shall find,
but by ev - 'ry word,
there am I in their midst;

and all these things shall be add - ed un - to you;
knock, and the door shall be o - pened un - to you;
that comes forth from the mouth of God;
and what - so - ev - er you ask I will do;

Al - le - lu, al - le - lu - ia.

2. *Optional Refrain, Descant, or Canon:*

Al - le - lu - ia, al - le - lu - ia,

al - le - lu - ia, al - le - lu, al - le - lu - ia.

*May be sung as a two-voice canon.

Text: Matthew 6:33, 7:7; adapt. by Karen Lafferty, b.1948
Tune: SEEK YE FIRST, Irregular; Karen Lafferty, b.1948
© 1972, CCCM Music/Universal Music–Brentwood Benson Publishing (admin. CapitolCMGPublishing.com)

271 Lord of All Hopefulness

1. Lord of all hope-ful-ness, Lord of all joy,
2. Lord of all ea-ger-ness, Lord of all faith,
3. Lord of all kind-li-ness, Lord of all grace,
4. Lord of all gen-tle-ness, Lord of all calm,

Whose trust, ev-er child-like, no cares could de-stroy,
Whose strong hands were skilled at the plane and the lathe,
Your hands swift to wel-come, your arms to em-brace,
Whose voice is con-tent-ment, whose pres-ence is balm,

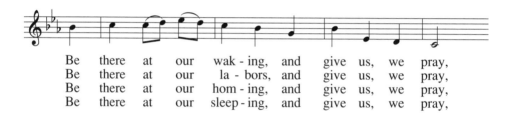

Be there at our wak-ing, and give us, we pray,
Be there at our la-bors, and give us, we pray,
Be there at our hom-ing, and give us, we pray,
Be there at our sleep-ing, and give us, we pray,

Your bliss in our hearts, Lord, at the break of the day.
Your strength in our hearts, Lord, at the noon of the day.
Your love in our hearts, Lord, at the eve of the day.
Your peace in our hearts, Lord, at the end of the day.

Text: Jan Struther, 1901–1953, © 1931, Oxford University Press
Tune: SLANE, 10 11 11 12; Irish melody; harm. by Erik Routley, 1917–1982, © 1975, Hope Publishing Company

Open My Eyes 272

Verses

1. O - pen my eyes, Lord. Help me to see your face.
2. O - pen my ears, Lord. Help me to hear your voice.
3. O - pen my heart, Lord. Help me to love like you.
4. I live with - in you. Deep in your heart, O Love.

O - pen my eyes, Lord. Help me to see. *(To verse 2)*
O - pen my ears, Lord. Help me to hear. *(To verse 3)*
O - pen my heart, Lord. Help me to love. *(To bridge)*
I live with - in you. Rest now in me.

Bridge

And the first shall be last, and our eyes are o - pened,

and we'll hear like nev-er be - fore. And we'll speak in new ways,

D.C.

and we'll see God's face in plac-es we've nev-er known.

Text: Mark 8:22-25; Jesse Manibusan, b.1958
Tune: Jesse Manibusan, b.1958
© 1988, 1998, 1999, Jesse Manibusan. Published by Spirit & Song, a div. of OCP.

Take, O Take Me As I Am 273

Take, O take me as I am; sum - mon out what I shall

be; set your seal up-on my heart and live in me.

Text: John L. Bell, b.1949
Tune: John L. Bell, b.1949
© 1995, Iona Community, GIA Publications, Inc., agent

274 O Lord, Hear My Prayer / Señor, Ten Piedad

Ostinato Chorale

O   Lord,   hear my prayer,   O   Lord,   hear my prayer:
*The Lord   is   my song,   the Lord   is   my praise:
Se - *ñor,* *ten pie - dad,* *Se* - *ñor,* *ten pie - dad:*

when   I   call   an - swer me.   O Lord, hear my prayer,   O
all   my   hope comes from God. The Lord is   my song,   the
si   *te in - vo - co,* *ó - ye - me.* *Se - ñor, ten pie - dad, Se -*

Last time

Lord, hear my prayer. Come   and lis - ten to me.   O
Lord   is   my praise: God,   the well-spring of life.   The
ñor, ten pie - dad: Ven, y es - cu - cha mi voz.   *Se -*

*Alternate text

Text: Psalm 102; Taizé Community, 1982
Tune: Jacques Berthier, 1923–1994
© 1982, 2011, Les Presses de Taizé, GIA Publications, Inc., agent

275 All Are Welcome

1. Let us   build   a house   where love   can   dwell   And
2. Let us   build   a house   where proph - ets   speak, And
3. Let us   build   a house   where love   is   found In
4. Let us   build   a house   where hands   will   reach Be -
5. Let us   build   a house   where all   are   named, Their

all   can   safe - ly   live,   A   place   where saints and
words are   strong and true,   Where all   God's chil - dren
wa -   ter, wine and wheat: A   ban - quet hall   on
yond   the   wood and stone   To heal   and strength - en,
songs and   vi - sions heard   And loved   and treas - ured,

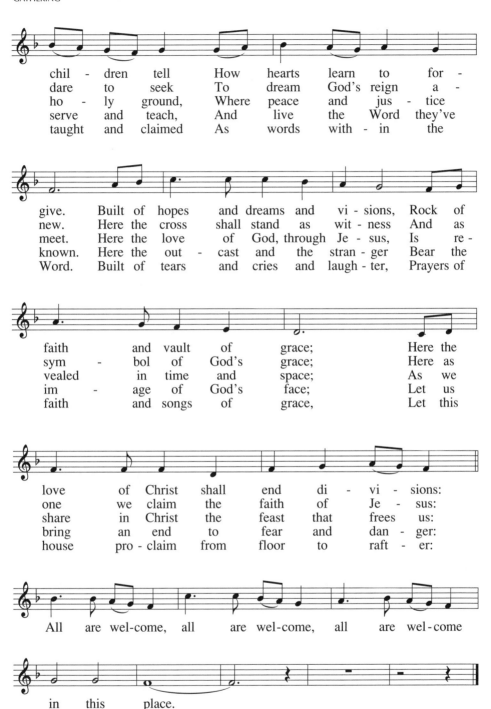

chil - dren tell How hearts learn to for -
dare to seek To dream God's reign a -
ho - ly ground, Where peace and jus - tice
serve and teach, And live the Word they've
taught and claimed As words with - in the

give. Built of hopes and dreams and vi - sions, Rock of
new. Here the cross shall stand as wit - ness And as
meet. Here the love of God, through Je - sus, Is re -
known. Here the out - cast and the stran - ger Bear the
Word. Built of tears and cries and laugh - ter, Prayers of

faith and vault of grace; Here the
sym - bol of God's grace; Here as
vealed in time and space; As we
im - age of God's face; Let us
faith and songs of grace, Let this

love of Christ shall end di - vi - sions:
one we claim the faith of Je - sus:
share in Christ the feast that frees us:
bring an end to fear and dan - ger:
house pro - claim from floor to raft - er:

All are wel-come, all are wel-come, all are wel-come

in this place.

Text: Marty Haugen, b.1950
Tune: TWO OAKS, 9 6 8 6 8 7 10 with refrain; Marty Haugen, b.1950
© 1994, GIA Publications, Inc.

276 All Who Hunger, Gather Gladly

1. All who hun - ger, gath - er glad - ly;
2. All who hun - ger, nev - er stran - gers;
3. All who hun - ger, sing to - geth - er;

Ho - ly man - na is our bread. Come from wil - der -
Seek - er, be a wel-come guest. Come from rest - less -
Je - sus Christ is liv - ing bread. Come from lone - li -

ness and wan - d'ring. Here, in truth, we will be fed.
ness and roam - ing. Here, in joy, we keep the feast.
ness and long - ing. Here, in peace, we have been led.

You that yearn for days of full - ness,
We that once were lost and scat - tered
Blest are those who from this ta - ble

All a - round us is our food. Taste and see the
In com - mun - ion's love have stood. Taste and see the
Live their days in grat - i - tude. Taste and see the

grace e - ter - nal. Taste and see that God is good.
grace e - ter - nal. Taste and see that God is good.
grace e - ter - nal. Taste and see that God is good.

Text: Sylvia G. Dunstan, 1955–1993, © 1991, GIA Publications, Inc.
Tune: HOLY MANNA, 8 7 8 7 D; William Moore, fl.1830; harm. by Charles Anders, b.1929, © 1969, *Contemporary Worship 1: Hymns*

Gather Your People 277

Refrain

Gath-er your peo-ple, O Lord. Gath-er your peo-ple, O Lord. One bread, one bod-y, one spir-it of love. Gath-er your peo-ple, O Lord.

Verses

1. Draw us forth to the ta-ble of life:
2. We are parts of the bod-y of Christ,
3. No more harm on the moun-tain of God;
4. Wash us, Lord, in the wa-ters of life;

broth-ers and sis-ters, each of us called to
need-ing each oth-er, each of the gifts the
swords in-to plow-shares. Free us, O Lord, from
wa-ters of mer-cy, wa-ters of hope that

walk in your light.
Spir-it pro-vides.
hard-ness of heart.
flow from your side.

D.C.

Text: 1 Corinthians 12, Isaiah 2:3–4, 11:9; Bob Hurd, b.1950
Tune: Bob Hurd. b.1950; acc. by Dominic MacAller, b.1959
© 1991, Bob Hurd. Published by OCP.

278 Gather Us In

1. Here in this place new light is stream - ing,
2. We are the young— our lives are a mys - t'ry,
3. Here we will take the wine and the wa - ter,

Now is the dark - ness van - ished a - way,
We are the old— who yearn for your face,
Here we will take the bread of new birth,

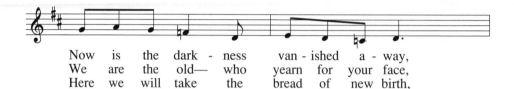

See in this space our fears and our dream - ings,
We have been sung through - out all of his - t'ry,
Here you shall call your sons and your daugh - ters,

Brought here to you in the light of this day.
Called to be light to the whole hu - man race.
Call us a - new to be salt for the earth.

Gath - er us in— the lost and for - sak - en,
Gath - er us in— the rich and the haugh - ty,
Give us to drink the wine of com - pas - sion,

Gath - er us in— the blind and the lame;
Gath - er us in— the proud and the strong;
Give us to eat the bread that is you;

Call to us now, and we shall a - wak - en,
Give us a heart so meek and so low - ly,
Nour - ish us well, and teach us to fash - ion

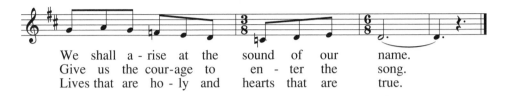

We shall a - rise at the sound of our name.
Give us the cour-age to en - ter the song.
Lives that are ho - ly and hearts that are true.

Text: Marty Haugen, b.1950
Tune: GATHER US IN, 10 9 10 10 D; Marty Haugen, b.1950
© 1982, GIA Publications, Inc.

I Come with Joy   279

1. I come with joy, a child of God, For -
2. I come with Chris - tians far and near To
3. As Christ breaks bread, and bids us share, Each
4. The Spir - it of the ris - en Christ, Un -
5. To - geth - er met, to - geth - er bound By

giv - en, loved, and free, The life of Je - sus
find, as all are fed, The new com - mu - ni -
proud di - vi - sion ends. The love that made us,
seen, but ev - er near, Is in such friend - ship
all that God has done, We'll go with joy, to

to re - call, In love laid down for me.
ty of love In Christ's com - mu - nion bread.
makes us one, And strang - ers now are friends.
bet - ter known, A - live a - mong us here.
give the world The love that makes us one.

Text: Brian Wren, b.1936, © 1971, rev. 1995, Hope Publishing Company
Tune: LAND OF REST, CM; American; adapt. by Annabel M. Buchanan, 1888–1983, © 1938 (renewed), this arr. © 2011, The H.W. Gray Company

280 All People That on Earth Do Dwell

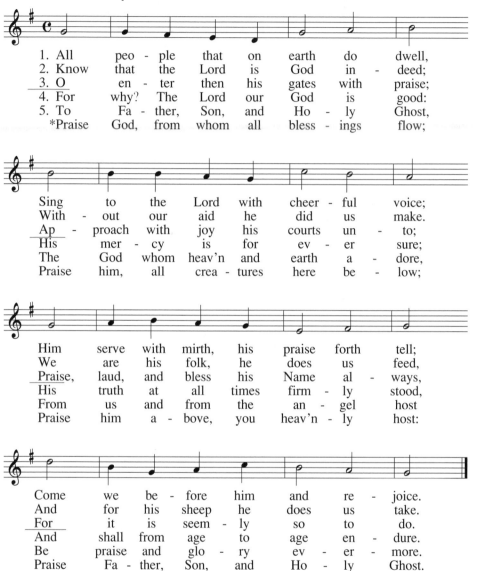

1. All peo - ple that on earth do dwell,
2. Know that the Lord is God in - deed;
3. O en - ter then his gates with praise;
4. For why? The Lord our God is good:
5. To Fa - ther, Son, and Ho - ly Ghost,
*Praise God, from whom all bless - ings flow;

Sing to the Lord with cheer - ful voice;
With - out our aid he did us make.
Ap - proach with joy his courts un - to;
His mer - cy is for ev - er sure;
The God whom heav'n and earth a - dore,
Praise him, all crea - tures here be - low;

Him serve with mirth, his praise forth tell;
We are his folk, he does us feed,
Praise, laud, and bless his Name al - ways,
His truth at all times firm - ly stood,
From us and from the an - gel host
Praise him a - bove, you heav'n - ly host:

Come we be - fore him and re - joice.
And for his sheep he does us take.
For it is seem - ly so to do.
And shall from age to age en - dure.
Be praise and glo - ry ev - er - more.
Praise Fa - ther, Son, and Ho - ly Ghost.

* May be sung alone or as an alternate to stanza 5.

Text: Psalm 100; William Kethe, d. c.1593, alt.; doxology, Thomas Ken, 1637–1711
Tune: OLD HUNDREDTH, LM; Louis Bourgeois, c.1510–1561

Uyai Mose / Come All You People 281

U - ya - i mo - se, ti - na - ma - te Mwa - ri,
Come all you peo - ple, come and praise your Mak - er,

U - ya - i mo - se, ti - na - ma - te Mwa - ri,
Come all you peo - ple, come and praise your Mak - er,

U - ya - i mo - se, ti - na - ma - te Mwa - ri,
Come all you peo - ple, come and praise your Mak - er,

U - ya - i mo - se zvi - no.
Come now and wor - ship the Lord.

Text: Alexander Gondo
Tune: Alexander Gondo; arr. by John L. Bell, b.1949, © 1994, Iona Community, GIA Publications, Inc., agent

Morning Has Broken 282

1. Morn - ing has bro - ken Like the first morn - ing, Black-bird has
2. Sweet the rain's new fall Sun - lit from heav - en, Like the first
3. Mine is the sun - light! Mine is the morn - ing Born of the

spo - ken Like the first bird. Praise for the sing - ing! Praise for the
dew - fall On the first grass. Praise for the sweet - ness Of the wet
one light E - den saw play! Praise with e - la - tion, Praise ev - 'ry

morn - ing! Praise for them, spring - ing Fresh from the Word!
gar - den, Sprung in com - plete - ness Where his feet pass.
morn - ing, God's re - cre - a - tion Of the new day!

Text: Eleanor Farjeon, 1881–1965, *The Children's Bells*, © David Higham Assoc. Ltd.
Tune: BUNESSAN, 5 5 5 4 D; Gaelic melody; acc. by Robert J. Batastini, b.1942, © 1999, GIA Publications, Inc.

283 Good Morning, God

1. Good morn-ing, God, the night is gone.
2. God, grant that in the morn-ing light

We bring to you a morn-ing song.
We see things clear - ly and a - right.

Now chase the shades of night a - way
God, as we greet this fresh new day

And turn the dark - ness in - to day.
Take an - ger, fear, and doubt a - way.

Text: Ken Medema, alt., © 1988, Brier Patch Music
Tune: O WALY WALY, LM; English traditional; acc. by Robert J. Batastini, b.1942, © 2000, GIA Publications, Inc.

284 At Evening

1. Now it is eve - ning: Lights of the cit - y
2. Now it is eve - ning: Lit - tle ones sleep - ing
3. Now it is eve - ning: Food on the ta - ble
4. Now it is eve - ning: Here in our meet - ing

Bid us re - mem - ber Christ is our Light.
Bid us re - mem - ber Christ is our Peace.
Bids us re - mem - ber Christ is our Life.
May we re - mem - ber Christ is our Friend.

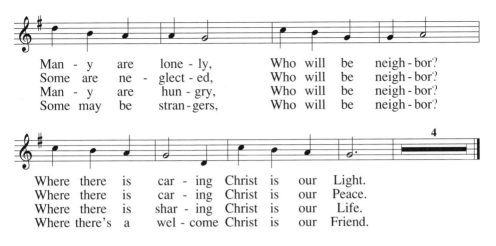

Man - y   are   lone - ly,   Who will be   neigh - bor?
Some are   ne - glect - ed,   Who will be   neigh - bor?
Man - y   are   hun - gry,   Who will be   neigh - bor?
Some may   be   stran - gers,   Who will be   neigh - bor?

Where there is   car - ing Christ is   our   Light.
Where there is   car - ing Christ is   our   Peace.
Where there is   shar - ing Christ is   our   Life.
Where there's a   wel - come Christ is   our   Friend.

Text: Fred Pratt Green, 1903–2000, © 1974, Hope Publishing Company
Tune: EVENING HYMN, 5 5 5 4 D; David Haas, b.1957, © 1985, GIA Publications, Inc.

All Night, All Day   285

Refrain

All night, all   day,   an - gels watch - ing o - ver me, my Lord.

All night, all   day,   an - gels watch - ing o - ver me.

Verses

1. Now   I   lay   me   down   to   sleep.
2. Lord, stay with me   through the   night.

An - gels watch - ing o - ver me, my Lord.   Pray the Lord my
An - gels watch - ing o - ver me, my Lord.   Wake me with the

D.C.

soul   will   keep.   An - gels   watch - ing o - ver   me.
morn - ing   light.   An - gels   watch - ing o - ver   me.

Text: African American traditional
Tune: ALL NIGHT, ALL DAY, 7 9 7 7 with refrain; African American traditional; acc. by Robert J. Batastini, b.1942, © 2000, GIA Publications, Inc.

286   Christ Is the King!

1. Christ is the King! O friends, re - joice;
2. O mag - ni - fy the Lord, and raise
3. They with a faith for ev - er new
4. O Chris - tian wom - en, Chris - tian men,
5. Christ through all a - ges is the same;

Broth - ers and sis - ters, with one voice
An - thems of joy and ho - ly praise
Fol - lowed the King, and round him drew
All the world o - ver, seek a - gain
Place the same hope in his great name;

Let the world know he is your choice.
For Christ's brave saints of an - cient days.
Thou - sands of men and wom - en true.
The Way dis - ci - ples fol - lowed then.
With the same faith his word pro - claim.

Al - le - lu - ia, al - le - lu - ia, al - le - lu - ia.

6. Let Love's all reconciling might
Your scattered companies unite
In service to the Lord of light.
Alleluia, alleluia, alleluia.

7. So shall the Church at last be one;
So shall God's will on earth be done,
New lamps be lit, new tasks begun.
Alleluia, alleluia, alleluia.

Text: George K. A. Bell, 1883–1958, alt., © Oxford University Press
Tune: GELOBT SEI GOTT, 888 with alleluias; Melchior Vulpius, c.1570–1615

We See the Lord 287

1. We see the Lord, we see the Lord, and he is
2. We see the Lord, we see the Lord, ⁊ and God's
3. We hear the Lord, we hear the Lord, ⁊ and God's
4. We bless the Lord, we bless the Lord, ⁊ and as

high and lift - ed up, and his train fills the Tem-ple, he is
face shines forth as a light in the Tem-ple, and God's
Word is - sues forth and re - sounds through the Tem-ple, and God's
in - cense goes up, so our prayers fill the Tem-ple, and as

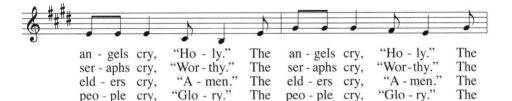

high and lift - ed up, and his train fills the Tem-ple. The
face shines forth as a light in the Tem-ple. The
Word is - sues forth and re - sounds through the Tem-ple. The
in - cense goes up, so our prayers fill the Tem-ple. The

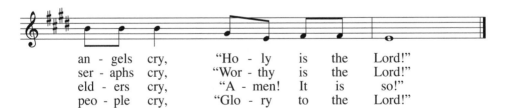

an - gels cry, "Ho - ly." The an - gels cry, "Ho - ly." The
ser - aphs cry, "Wor-thy." The ser - aphs cry, "Wor-thy." The
eld - ers cry, "A - men." The eld - ers cry, "A - men." The
peo - ple cry, "Glo - ry." The peo - ple cry, "Glo - ry." The

an - gels cry, "Ho - ly is the Lord!"
ser - aphs cry, "Wor - thy is the Lord!"
eld - ers cry, "A - men! It is so!"
peo - ple cry, "Glo - ry to the Lord!"

Text: Vs. 1, Isaiah 6:1–3; vss. 2–4, James E. Byrne, © 1973
Tune: Traditional; arr. by Charles High, © 1978, Songs of the Sword of the Spirit/The Word of God Music; acc. by Robert J. Batastini, b.1942,
© 1989, GIA Publications, Inc.

288 We Sing of the Saints

1. We sing of the saints filled with Spir-it and grace, Blest wom-en and
2. *(Optional verse for saint's day)*
3. We, too, have been cho-sen to fol-low the way Of good-ness and

men through all time, from each place. God chose them, the ho-ly, the

truth in our stud-y and play, We raise up our song, liv-ing

hum-ble, the wise To spread the Good News of sal-va-tion in Christ.

saints here be-low, With heav-en-ly saints, as our praise ev-er flows.

Optional Verses for Saint's Days

2. Feasts of Mary
A lowly, young woman God's mother would be,
The first true believing disciple was she.
From cradle to cross, she would follow her Son
And share in the life everlasting he won.

Feasts of Joseph
A carpenter, upright and faithful, was called
To care for young Jesus, a child weak and small.
To teach and to guide, to embrace him in love,
Reminding him here of the Father above.

Feasts of John the Baptist
A prophet and herald who made straight the way
For Jesus to come, bringing mercy's new day.
He preached to the people to change and repent,
Preparing them as the Messiah was sent.

St. Patrick (March 17)
From Britain to Ireland strong Patrick returned,
He baptized and preached in the name of our Lord.
He used simple clover to show God was One,
To teach of the Father and Spirit and Son.

St. Kateri Tekakwitha (July 14)
The "Lily of Mohawks," Kateri was called
For sharing God's love with the great and the small,
She bore the name "Christian" with honor and pride,
And now her name, "Blessed" is known far and wide.

St. Augustine (August 28)
A great, holy man, born on Africa's shores
Augustine, at first, loved the worldly life more;
He found later on, Jesus Christ, the true Way,
And chose the true Gospel to live and proclaim.

Archangels (September 29)
Of Gabriel, Raphael, Michael we sing,
God's messengers; joyful, glad tidings they bring;
Protecting the Church, and announcing the time
When Christ shall return in his glory sublime.

St. Francis of Assisi (October 4)
Saint Francis was born a rich, noble young man,
But God had in mind a much different plan;
So Francis left status and money behind,
To help many people God's true will to find.

St. Teresa of Jesus (October 15)
A woman of wisdom, of faith and of prayer,
Teresa would speak up when others didn't dare.
She challenged the Church to renew and revive;
Her great love of Jesus was always her guide.

All Saints (November 1)
There are many saints whom we don't know by name,
For God works through people who never find fame.
But, gathered together, they now sing God's might,
With martyrs and prophets, in heavenly light.

All Souls (November 2)
We honor the mem'ry of those now at rest,
Who followed the Gospel, whose lives were so blest;
From fam'lies and friendships, they make heaven seem
More home-like for us, in our prayers and our dreams.

St. Nicholas (December 6)
A bishop, a friend of the poor and the weak,
Of orphans and children, the hungry, the meek;
To help those in need, to return them to health,
Saint Nicholas used all his power and wealth.

St. Juan Diego (December 9)
This poor Aztec native lived in Mexico;
Was given a sign: roses blooming in snow.
The Mother of God to Diego appeared,
So Jesus her Son would be always revered.

St. Lucy (December 13)
Her feast is in Advent, her name means "the light,"
She died for upholding what she thought was right;
St. Lucy took care of the poor and the frail;
Her witness was brave and her faith never failed.

Text: Alan J. Hommerding, b.1956, © 1994, World Library Publications
Tune: ZIE GINDS KOMT DE STOOMBOOT, 11 11 11 11; traditional Dutch melody; acc. by Karl A. Pölm-Faudré, © 1984, World Library Publications

289 Litany of the Saints

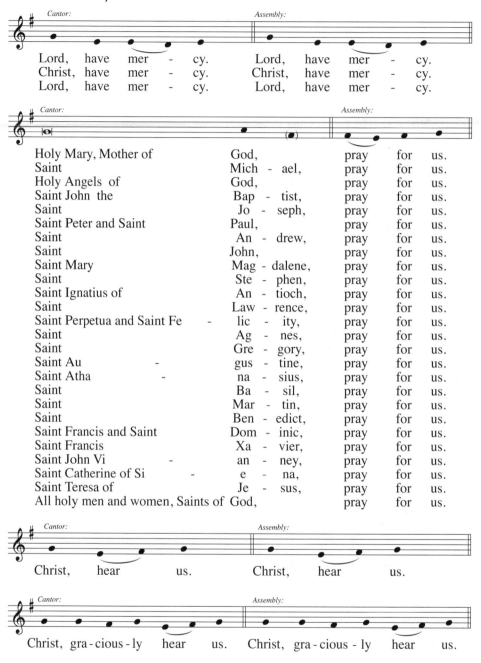

Cantor: Lord, have mer - cy. *Assembly:* Lord, have mer - cy.
Christ, have mer - cy. Christ, have mer - cy.
Lord, have mer - cy. Lord, have mer - cy.

		pray for us.
Holy Mary, Mother of	God,	pray for us.
Saint	Mich - ael,	pray for us.
Holy Angels of	God,	pray for us.
Saint John the	Bap - tist,	pray for us.
Saint	Jo - seph,	pray for us.
Saint Peter and Saint	Paul,	pray for us.
Saint	An - drew,	pray for us.
Saint	John,	pray for us.
Saint Mary	Mag - dalene,	pray for us.
Saint	Ste - phen,	pray for us.
Saint Ignatius of	An - tioch,	pray for us.
Saint	Law - rence,	pray for us.
Saint Perpetua and Saint Fe -	lic - ity,	pray for us.
Saint	Ag - nes,	pray for us.
Saint	Gre - gory,	pray for us.
Saint Au -	gus - tine,	pray for us.
Saint Atha -	na - sius,	pray for us.
Saint	Ba - sil,	pray for us.
Saint	Mar - tin,	pray for us.
Saint	Ben - edict,	pray for us.
Saint Francis and Saint	Dom - inic,	pray for us.
Saint Francis	Xa - vier,	pray for us.
Saint John Vi -	an - ney,	pray for us.
Saint Catherine of Si -	e - na,	pray for us.
Saint Teresa of	Je - sus,	pray for us.
All holy men and women, Saints of	God,	pray for us.

Cantor: Christ, hear us. *Assembly:* Christ, hear us.

Cantor: Christ, gra - cious - ly hear us. *Assembly:* Christ, gra - cious - ly hear us.

Text: *Litany of the Saints, Roman Missal*
Music: *Litany of the Saints, Roman Missal*
© 2010, ICEL

When the Saints Go Marching In   290

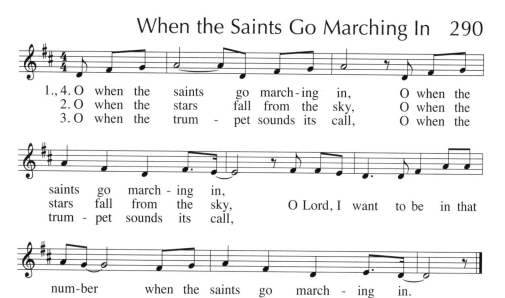

1., 4. O when the saints go march-ing in,   O when the
2. O when the stars fall from the sky,   O when the
3. O when the trum - pet sounds its call,   O when the

saints go march - ing in,
stars fall from the sky,   O Lord, I want to be in that
trum - pet sounds its call,

num-ber when the saints go march - ing in.

Text: African American spiritual
Tune: WHEN THE SAINTS, 88 10 7; African American spiritual; arr. by Stephen Key, © 2000, GIA Publications, Inc.

291 Blessed Feasts of Blessed Martyrs

1. Bless - ed feasts of bless - ed mar - tyrs, Ho - ly wom - en,
2. Faith pre - vail - ing, hope un - fail - ing, Lov - ing Christ with
3. There-fore, all that reign in glo - ry, Strong and sure with

ho - ly men, With our love and ad - mi - ra - tion,
sin - gle heart, Thus they, glo - rious and vic - to - rious,
Christ on high, Join to ours your sup - pli - ca - tion

Greet we your re - turn a - gain. Wor - thy deeds are
Brave - ly bore the mar - tyr's part, By con-tempt of
When be - fore him we draw nigh, Pray - ing that, this

theirs, and won-ders, Wor - thy of the name they bore;
ev - 'ry an-guish, By un - yield - ing bat - tle done;
life com - plet - ed, All its fleet - ing mo - ments past,

We, with joy - ful praise and sing - ing,
Vic - tors at the last, they tri - umph,
By his grace we may be wor - thy

Hon - or them for ev - er - more.
With the host of an - gels one.
Of e - ter - nal bliss at last.

Text: *O beata beatorum*, Latin, 12th. C.; tr. John M. Neale, 1818–1866, alt.
Tune: HYMN TO JOY, 8 7 8 7 D; arr. from Ludwig van Beethoven, 1770–1827, by Edward Hodges, 1796–1867

Ye Watchers and Ye Holy Ones 292

1. Ye watch-ers and ye ho-ly ones, Bright ser-aphs, cher-u-bim, and thrones, Raise the glad strain: "Al-le-lu-ia!" Cry out, do-min-ions, prince-doms, pow'rs, Vir - tues, arch-an-gels, an-gels' choirs: "Al-le-lu-ia! Al-le-lu-ia!" Al-le-lu-ia, al-le-lu-ia, al-le-lu - ia!

2. O high-er than the cher-u-bim, More glo-rious than the ser-a-phim, Lead their prais-es: "Al-le-lu-ia!" O bear-er of the e-ter-nal Word, Most gra-cious, mag-ni-fy the Lord: "Al-le-lu-ia! Al-le-lu-ia!" Al-le-lu-ia, al-le-lu-ia, al-le-lu - ia!

3. Re-spond, ye souls in end-less rest, Ye pa-tri-archs and proph-ets blest: "Al-le-lu-ia, Al-le-lu-ia!" Ye ho-ly twelve, ye mar-tyrs strong, All saints tri-um-phant, raise the song: "Al-le-lu-ia! Al-le-lu-ia!" Al-le-lu-ia, al-le-lu-ia, al-le-lu - ia!

4. O friends, in glad-ness let us sing, Su-per-nal an-thems ech-o-ing: "Al-le-lu-ia, Al-le-lu-ia!" To God the Fa-ther, God the Son, And God the Spir-it, Three in One: "Al-le-lu-ia! Al-le-lu-ia!" Al-le-lu-ia, al-le-lu-ia, al-le-lu - ia!

Text: John A. Riley, 1858–1945
Tune: LASST UNS ERFREUEN, LM with alleluias; *Geistliche Kirchengesänge*, Cologne, 1623; harm. by Ralph Vaughan Williams, 1872–1958

293   Lift High the Cross

Lift high the cross, the love of Christ pro-claim till
all the world a-dore his sa-cred name.

1. Come, Chris-tians, fol-low where our Sav-ior trod, Our
2. Led on their way by this tri-um-phant sign, The
3. Each new-born ser-vant of the Cru-ci-fied Bears
4. O Lord, once lift-ed on the glo-rious tree, Your
5. So shall our song of tri-umph ev-er be: Praise

D.C.

King vic-to-rious, Christ, the Son of God.
hosts of God in con-qu'ring ranks com-bine.
on the brow the seal of him who died.
death has bought us life e-ter-nal-ly.
to the Cru-ci-fied for vic-to-ry!

Text: 1 Corinthians 1:18; George W. Kitchin, 1827–1912, and Michael R. Newbolt, 1874–1956, alt.
Tune: CRUCIFER, 10 10 with refrain; Sydney H. Nicholson, 1875–1947
© 1974, Hope Publishing Company

Sing of Mary, Pure and Lowly 294

1. Sing of Mar - y, pure and low - ly, Vir - gin Moth - er
   un - de - filed. Sing of God's own Son most ho - ly,
   Who be - came her lit - tle child. Fair - est Child of
   fair - est Moth - er, God the Lord who came to earth,
   Word - made - flesh, our ver - y broth - er,
   Takes our na - ture by his birth.

2. Sing of Je - sus, son of Mar - y, In the home at
   Naz - a - reth. Toil and la - bor can - not wea - ry
   Love en - dur - ing un - to death. Con - stant was the
   love he gave her, Though he went forth from her side,
   Forth to preach, and heal, and suf - fer,
   Till on Cal - va - ry he died.

3. Glo - ry be to God the Fa - ther; Glo - ry be to
   God the Son; Glo - ry be to God the Spir - it;
   Glo - ry to the Three in One. From the heart of
   bless - ed Mar - y, From all saints the song as - cends,
   And the Church the strain re - ech - oes
   Un - to earth's re - mot - est ends.

Text: Roland F. Palmer, 1891–1985, © Estate of Roland Palmer
Tune: PLEADING SAVIOR, 8 7 8 7 D; *Christian Lyre*, 1830; harm. by Richard Proulx, 1937–2010, © 1986, GIA Publications, Inc.

295 Ave Maria

Verses

1. Hail Mar - y full of grace, the
2. Ho - ly Mar - y moth-er of God, the

Lord is with you.
Lord is with you.

Bless - ed are you a - mong all wom-en,
Pray for us sin - ners, pray for us sin - ners,

Blest is the fruit of your womb.
Now and at the hour of our death.

Refrain

Je - sus, formed in your faith, A - ve Ma - rí - a al - le -

lu - ia. Je - sus, born in your love,

A - ve Ma - rí - a al - le - lu - ia.

Holy Is Your Name 296

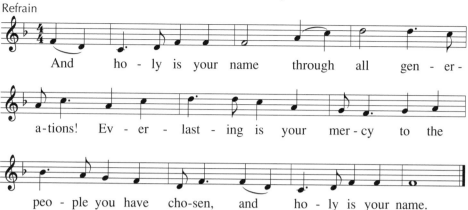

Refrain

And ho - ly is your name through all gen - er -
a - tions! Ev - er - last - ing is your mer - cy to the
peo - ple you have cho - sen, and ho - ly is your name.

Verses

1. My soul is filled with joy as I sing to God my savior:
   you have looked upon your servant, you have visited your people.

2. I am lowly as a child, but I know from this day forward
   that my name will be remembered, for all will call me blessed.

3. I proclaim the pow'r of God, you do marvels for your servants;
   though you scatter the proud hearted, and destroy the might of princes.

4. To the hungry you give food, send the rich away empty.
   In your mercy you are mindful of the people you have chosen.

5. In your love you now fulfill what you promised to your people.
   I will praise you, Lord, my savior, everlasting is your mercy.

Text: Luke 1:46–55, David Haas, b.1957
Tune: WILD MOUNTAIN THYME, Irregular; Irish traditional; arr. by David Haas, b.1957
© 1989, GIA Publications, Inc.

297 Immaculate Mary

1. Im - mac - u - late Mar - y, your prais - es we sing;
2. Pre - des - tined for Christ by e - ter - nal de - cree,
3. To you by an an - gel, the Lord God made known
4. Most blest of all wom - en, you heard and be - lieved;
5. The an - gels re - joiced when you brought forth God's Son;

You reign now in splen - dor with Je - sus our King.
God willed you both vir - gin and moth - er to be.
The grace of the Spir - it, the gift of the Son.
Most blest is the fruit of your womb then con - ceived.
Your joy is the joy of all a - ges to come.

A - ve, a - ve, a - ve, Ma - rí - a.

A - ve, a - ve, Ma - rí - a.

6. Your child is the Savior, all hope lies in him:
   He gives us new life and redeems us from sin.

7. In glory for ever now close to your Son,
   All ages will praise you for all God has done.

Text: St. 1, Jeremiah Cummings, 1814–1866, alt.; sts. 2–7, Brian Foley, 1919–2000, © 1971, Faber Music Ltd.
Tune: LOURDES HYMN, 11 11 with refrain; French melody, Grenoble, 1882

Regina Caeli / O Queen of Heaven 298

Re - gí - na cae - li, lae - tá - re, al - le - lú - ia,
O Queen of heav - en, be joy - ful, al - le - lu - ia,

Qui - a quem me - ru - í - sti por - tá - re, al - le - lú - ia,
For he whom you have hum - bly borne for us, al - le - lu - ia,

Re - sur - ré - xit si - cut di - xit, al - le - lú - ia,
Has a - ris - en, as he prom - ised, al - le - lu - ia,

O - ra pro no - bis De - um, al - le - lú - ia.
Of - fer now our prayer to God, al - le - lu - ia.

Text: Latin, 12th C.; tr. by C. Winfred Douglas, 1867–1944, alt.
Tune: REGINA CAELI, Irregular; Mode VI; acc. by Robert LeBlanc, OSB, b.1948, © 1986, GIA Publications, Inc.

Be Joyful, Mary 299

1. Be joy - ful, Mar - y, heav'n - ly Queen,
2. The Son you bore by heav - en's grace, Be
3. The Lord has ris - en from the dead, *Gau -*
4. Now pray to God, O Vir - gin fair,

joy - ful, Mar - y! Your grief is changed to joy se - rene,
de, Ma - rí - a! Did by his death our guilt e - rase,
He rose in glo - ry as he said,
That he our souls to heav - en bear,

Al - le - lu - ia!
Al - le - lu - ia! Re - joice, re - joice, O Mar - y!
Al - le - lu - ia! *Lae - tá - re, O Ma - rí - a!*
Al - le - lu - ia!

Text: *Regina caeli jubila*; Latin, 17th C.; tr. anon. in *Psallite,* 1901
Tune: REGINA CAELI, 8 5 8 4 7; Leisentritt's *Gesangbuch,* 1584, alt.

300 Desde el Cielo / From the Heavens

Estribillo: Des - de_el cie - lo_u-na_her - mo - sa ma - ña - na,
1. Su - pli - can - te jun - ta - ba las ma - nos,
2. Su lle - ga - da lle - nó de_a - le - grí - a,
3. Jun - to_al mon - te pa - sa - ba Juan Die - go,

Refrain: From the heav'ns on a beau - ti - ful morn - ing,
1. She was clasp - ing her hands, soft - ly pray - ing,
2. Her ar - ri - val brought joy o - ver - flow - ing,
3. From the hill - side Juan Die - go was round - ing,

Des - de_el cie - lo_u-na_her - mo - sa ma - ña - na,
Su - pli - can - te jun - ta - ba las ma - nos.
Su lle - ga - da lle - nó de_a - le - grí - a,
Jun - to_al mon - te pa - sa - ba Juan Die - go.

From the heav'ns on a beau - ti - ful morn - ing,
She was clasp - ing her hands, soft - ly pray - ing,
Her ar - ri - val brought joy o - ver - flow - ing,
From the hill - side Juan Die - go was round - ing,

La Gua - da - lu - pa - na, la Gua - da - lu - pa - na,
Y_e - ran me - xi - ca - nos, y_e - ran me - xi - ca - nos,
De paz y_ar - mo - ní - a, de paz y_ar - mo - ní - a,
Y_a - cer - có - se lue - go, y_a - cer - có - se lue - go,

Ra - diant light was pour - ing, ra - diant light was pour - ing,
Face and pos - ture say - ing, face and pos - ture say - ing,
Peace and con - cord grow - ing, peace and con - cord grow - ing,
Mu - sic sweet - ly sound - ing, mu - sic sweet - ly sound - ing,

1. | 2.

La Gua - da - lu - pa - na ba - jó_al Te - pe - yac. yac.
Y_e - ran me - xi - ca - nos su por - te_y su faz. faz.
De paz y_ar - mo - ní - a to-do_el A - ná - huac. huac.
Y_a - cer - có - se lue - go al o - ír can - tar. tar.

La Gua - da - lu - pa - na came to Te - pe - yac. yac.
She was Me - xi - ca - na, like the peo-ple there. there.
Peace and con-cord grow-ing in the A - ná - huac. huac.
Mu - sic sweet-ly sound-ing filled the cool, crisp air. air.

4. "Juan Dieguito," la Virgen le dijo,
   "Juan Dieguito," la Virgen le dijo,
   "Este cerro_elijo, este cerro_elijo,
   Este cerro_elijo para_hacer mi_altar."
   "Este cerro_elijo, este cerro_elijo,
   Este cerro_elijo para_hacer mi_altar."

5. Y_en la tilma_entre rosas pintadas,
   Y_en la tilma_entre rosas pintadas,
   Su_imagen amada, su_imagen amada,
   Su_imagen amada se dignó dejar.
   Su_imagen amada, su_imagen amada,
   Su_imagen amada se dignó dejar.

6. Desde_entonces para_el Mexicano,
   Desde_entonces para la Mexicana,
   Ser Guadalupano, ser Guadalupana,
   Ser Guadalupanos es algo_esencial.
   Ser Guadalupano, ser Guadalupana,
   Ser Guadalupanos es algo_esencial.

7. Madrecita de los Mexicanos,*
   Madrecita de los Mexicanos,
   Que_estás en el cielo, que_estás en
     el cielo,
   Que_estás en el cielo, ruega_a Dios
     por nos.
   Que_estás en el cielo, que_estás en
     el cielo,
   Que_estás en el cielo, ruega_a Dios
     por nos.

8. En sus penas se postra de_hinojos,
   En sus penas se postra de_hinojos,
   Y_eleva sus ojos, y_eleva sus ojos,
   Y_eleva sus ojos hacia_el Tepeyac.
   Y_eleva sus ojos, y_eleva sus ojos,
   Y_eleva sus ojos hacia_el Tepeyac.

4. *"Juan Dieguito," the Virgin called gently.*
   "Juan Dieguito," the Virgin called gently.
   Telling him intently, telling him intently,
   "This hill I have chosen for my holy shrine."
   Telling him intently, telling him intently,
   "This hill I have chosen for my holy shrine."

5. *Roses fell from his cloak, brightly tinted,*
   Roses fell from his cloak, brightly tinted,
   Leaving there imprinted, leaving there
     imprinted,
   Leaving there the image of the Virgin fair.
   Leaving there imprinted, leaving there
     imprinted
   Leaving there the image of the Virgin fair.

6. *From that time forward, each Mexicano,*
   From that time forward, each Mexicana,
   True Guadalupano, true Guadalupana,
   True Guadalupanos all are born to be.
   True Guadalupano, true Guadalupana,
   True Guadalupanos all are born to be.

7. *Madrecita† to all peoples given,*
   Madrecita to all peoples given,
   As the Queen of Heaven, as the Queen
     of Heaven,
   As the Queen of Heaven, kindly pray
     for us.
   As the Queen of Heaven, as the Queen
     of Heaven,
   As the Queen of Heaven, kindly pray
     for us.

8. *We approach you in love, humbly kneeling,*
   We approach you in love, humbly kneeling,
   Earnestly appealing, earnestly appealing,
   Lifting up our eyes and hearts to Tepeyac.
   Earnestly appealing, earnestly appealing,
   Lifting up our eyes and hearts to Tepeyac.

Texto alternativo / alternate text: Madrecita de todos nosotros (2x)
†Dearest Mother

Text: Traditional; tr. by Mary Louise Bringle, b.1953, © 2005, GIA Publications, Inc.
Tune: APARACIONES GUADALUPANAS, 10 10 12 11 D; traditional; harm. by Ronald F. Krisman, b.1946,
   © 2005, GIA Publications, Inc.

301 Adiós, Reina del Cielo / Adiós, O Queen of Heaven

Estribillo: A - diós, Rei - na del cie - lo, Ma - dre del Sal - va - dor.
1. De tu di - vi - no ros - tro me a - le - jo con pe - sar,
2. A - diós, Rei - na del cie - lo, Ma - dre del Sal - va - dor,
3. De tu di - vi - no ros - tro la be - lle - za al de - jar,

Refrain: A - diós, O Queen of heav - en and Moth - er of our Lord.
1. The time has come to leave you, whose im - age is sub - lime;
2. A - diós, O Queen of heav - en and Moth - er of our Lord,
3. Your beau - ty is e - ter - nal, be - fit - ting heav - en's Queen;

A - diós, oh Ma - dre mí - a. A - diós, a - diós, a - diós.
Per - mí - te - me que vuel - va tus plan - tas a be - sar.
Dul - ce pren - da a - do - ra - da de mi sin - ce - ro a - mor.
Per - mí - te - me que vuel - va tus plan - tas a be - sar.

A - diós, fare - well, your chil - dren now sing with one ac - cord.
We thank you for ac - cept - ing your part in God's de - sign.
With o - pen hearts we greet you, our love for you out - poured.
Your love in - spires and moves us like noth - ing we have seen.

4. A dejarte, oh María, no acierta el corazón:
   Te lo entrego, Señora, dame tu bendición.

5. Adiós, Hija del Padre; Madre del Hijo, adiós.
   Del Espíritu Santo, oh casta Esposa, adiós.

6. Adiós, oh Madre Virgen, más pura que la luz:
   Jamás, jamás me olvides delante de Jesús.

7. Adiós, del cielo encanto, mi delicia y mi amor,
   Adiós, oh Madre mía. Adiós, adiós, adiós.

4. *Implant in us, O Mary, your gifts from heav'n above:*
   We trust you, noble Lady, to bless us with your love.

5. *Graced daughter of the Father and mother of God's Son,*
   Chaste spouse of God the Spirit, blest by the Three in One.

6. *Farewell, O Virgin Mother, God's handmaid pure as light:*
   Remind your Son, dear Mary, to keep us in his sight.

7. *Adiós, delight of heaven, your praise we long to tell;*
   Adiós, our blessed Mother, we fondly say farewell.

Text: Traditional; tr. by Jill Switzer Wolf, b.1976, and J. Eduardo Wolf, b.1971, © 2012, GIA Publications, Inc.
Tune: Traditional; harm. by Ronald F. Krisman, b.1946, © 2012, GIA Publications, Inc.

Hail, Holy Queen Enthroned Above 302

1. Hail, ho - ly Queen en - throned a - bove, O Ma - rí - a. Hail,
2. The cause of joy to all be - low, O Ma - rí - a. The
3. O gen - tle, lov - ing, ho - ly one, O Ma - rí - a. The

Queen of mer - cy and of love, O Ma - rí - a.
spring through which all grac - es flow, O Ma - rí - a.
God of light be - came your Son, O Ma - rí - a.

Tri - umph, all ye Cher - u - bim; Sing with us, ye
An - gels, all your prais - es bring; Earth and heav - en,
Tri - umph, all ye Cher - u - bim; Sing with us, ye

Ser - a - phim. Heav'n and earth re - sound the hymn:
with us sing; All cre - a - tion ech - o - ing:
Ser - a - phim. Heav'n and earth re - sound the hymn:

Sal - ve, Sal - ve, Sal - ve Re - gí - na.

Text: *Salve Regina, mater misericordiae*; c.1080; tr. *Roman Hymnal*, 1884; st. 2–3, adapt. by M. Owen Lee, CSB, b.1930
Tune: SALVE REGINA COELITUM, 8 4 8 4 777 4 5; *Choralmelodien zum Heiligen Gesänge*, 1808; harm. by Healey Willan, 1880–1968,
© Willis Music Co.

303 Mañanitas a la Virgen de Guadalupe / Morning Praises to the Virgin of Guadalupe

Verses 1–4

1. Oh Vir - gen, la más her - mo - sa del Va -
2. Re - ci - be, Ma - dre que - ri - da, nues - tra
3. Re - ci - be, Ma - dre que - ri - da, nues - tra
4. Tú bri - llas - te, Vir - gen San - ta, co - mo_es -

1. *Bless-ed Vir - gin, O most love - ly of the*
2. *Bless-ed Moth - er, most be - lov - ed, how we*
3. *Bless-ed Moth - er, full of grac - es, here we*
4. *Ho - ly Vir - gin, you are shin - ing like the*

lle de A - ná - huac, Tus hi - jos muy de ma -
fe - li - ci - ta - ción, Hoy por ser el día tan
fe - li - ci - ta - ción: Mi - ra - mos a - quí pos -
tre - lla ma - ti - nal, A - nun - cian - do la_al - bo -

A - ná -huac, we sing: As your chil - dren come to
hon - or you this day, When you ten - der - ly ap -
kneel in hum - ble prayer: Look up - on us with your
bright - est morn -ing star. As the sky be - gins to

ña - na te vie - nen a sa - lu - dar.
gran - de de tu tier - na_a - pa - ri - ción.
tra - dos y da - nos tu ben - di - ción.
ra - da que_i - ba pron - to_a co - men - zar.

greet you, our morn - ing prais - es we bring.
peared, bring - ing hope and light for our way.
fa - vor, and show - er all with your care.
light - en we see how ra - diant you are.

Refrain

Des - pier - ta, Ma-dre, des - pier-ta, mi - ra que ya_a - ma - ne - ció;
A - wake, Moth-er, now a - wak-en as day-light comes in - to view.

[1.–3.]

Mi-ra_es - te ra - mo de flo - res que pa - ra ti trai-go yo.
See this bright bou-quet of flow-ers we bring to of - fer to you.

yo.
you.

4. | Verse 5

5. Ya viene al-bo - ran-do el dí - a, qué lin-
El ce - rro del Te - pe - yac es-co-
5. *The dawn is spread-ing its col-ors to sa-*
In Te - pe-yac, on a hill-side, you have

da es - tá la ma - ña - na, Sa - lu - de-
gis - te por mo - ra - da, Por e - so
lute you, fair Ma - don - na. We, too, would
graced us, fair Ma - don - na. For choos - ing

mos a Ma - rí - a: bue-nos dí - as, Gua-da-lu - pa-na.
te sa - lu - da - mos, bue-nos dí - as, Gua-da-lu - pa-na.
of - fer our prais - es as we greet you, Gua-da-lu - pa-na.
this as your dwell - ing, we now hail you, Gua-da-lu - pa-na.

Ya vie - ne a-ma - ne-cien - do, ya la
The morn - ing light is break - ing with the

luz del dí - a nos dio; Le - ván - ta - te, Vir-gen-
daz - zling gift of the sun. Now a - rise, O dear - est

ci - ta, mi - ra que ya a - ma - ne - ció.
Vir - gin: for a new day has be - gun!

Text: Traditional; tr. by Mary Louise Bringle, b.1953, © 2012, GIA Publications, Inc.
Tune: Traditional; harm. by Ronald F. Krisman, b.1946, © 2012, GIA Publications, Inc.

304 Magnificat / Sing Out, My Soul

Canon

1. Ma - gní - fi - cat, ma - gní - fi - cat,
Sing out, my soul. *Sing out, my soul.*

2. Ma - gní - fi - cat á - ni - ma
Sing out and glo-ri-fy the

me - a Dó - mi - num. Ma - gní - fi - cat,
Lord who sets us free. *Sing out, my soul.*

3. ma - gní - fi - cat,
Sing out, my soul.

4. Ma - gní - fi - cat á - ni - ma me - a!
Sing out and glo - ri - fy the Lord God!

Text: Luke 1:46, *My soul magnifies the Lord;* Taizé Community, 1978
Tune: Jacques Berthier, 1923–1994
© 1979, Les Presses de Taizé, GIA Publications, Inc., agent

305 Steal Away to Jesus

Refrain

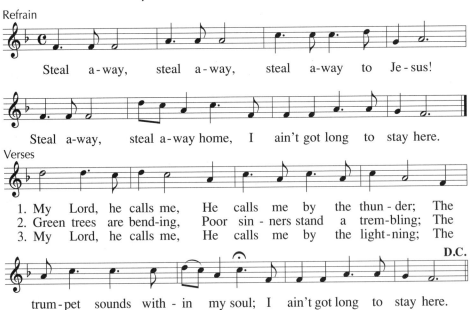

Steal a - way, steal a - way, steal a - way to Je - sus!

Steal a - way, steal a - way home, I ain't got long to stay here.

Verses

1. My Lord, he calls me, He calls me by the thun - der; The
2. Green trees are bend-ing, Poor sin - ners stand a trem - bling; The
3. My Lord, he calls me, He calls me by the light-ning; The

D.C.

trum - pet sounds with - in my soul; I ain't got long to stay here.

Text: African American spiritual
Tune: African American spiritual

Soon and Very Soon 306

1. Soon and ver - y soon we are goin' to see the King,
2. No more cry - in' there, we are goin' to see the King,
3. No more dy - in' there, we are goin' to see the King,
4. Soon and ver - y soon we are goin' to see the King,

Soon and ver - y soon we are goin' to see the King,
No more cry - in' there, we are goin' to see the King,
No more dy - in' there, we are goin' to see the King,
Soon and ver - y soon we are goin' to see the King,

Soon and ver - y soon we are goin' to see the King.
No more cry - in' there, we are goin' to see the King.
No more dy - in' there, we are goin' to see the King. Hal-le -
Soon and ver - y soon we are goin' to see the King.

1., 2.

lu - jah, hal - le - lu - jah, we're goin' to see the King!

3., 4.

Hal - le - lu - jah, hal - le - lu -

jah, hal - le - lu - jah, hal - le - lu - jah.

Text: Andraé Crouch, b.1942
Tune: SOON AND VERY SOON, 12 12 12 14; Andraé Crouch, b.1942
© 1976, Crouch Music/Bud John Songs (admin. CapitolCMGPublishing.com)

307 Jerusalem, My Happy Home

1. Je - ru - sa - lem, my hap - py home, When
2. Your saints are crowned with glo - ry great; They
3. There Da - vid stands with harp in hand As
4. Our La - dy sings Ma - gni - fi - cat With
5. There Mag - da - lene has left her tears, And
6. Je - ru - sa - lem, Je - ru - sa - lem, God

shall I with you be? When shall my sor - rows
see God face to face; They tri - umph still, they
mas - ter of the choir: Ten thou - sand times would
tune sur - pass - ing sweet; And all the vir - gins
cheer - ful - ly does sing With bless - ed saints, whose
grant that I may see Your end - less joy, and

have an end? Your joys when shall I see?
still re - joice In that most ho - ly place.
we be blessed Who might this mu - sic hear.
join the song While sit - ting at her feet.
har - mo - ny In ev - 'ry street does ring.
of the same Par - tak - er ev - er be!

Text: F.B.P., 16th C., alt.
Tune: LAND OF REST, CM; American melody; harm. by Richard Proulx, 1937–2010, © 1975, GIA Publications, Inc.

Shall We Gather at the River 308

1. Shall we gath - er at the riv - er, Where bright
2. On the mar - gin of the riv - er, Wash - ing
3. Ere we reach the shin - ing riv - er, Lay we
4. Soon we'll reach the shin - ing riv - er, Soon our

an - gel feet have trod, With its crys - tal tide for
up its sil - ver spray, We will walk and wor - ship
ev - 'ry bur - den down; Grace our spir - its will de -
pil-grim-age will cease; Soon our hap - py hearts will

ev - er Flow-ing by the throne of God?
ev - er, All the hap - py gold - en day.
liv - er, And pro - vide a robe and crown.
quiv - er With the mel - o - dy of peace.

Yes, we'll gath - er at the riv - er, The beau - ti - ful, the

beau-ti - ful riv - er, Gath - er with the saints at the

riv - er That flows by the throne of God.

Text: Robert Lowry, 1826–1899
Tune: HANSON PLACE, 8 7 8 7 with refrain; Robert Lowry, 1826–1899

309 Christ Will Be Your Strength

Christ will be your strength! Learn to know and fol-low him!

Text: David Haas, b.1957
Tune: David Haas, b.1957
© 1988, GIA Publications, Inc.

310 You Have Put on Christ

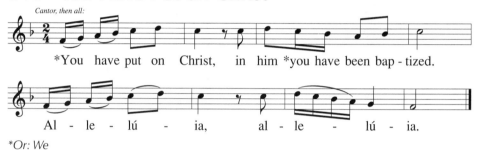

Cantor, then all:

*You have put on Christ, in him *you have been bap - tized.

Al - le - lú - ia, al - le - lú - ia.

Or: We

Text: ICEL, © 1969
Music: Howard Hughes, SM, © 1977, ICEL

311 Baptized in Water

1. Bap - tized in wa - ter, Sealed by the Spir - it, Cleansed by the
2. Bap - tized in wa - ter, Sealed by the Spir - it, Dead in the
3. Bap - tized in wa - ter, Sealed by the Spir - it, Marked with the

blood of Christ our King: Heirs of sal - va - tion, Trust-ing his
tomb with Christ our King: One with his ris - ing, Freed and for-
sign of Christ our King: Born of one Fa - ther, We are his

prom - ise, Faith - ful - ly now God's praise we sing.
giv - en, Thank-ful - ly now God's praise we sing.
chil - dren, Joy - ful - ly now God's praise we sing.

Text: Michael Saward, b.1932, © 1982, The Jubilate Group (admin. by Hope Publishing Company)
Tune: BUNESSAN, 5 5 8 D; Gaelic melody; acc. by Marty Haugen, b.1950, © 1987, GIA Publications, Inc.

Sweet Refreshment 312

Refrain

Cantor: Come to the wa-ter. *All:* Come to the wa-ter. *Cantor:* Drink of it free-ly.

All: Drink of it free-ly. *Cantor:* Taste God's own Spir-it. *All:* Taste God's own

Spir-it. *Cantor:* Sweet re - fresh-ment. *All:* Sweet re - fresh-ment.

Verses

Cantor:
1. At the dawn of cre - a - tion, your
2. When your peo - ple were cap - tive, you
3. In the wa - ters of Jor - dan, your
4. Liv - ing wa - ters, e - ter - nal,

Spir - it, O God, moved on the wa - ters. You
led them, O God, led them from bond - age. You
Son was bap - tized; with Spir - it a - noint - ed, that
quench ev - 'ry thirst, cleanse ev - 'ry soul.

D.C.

breathed and the wa - ters were life.
led them through wa - ters to life.
we might be raised to new life.
You are the foun - tain of life.

Text: Based on *Blessing of Water,* Easter Vigil; adapt. by Bob Moore, b.1962
Tune: Bob Moore, b.1962
© 1999, GIA Publications, Inc.

313 Wade in the Water

Refrain

Wade in the wa-ter, wade in the wa-ter, chil-dren,

wade in the wa-ter, God's a gon-na trou-ble the wa-ter.

Verses

Cantor:

1. See that host all dressed in white,
2. See that band all dressed in red,
3. Look o - ver yon - der, what do I see?
4. If you don't be - lieve I've been re - deemed,

All:

God's a gon - na trou - ble the wa - ter;

Cantor:

The lead - er looks like the Is - ra - el - ite,
Looks like the band that Mo - ses led,
The Ho - ly Ghost a com - in' on me,
Just fol - low me down to Jor - dan's stream,

All:

D.C.

God's a gon - na trou - ble the wa - ter.

Text: African American spiritual
Tune: African American spiritual; harm. by Diana Kodner, b.1957, © 1994, GIA Publications, Inc.

Taste and See   314

Refrain

Taste and see, taste and see the good-ness of the Lord. O taste and see, taste and see the good-ness of the Lord, of the Lord.

Verses

1. I will bless the Lord at all times.
2. Glo-ri-fy the Lord with me.
3. Wor-ship the Lord, all you peo-ple.

Praise shall al-ways be on my lips;
To-geth-er let us all praise God's name.
You'll want for noth-ing if you ask.

my soul shall glo-ry in the Lord
I called the Lord who an-swered me;
Taste and see that the Lord is good;

for God has been so good to me.
from all my trou-bles I was set free.
in God we need put all our trust.

D.C.

Text: Psalm 34; James E. Moore, Jr., b.1951
Tune: James E. Moore, Jr., b.1951
© 1983, GIA Publications, Inc.

315 I Am the Bread of Life / Yo Soy el Pan de Vida

Verses

1.____ I am the Bread of life. You who
2. The bread that____ I will give is my
3. Un - less____ you____ eat of the
4.____ I am the Res - ur - rec - tion,____
5.____ Yes, Lord,____ we be - lieve that____

1.____ Yo soy el Pan de Vi - da. A mí
2. El pan que____ yo da - ré es mi
3.____ Si us - te - des no co - men la____
4. Yo soy la____ Re - su - rrec-ción,____
5.____ Sí, Se - ñor, cre - e - mos que____

come to me shall not hun - ger;____ and who be -
flesh for the life of the world,____ and if you
flesh of the Son of Man____ and____
I____ am the life.____ If you be -
you____ are the Christ,____ the____

ven - gan:____ no ten -drán ham - bre.____ En mí
car - ne, la vi - da del mun - do.____ Los que
car - ne del Hi - jo del Hom - bre,____ y no
Yo____ soy la Vi - da.____ Si en
tú e - res____ el Me - sí - as,____ el____

lieve in me shall not thirst.____ No one can come to
eat____ of this bread,____ you shall__ live for
drink____ of his blood,- and drink____ of his
lieve____ in____ me,____ e - ven__ though you
Son____ of____ God,____ Who____ has__

cre - an:__ no ten -drán sed.____ Na - die__ vie - ne a
co - men__ de es - te pan____ vi - vi - rán por
be - ben__ de su san -gre, no be - ben__ de su
mí us - te - des cre - en,____ aun -que__ ha - yan
Hi - jo de Dios,_ que has ve - ni -do al

me   un - less   the   Fa - ther   beck - ons.
ev - er,_____   you   shall   live   for   ev - er.
blood,   you   shall   not have life with - in   you.
die,_____   you   shall   live   for   ev - er.
come   in - to_____   the_____ world.____

mí   *si mi Pa - dre*   *no lo_a - tra - e.*
*siem - pre,*_____   *vi - vi - rán*   *por siem - pre.*
san - gre,   *no po -drán*   *te - ner*   *mi*   *vi - da.*
*muer - to,*_____   *vi - vi - rán*   *por siem - pre.*
*mun - do*_____   *pa - ra*   *re - di - mir - nos.*

Refrain

And I will raise   you up,   and I will
Yo los re - su - ci - ta - ré,   Yo los re -

raise   you   up,   and I will raise   you
su - ci - ta - ré,   Yo los re - su - ci - ta -

up   on   the   last   day.
ré   en   el   dí - a   fi - nal.

Text: John 6 and 11; Suzanne Toolan, RSM, b.1927; tr. anon., rev. by Ronald F. Krisman, b.1946
Tune: BREAD OF LIFE, Irregular with refrain; Suzanne Toolan, RSM, b.1927

316 I Receive the Living God

Refrain

I re - ceive the liv - ing God, And my heart is full of joy. I re - ceive the liv-ing God, And my heart is full of joy.

Verses

1. Je - sus says: I am the Bread Sent to
2. Je - sus says: I am the Vine, Far from
3. Je - sus says: I am the Way, And my
4. Je - sus says: I am the Truth. If you
5. Je - sus says: I am the Life, Raised in
6. Je - sus says: I am the Day, Shin - ing

you from God Most High. Take and eat, and you will
whom no life can grow. If you join your - self to
path is straight and true. Fol - low me to where I
fol - low close to me, You will know me in your
tri - umph from the dead. As one Bod - y now re -
bright - ly through your night. Wel - come me, and you will

D.C.

live; You need nev - er fear to die.
me, A rich har - vest you will know.
lead; There my Fa - ther waits for you.
heart, And my word will make you free.
main, Mem - bers joined to me, the Head.
walk By the Spir - it's guid - ing light.

7. Jesus says: I am the Love
   Which can bind you close to me.
   Those who know this gift I bring
   Will find true community.

8. Jesus says: I am the Peace
   Which the world cannot bestow.
   Learn to love and live in me,
   And in you my Reign will grow.

9. Jesus says: I am the Lamb,
   And my death set sinners free.
   Those who drink the cup I drink
   Must take up this work with me.

Text: Vss. 1–3, 5–9, Bernard Geoffroy, b.1946; tr. by Ronald F. Krisman, b.1946, © 2011, GIA Publications, Inc.; vs. 4, anonymous
Tune: LIVING GOD, 7 7 7 7 with refrain; Dom Clément Jacob, OSB, 1906–1977, adapt.; harm. by Richard Proulx, 1937–2010, © 1986, GIA Publications, Inc.

One Bread, One Body   317

Text: 1 Corinthians 10:16–17, 12:4, 12–13, 20; Galatians 3:28; Ephesians 4:46; the *Didache* 9; John Foley, SJ, b.1939
Tune: ONE BREAD, ONE BODY, 4 4 6 with refrain; John Foley, SJ, b.1939
© 1978, John B. Foley, SJ. Published by OCP.

318 Pan de Vida

Refrain

*Pan de Vi - da, cuer-po del Se - ñor,

cup of bless - ing, blood of Christ the Lord.

At this ta - ble the last shall be first, ***po-*

der es ser - vir, por-que Dios es a - mor.

Verses

1. We are the dwell-ing of God,
***2. Us - te - des me lla - man "Se - ñor,"** *me in-*
3. There is no Jew or Greek,

fra - gile and wound-ed and weak. We are the
cli - no a la - var - les los pies. Ha - gan lo
there is no slave or free; there is no

bod - y of Christ, called to be the com -
mis - mo, hu - mil - des, sir - vién - do - se
wom-an or man; on - ly heirs of the

D.C.

pas - sion of God.
u - nos a o - tros.
prom - ise of God.

*Bread of Life, body of the Lord,   **power is for service, because God is Love.
***You call me "Lord," and I bow to wash your feet:
you must do the same, humbly serving each other.

Text: John 13:13–14, Galatians 3:28–29; Bob Hurd, b.1950, and Pia Moriarty, b.1948
Tune: Bob Hurd, b.1950; acc. by Craig Kingsbury, b.1952
© 1988, Bob Hurd and Pia Moriarty. Published by OCP.

Now We Remain 319

Refrain

We hold the death of the Lord deep in our hearts. Liv-ing, now we re-main with Je-sus, the Christ.

Verses

1. Once we were peo-ple a-fraid, lost in the night. Then by your cross we were saved— Dead be-came liv-ing, Life from your giv-ing.

2. Some-thing which we have known, some-thing we've touched, What we have seen with our eyes; This we have heard: Life-giv-ing Word.

3. He chose to give of him-self, be-came our bread: Bro-ken, that we might live— Love be-yond love, Pain for our pain.

4. We are the pres-ence of God; this is our call: Now to be-come bread and wine— Food for the hun-gry, Life for the wea-ry.

For to live with the Lord, we must die with the Lord.

Text: Corinthians, 1 John, 2 Timothy; David Haas, b.1957
Tune: David Haas, b.1957
© 1983, GIA Publications, Inc.

320 Take and Eat

Refrain

Take and eat; take and eat: this is my bod-y giv-en up for you. Take and drink; take and drink: this is my blood giv-en up for you.

Verses

1. I am the Word that spoke and light was made;
2. I am the way that leads the ex-ile home;
3. I am the Lamb that takes a-way your sin;
4. I am the cor-ner-stone that God has laid;
5. I am the light that came in-to the world;
6. I am the first and last, the Liv-ing One;

I am the seed that died to be re-born;
I am the truth that sets the cap-tive free;
I am the gate that guards you night and day;
A cho-sen stone and pre-cious in his eyes;
I am the light that dark-ness can-not hide;
I am the Lord who died that you might live;

I am the bread that comes from heav'n a-bove;
I am the life that rais-es up the dead;
You are my flock: you know the shep-herd's voice;
You are God's dwell-ing place, on me you rest;
I am the morn-ing star that nev-er sets;
I am the bride-groom, this my wed-ding song;

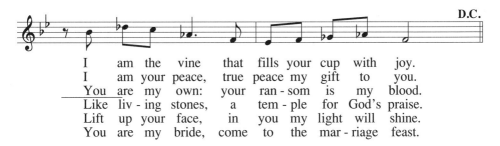

D.C.

I am the vine that fills your cup with joy.
I am your peace, true peace my gift to you.
You are my own: your ran-som is my blood.
Like liv-ing stones, a tem-ple for God's praise.
Lift up your face, in you my light will shine.
You are my bride, come to the mar-riage feast.

Text: Verse text, James Quinn, SJ, 1919–2010, © 1989. Used by permission of Selah Publishing Co., Inc.; refrain text, Michael Joncas, b.1951,
   © 1989, GIA Publications, Inc.
Tune: CORPUS DOMINI, 10 10 10 10 with refrain; Michael Joncas, b.1951, © 1989, GIA Publications, Inc.

We Come to Your Table   321

Verses

Cantor: All:

1. Gen - tle   Je - sus,   ris - en   Lord,
2. Bring - ing   gifts   of   all   we   are.
3. In   your   bod - y   we   find   life,   we come to your
4. In   your   bod - y   we   are   one,
5. Je - sus   Sav - ior,   liv - ing   bread!
6. You   in - vite   us,   we   re - joice!

Cantor:

          with   our   hearts   so   full   of   joy,
          gifts   of   life   and   love   and   joy,
ta - ble; life   you   give   for   us   to   share.
          one   with   you   and   one   an - oth - er.
          Bread   of   heav - en,   bread   of   hope,
          We   re - mem - ber,   we   give   thanks!

All: Refrain

we   come   to   your   ta - ble.   We   come,   we   come,

we   come   to   your   ta - ble.   We   come,   we   come,

we   come   to   your   ta - ble.

Text: Carey Landry, b.1944
Tune: Carey Landry, b.1944
© 1973, OCP

322 Song of the Body of Christ / Canción del Cuerpo de Cristo

Refrain

We come to share our sto-ry, we
Hoy ve - ni - mos a con - tar nues-tra his - to - ria, com - par-

come to break the bread, We come to
tien - do el pan ce - les - tial. Hoy ve - ni - mos jun - tos

know our ris - ing from the dead.
a ce - le - brar tu mis - te - rio pas - cual.

Verses

1. We come as your peo - ple, we
2. We are called to heal the bro - ken, to be
3. Bread of life and cup of prom - ise, in this
4. You will lead and we shall fol - low, you will
5. We will live and sing: "A - lo - ha," "Al - le -
(live and sing your prais - es,)

come as your own, u - nit - ed with each
hope for the poor, we are called to feed the
meal we all are one. In our dy - ing and our
be the breath of life; liv-ing wa - ter, we are
lu - ia" is our song. May we live in love and

D.C.

oth - er, love finds a home.
hun - gry at our door.
ris - ing, may your king - dom come.
thirst - ing for your light.
peace our whole life long.

Estrofas

1. Hoy ve - ni - mos por - que so - mos tu pue - blo, re - na -
2. A sa - nar al en - fer - mo nos lla - mas, al an -
3. Pan de vi - da y san - gre de la a - lian - za, haz - nos
4. Nos guia - rás y te se - gui - re - mos. Nues - tro a -
5. Vi - vi - re - mos can - tan - do "A - lo - ja." "A - le -

ci - dos por tu per - dón, re - u - ni - dos
sio - so, tu es - pe - ran - za tra - er, y al ham - brien - to,
u - no en es - ta co - mu - nión. Que tu rei - no
lien - to vi - tal tú se - rás. Nues - tra luz, en el
lu - ya" es nues - tra can - ción. Que vi - va - mos por

D.C.

en tu a - mor, y de un co - ra - zón.
nues - tro a - li - men - to o - fre - cer.
ven - ga en nues - tra trans - for - ma - ción.
dí - a y en la no - che bri - lla - rás.
siem - pre en paz y fra - ter - na u - nión.

Text: David Haas, b.1957, Spanish translation by Donna Peña, b.1955, and Ronald F. Krisman, b.1946
Tune: NO KE ANO' AHI AHI, Irregular, Hawaiian traditional, arr. by David Haas, b.1957
© 1989, tr. 2004, GIA Publications, Inc.

323 You Satisfy the Hungry Heart

Refrain

You sat - is - fy the hun - gry heart With
gift of fin - est wheat; Come give to us, O
sav - ing Lord, The bread of life to eat.

Verses

1. As when the shep - herd calls his sheep, They
2. With joy - ful lips we sing to you Our
3. Is not the cup we bless and share The
4. The mys - t'ry of your pres - ence, Lord, No
5. You give your - self to us, O Lord; Then

know and heed his voice; So when you call your
praise and grat - i - tude, That you should count us
blood of Christ out - poured? Do not one cup, one
mor - tal tongue can tell: Whom all the world can -
self - less let us be, To serve each oth - er

D.C.

fam - 'ly, Lord, We fol - low and re - joice.
wor - thy, Lord, To share this heav'n - ly food.
loaf, de - clare Our one - ness in the Lord?
not con - tain Comes in our hearts to dwell.
in your name In truth and char - i - ty.

Text: Omer Westendorf, 1916–1997
Tune: BICENTENNIAL, CM with refrain; Robert E. Kreutz, 1922–1996
© 1977, Archdiocese of Philadelphia. Published by International Liturgy Publications

Behold the Lamb 324

Verses

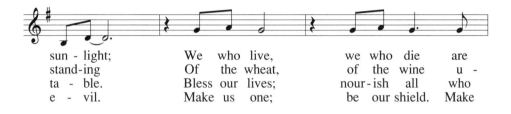

1. Those who were in the dark are thank-ful for the
2. Peace-ful now, those whose hearts are blessed with un - der -
3. Gen - tle one, Child of God, join with us at this
4. Lord of all, give us light. De - liv - er us from

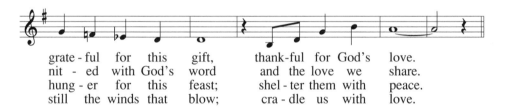

sun - light; We who live, we who die are
stand-ing Of the wheat, of the wine u -
ta - ble. Bless our lives; nour-ish all who
e - vil. Make us one; be our shield. Make

grate - ful for this gift, thank-ful for God's love.
nit - ed with God's word and the love we share.
hung - er for this feast; shel - ter them with peace.
still the winds that blow; cra - dle us with love.

Refrain

Be - hold, be - hold the Lamb of God. All who eat,

all who drink shall live; and all, all who dwell in

God, shall come to know God's glo-ry!

Text: Martin Willett, b.1960, alt.
Tune: Martin Willett, b.1960; acc. by Craig S. Kingsbury, b.1952
© 1984, OCP

325 Bread of Life from Heaven /
Pan de Vida Eterna

Refrain

Bread of life from heav-en, your blood and bod - y giv-en, we
Pan de vi - da_e - ter - na, nos das tu cuer - po_y san-gre.

eat this bread and drink this cup un - til you come a - gain.
Has - ta que vuel - vas tú, Se - ñor, co - me - mos en tu_a -mor.

Verses

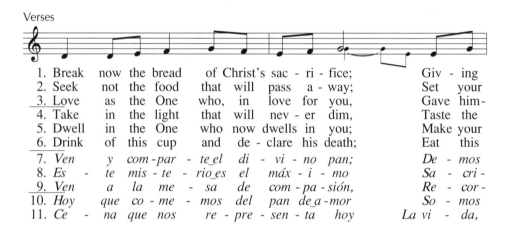

1. Break now the bread of Christ's sac - ri - fice; Giv - ing
2. Seek not the food that will pass a - way; Set your
3. Love as the One who, in love for you, Gave him-
4. Take in the light that will nev - er dim, Taste the
5. Dwell in the One who now dwells in you; Make your
6. Drink of this cup and de - clare his death; Eat this
7. *Ven y com - par - te_el di - vi - no pan; De - mos*
8. *Es - te mis - te - rio_es el máx - i - mo Sa - cri -*
9. *Ven a la me - sa de com - pa - sión, Re - cor -*
10. *Hoy que co - me - mos del pan de_a -mor So - mos*
11. *Ce - na que nos re - pre - sen - ta hoy La vi - da,*

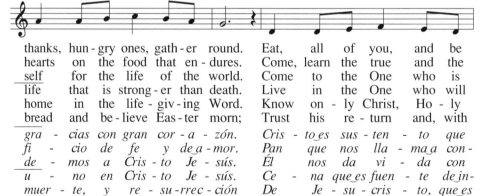

thanks, hun - gry ones, gath - er round. Eat, all of you, and be
hearts on the food that en - dures. Come, learn the true and the
self for the life of the world. Come to the One who is
life that is strong - er than death. Live in the One who will
home in the life - giv - ing Word. Know on - ly Christ, Ho - ly
bread and be - lieve Eas-ter morn; Trust his re - turn and, with
gra - cias con gran cor - a - zón. Cris - to_es sus - ten - to que
fi - cio de fe y de_a -mor. Pan que nos lla - ma_a con -
de - mos a Cris - to Je - sús. Él nos da vi - da con
u - no en Cris - to Je - sús. Ce - na que_es fuen - te de_in -
muer - te, y re - su - rrec - ción De Je - su - cris - to, que_es

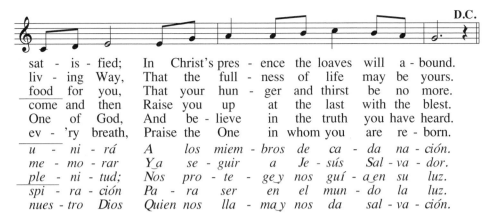

sat - is - fied; In Christ's pres - ence the loaves will a - bound.
liv - ing Way, That the full - ness of life may be yours.
food for you, That your hun - ger and thirst be no more.
come and then Raise you up at the last with the blest.
One of God, And be - lieve in the truth you have heard.
ev - 'ry breath, Praise the One in whom you are re - born.

_u_ - _ni_ - _rá_ _A los miem_ - _bros de ca_ - _da na_ - _ción._
_me_ - _mo_ - _rar_ _Ya se_ - _guir a Je_ - _sús Sal_ - _va_ - _dor._
ple - _ni_ - _tud;_ _Nos pro_ - _te_ - _ge_y _nos guí_ - _a_en _su luz._
spi - _ra_ - _ción_ _Pa_ - _ra ser en el mun_ - _do la luz._
nues - _tro Dios_ _Quien nos lla_ - _ma_y _nos da sal_ - _va_ - _ción._

Text: Based on John 6; adapt. by Susan R. Briehl, b.1952; Spanish by Jaime Cortez, b.1963
Tune: ARGENTINE SANTO, 9 9 9 9 with refrain; Argentine melody; adapt. and verses by Marty Haugen, b.1950
© 2001, GIA Publications, Inc.

Eat This Bread / Coman de Este Pan 326

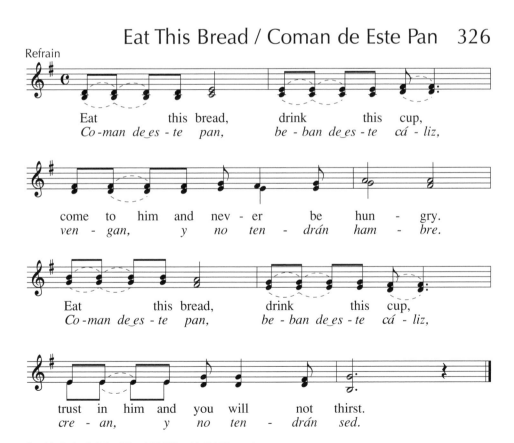

Eat this bread, drink this cup,
_Co_ -_man de_es - _te pan,_ _be_ - _ban de_es - _te cá_ - _liz,_

come to him and nev - er be hun - gry.
ven - _gan,_ _y no ten_ - _drán ham_ - _bre._

Eat this bread, drink this cup,
_Co_ -_man de_es - _te pan,_ _be_ - _ban de_es - _te cá_ - _liz,_

trust in him and you will not thirst.
cre - _an,_ _y no ten_ - _drán sed._

Text: John 6; adapt. by Robert J. Batastini, b.1942, and the Taizé Community
Tune: Jacques Berthier, 1923–1994
© 1984, tr. 2005, Les Presses de Taizé, GIA Publications, Inc., agent

327 Gusten y Vean / Taste and See

Refrain

Gus-ten y ve-an, gus-ten y ve-an qué bue-no es el Señor, qué bue-no es el Se-ñor. Taste and see,
taste and see the good-ness of the Lord.

Verses

Cantor:

1. Ven - gan los ham-brien - tos:
2. Ven - gan los se - dien - tos:
3. Ven - gan los po - bres:
4. Ven - gan los do - lien - tos: *All:* ¡Gus-ten y ve - an!
5. Ven - gan los que su - fren:
6. Ven - gan los can - sa - dos:
7. Ven - gan a la me - sa:

Cantor:

Come all who hun - ger:
All you who thirst:
Come all you poor ones:
All who are griev - ing: *All:* Taste and see the
Come all who suf - fer:
All who are wea - ry:
Come to the ta - ble:

D.C.

good-ness of the Lord, the good-ness of the Lord.

Psalm 34 Verses

1. I will bless the Lord at all times,
   God's praise always on my lips;
   in the Lord my soul shall make its boast.
   The humble shall hear and be glad.

2. Glorify the Lord with me.
   Together let us praise God's name.
   I sought the Lord and was heard;
   from all my terrors set free.

3. Look towards God and be radiant;
   let your faces not be abashed.
   When the poor cry out the Lord hears them
   and rescues them from all their distress.

4. The angel of the Lord is encamped
   around those who fear God, to rescue them.
   Taste and see that the Lord is good.
   They are happy who seek refuge in God.

1. *Bendigo al Señor en todo momento,*
   su alabanza está siempre en mi boca;
   mi alma se gloria en el Señor:
   que los humildes lo escuchen y se alegren.

2. *Proclamen conmigo la grandeza del Señor,*
   ensalcemos juntos su nombre.
   Yo consulté al Señor y me respondió,
   me libró de todas mis ansias.

3. *Contémplenlo, y quedarán radiantes,*
   su rostro no se avergonzará.
   Si el afligido invoca al Señor,
   él lo escucha y lo salva de sus angustias.

4. *El ángel del Señor acampa*
   en torno a sus fieles, y los protege.
   Gusten y vean qué bueno es el Señor,
   dichoso el que se acoge a él.

Text: Based on Psalm 34; Tony E. Alonso, b.1980, © 2008, GIA Publications, Inc.; Psalm 34:2–9 verses, © 1963, 2000, The Grail,
GIA Publications, Inc., agent; Spanish tr. from *Leccionario, Edición Hispanoamérica*, © 1970, 1972, Conferencia Episcopal Española
Tune: Tony E. Alonso, b.1980, © 2008, 2010, GIA Publications, Inc.

328 Draw Near

Refrain

Draw near, draw near! Take the Bod-y
of your Lord. Draw near, draw near!
Drink the Blood for you out-poured.

Verses

1. Draw near and take the Bod-y of the Lord,
2. Christ, our Re-deem - er, God's e-ter-nal Son,
3. Let us ap-proach with faith-ful hearts sin-cere
4. With heav'n-ly bread Christ makes the hun-gry whole;

And drink with faith the Blood for you out-poured.
Has by his cross and blood the vic - t'ry won.
And claim the prom-ise of sal-va-tion here.
His liv-ing wa-ter fills the thirst-ing soul.

Saved by Christ's Bod - y and his ho-ly Blood, With
He spent his life for great-est and for least. Praise
Christ rules our hearts, and all his saints de-fends; He
Al - pha-O - me - ga, un-to whom shall bow All

D.C.

souls re-freshed we give our thanks to God.
Christ the Pas-chal Vic-tim, Christ the Priest.
gives be-liev-ers life that nev-er ends.
na - tions of the earth, be with us now.

Text: *Sancti, venite, Christi corpus sumite*, 7th C.; tr. by John M. Neale, 1818-1866, alt.
Tune: NEALE, 10 10 10 10 with refrain; Steven R. Janco, b.1961, © 1992, World Library Publications

At the Table of Jesus 329

Refrain

At the ta - ble of Je-sus we are nour - ished and fed By the
bless - ing cup and heav-en's liv - ing bread. At the
ta - ble of Je - sus earth and heav - en are wed. To a
hun - gry world, by our God we are led.

Verses

1. Where love and char - i - ty are found There God is a-mong us; God's
2. Now, as we gath-er all as one, Di - vi-sion is end-ed, com-
3. Joined with the an-gels and the saints, Be - hold-ing God's glo - ry and

1. good - ness a - bounds. As Christ gath - ers man - y as one,
2. mun - ion be - gun. Let fear, an - ger, ha - tred now end.
3. tast - ing God's grace, We'll sing praise in God's ho - ly place,

D.C.

1. Let our hearts be glad and re - flect God's love.
2. Let us dwell in love as our God in - tends.
3. And with heav - en's hosts we'll come face to face.

Text: Based on *Ubi Caritas*; Tony E. Alonso, b.1980
Tune: SIMPLE GIFTS, Irregular with refrain; Joseph Brackett, Jr., 1797–1882; arr. by Marty Haugen, b.1950
© 2010, GIA Publications, Inc.

330 Eucharistic Exposition and Benediction

EXPOSITION

*As the priest or deacon prepares the holy eucharist for adoration, the following or another suitable song (*I Am the Bread of Life / Yo Soy el Pan de Vida, *no. 315, or* Alleluia! Sing to Jesus, *no. 151) is sung:*

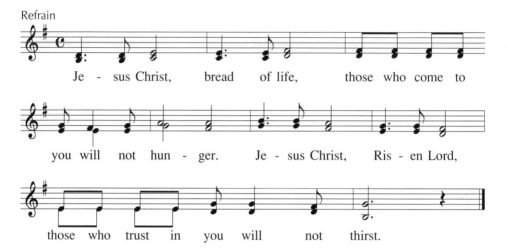

Refrain

Je - sus Christ, bread of life, those who come to
you will not hun - ger. Je - sus Christ, Ris - en Lord,
those who trust in you will not thirst.

Text: John 6; Taizé Community
Tune: Jacques Berthier, 1923–1994
© 1984, Les Presses de Taizé, GIA Publications, Inc., agent

ADORATION

During the adoration there are prayers, songs, Scripture readings, and possibly a homily. Silent prayer is also encouraged.

BENEDICTION

As the priest or deacon incenses the Blessed Sacrament, the following or another appropriate hymn or song may be sung.

331 Come Adore This Wondrous Presence / Tantum Ergo

1. Come a - dore this won - drous pres - ence; Bow to Christ, the
2. Glo - ry be to God the Fa - ther, Praise to his co -
1. *Tan - tum er - go Sa - cra - mén - tum Ve - ne - ré - mur*
2. *Ge - ni - tó - ri, Ge - ni - tó - que Laus et ju - bi -*

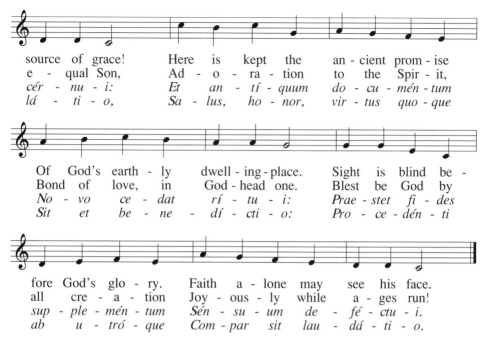

source of grace!   Here   is   kept   the   an - cient prom - ise
e - qual Son,   Ad - o - ra - tion   to   the   Spir - it,
cér - nu - i: Et   an - tí - quum   do - cu - mén - tum
lá - ti - o,   Sa - lus,   ho - nor,   vir - tus   quo - que

Of   God's   earth - ly   dwell - ing - place.   Sight   is   blind   be -
Bond   of   love,   in   God - head one.   Blest   be   God   by
No - vo   ce - dat   rí - tu - i: Prae - stet   fi - des
Sit   et   be - ne - dí - cti - o: Pro - ce - dén - ti

fore God's glo - ry.   Faith   a - lone   may   see   his   face.
all   cre - a - tion   Joy - ous - ly   while   a - ges   run!
sup - ple - mén - tum   Sén - su - um   de - fé - ctu - i.
ab   u - tró - que   Com - par   sit   lau - dá - ti - o.

Text: Thomas Aquinas, 1225–1274; tr. by James Quinn, SJ, 1919–2010, © 1969. Used by permission of Selah Publishing Co., Inc.
Tune: ST. THOMAS, 8 7 8 7 8 7; John F. Wade, 1711–1786

After a prayer, the priest or deacon blesses the assembly with the Blessed Sacrament.

REPOSITION

As the priest or deacon places the Blessed Sacrament in the tabernacle, the assembly sings or says the following:

Blessed be God.
Blessed be his holy name.
Blessed be Jesus Christ, true God and true man.
Blessed be the name of Jesus.
Blessed be his most sacred heart.
Blessed be his most precious blood.
Blessed be Jesus in the most holy sacrament of the altar.
Blessed be the Holy Spirit, the Paraclete.
Blessed be the great Mother of God, Mary most holy.
Blessed be her holy and immaculate conception.
Blessed be her glorious assumption.
Blessed be the name of Mary, virgin and mother.
Blessed be Saint Joseph, her most chaste spouse.
Blessed be God in his angels and in his saints.

A song of praise may be sung to conclude the celebration.

332　Healer of Our Every Ill

Refrain

Heal - er　of　our　ev - 'ry ill,　Light of each to - mor - row,

Give us peace be - yond our fear And hope be - yond our　sor　-　row.

Verses

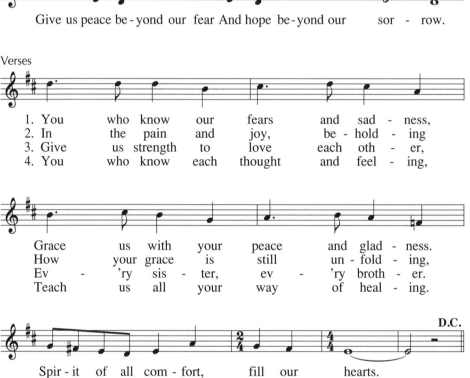

1. You　　who　know　our　　fears　and　sad - ness,
2. In　　the　pain　and　joy,　be - hold - ing
3. Give　　us　strength　to　love　each　oth - er,
4. You　　who　know　each　thought　and　feel - ing,

Grace　　us　with　your　peace　and　glad - ness.
How　　your grace　is　still　un - fold - ing,
Ev - 'ry sis - ter,　ev - 'ry broth - er.
Teach　us　all　your　way　of　heal - ing.

D.C.

Spir - it　of　all com - fort,　fill　our　hearts.
Give us　all your vi - sion,　God　of　love.
Spir - it　of　all kind - ness,　be　our　guide.
Spir - it　of com - pas - sion,　fill each　heart.

Text: Marty Haugen, b.1950
Tune: HEALER OF OUR EVERY ILL, 88 9 with refrain; Marty Haugen, b.1950
© 1987, GIA Publications, Inc.

When Jesus the Healer 333

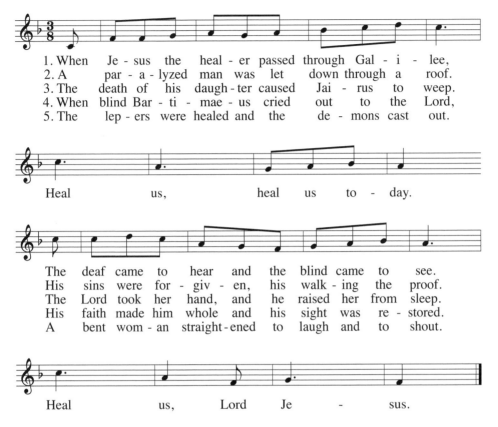

1. When Je - sus the heal - er passed through Gal - i - lee,
2. A par - a - lyzed man was let down through a roof.
3. The death of his daugh - ter caused Jai - rus to weep.
4. When blind Bar - ti - mae - us cried out to the Lord,
5. The lep - ers were healed and the de - mons cast out.

Heal us, heal us to - day.

The deaf came to hear and the blind came to see.
His sins were for - giv - en, his walk - ing the proof.
The Lord took her hand, and he raised her from sleep.
His faith made him whole and his sight was re - stored.
A bent wom - an straight - ened to laugh and to shout.

Heal us, Lord Je - sus.

Text: Peter D. Smith, b.1938
Tune: HEALER, 11 6 11 5; Peter D. Smith, b.1938; acc. by Robert N. Roth
© 1978, Stainer & Bell, Ltd. & Methodist Church (UK) Division of Education and Youth (Admin. by Hope Publishing Company)

For Health and Strength 334

Canon

1. For health and strength and dai - ly food,
2. For neigh - bors, friends, and fam - i - ly, We give you thanks, O God.
3. For faith and hope and lov - ing care,

Text: Vs. 1, traditional; vss. 2, 3, Bert Polman, © 1994, CRC Publications
Tune: FOR HEALTH AND STRENGTH, 8 6; anonymous; acc. by Robert J. Batastini, b.1942, © 2000, GIA Publications, Inc.

335   Final Blessing

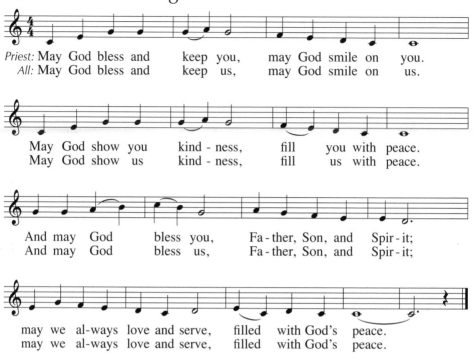

Priest: May God bless and keep you, may God smile on you.
All: May God bless and keep us, may God smile on us.

May God show you kind - ness, fill you with peace.
May God show us kind - ness, fill us with peace.

And may God bless you, Fa - ther, Son, and Spir - it;
And may God bless us, Fa - ther, Son, and Spir - it;

may we al - ways love and serve, filled with God's peace.
may we al - ways love and serve, filled with God's peace.

Text: Numbers 6:24–26; David Haas, b.1957, © 1997, GIA Publications, Inc.
Tune: ADORO TE DEVOTE, Mode V; adapt. by David Haas, b.1957, © 1997, GIA Publications, Inc.

336   Go Now in Peace

Canon

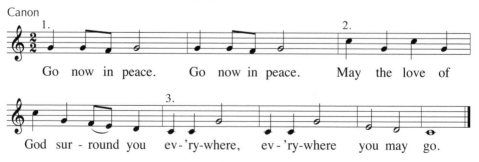

Go now in peace. Go now in peace. May the love of

God sur - round you ev - 'ry-where, ev - 'ry-where you may go.

Text: Natalie Sleeth, 1930–1992
Tune: Natalie Sleeth, 1930–1992; acc. by Robert J. Batastini, b.1942
© 1976, Hinshaw Music, Inc.

For Your Gracious Blessing 337

For your gra-cious bless-ing, for your won-drous word,

for your lov-ing kind-ness, we give thanks, O God.

Text: Traditional
Tune: Traditional; acc. by Robert N. Roth, © 2000, GIA Publications, Inc.

May the Lord, Mighty God 338

1., 3. May the Lord, might-y God, bless and
2. Lift your eyes and see God's face full of

keep you for-ev - er, grant you peace,
grace for - ev - er. May the Lord,

per - fect peace, cour-age in ev - 'ry en-deav - or.
might-y God, bless and keep you for-ev - er.

Text: Numbers 6:24-26; unknown
Tune: WEN-TI, Irregular; Chinese, Pao-chen Li; adapted by I-to Loh, b.1936, © 1983, Abingdon Press; acc. by Diana Kodner, b.1957, © 1993,
    GIA Publications, Inc.

339   Acknowledgments

3 Text: © 1963, 1993, The Grail, GIA Publications, Inc., agent

6 Text: © 1969, James Quinn, SJ, Selah Publishing Co., Inc., North American agent. www.selahpub.com.

50 Harm.: © 1989, The United Methodist Publishing House (admin. The Copyright Company, Nashville, TN). All rights reserved. International copyright secured. Used by permission.

51 Arr.: © 1990, Iona Community, GIA Publications, Inc., agent

53 Music: © 1984, Les Presses de Taizé, GIA Publications, Inc., agent

57 Music: © Verbum Forlong AB, Sweden

64 Music: © 1980, Les Presses de Taizé, GIA Publications, Inc., agent

65 Music: © 2001, World Library Publications. wlpmusic.com. All rights reserved..

109 Acc.: © 1975, GIA Publications, Inc.

111 © 1982, GIA Publications, Inc.

112 © 1984, Augsburg Fortress

113 © 1994, Les Presses de Taizé, GIA Publications, Inc., agent

114 Text: © David Higham Assoc. Ltd. Harm.: From *The Oxford Book of Carols*, © 1928, Oxford University Press. Reproduced by permission. All rights reserved.

115 © 1988, 1989, 1990, Christopher Walker. Published by OCP. 5536 NE Hassalo, Portland, OR 97213. All rights reserved. Used by permission.

116 © 1984, Les Presses de Taizé, GIA Publications, Inc., agent

117 © 2003, World Library Publication. wlpmusic.com. All rights reserved.

119 Text tr.: © 1985, The Church Pension Fund. Acc.: © 1986, GIA Publications, Inc.

120 Harm.: © 1994, GIA Publications, Inc.

124 © 1984, GIA Publications, Inc.

125 Tune: © 1979, 1988, Les Presses de Taizé, GIA Publications, Inc., agent

126 Harm.: © 1995, GIA Publications, Inc.

127 Tune tr. and arr.: © 1990, Iona Community, GIA Publications, Inc., agent

128 Harm.: © 1961, General Convention of the Episcopal Church, USA.

129 Text and tune: © 1945, Boosey and Co., Ltd. Copyright Renewed. Reprinted by permission of Boosey and Hawkes, Inc. Acc.: © 1993, GIA Publications, Inc.

135 Text tr.: © 1982, Peter J. Scagnelli. Published by World Library Publications. wlpmusic.com. All rights reserved. Acc.: © 1975, GIA Publications, Inc.

136 © 1990, 1991, GIA Publications, Inc.

137 Text trans.: © 1975, 2011, Peter J. Scagnelli. Published by World Library Publications.wlpmusic.com. All rights reserved.

138 Harm.: © 1986, GIA Publications, Inc.

139 Verse text and tune: © 2003, GIA Publications, Inc. Refrain text: © 1973, ICEL

143 Text: © 2000, World Library Publications. wlpmusic.com. All rights reserved. Harm. © 1986, GIA Publications, Inc.

144 © 1995, GIA Publications, Inc.

146 Harm.: From *Cantate Domino*, © 1980, World Council of Churches

147 © 1981, Les Presses de Taizé, GIA Publications, Inc., agent.

149 Acc.: © 2000, GIA Publications, Inc.

150 Harm.: © 1987, GIA Publications, Inc.

152 Text: © 2001, GIA Publications, Inc. Acc.: © 2000, GIA Publications, Inc.

153 © 1973, International Liturgy Publications, PO Box 50476, Nashville, TN 37205. www.ILPmusic.org

155 © 1984, Peace of Music Publishing AB, admin. Walton Music Corp., a div. of GIA Publications, Inc.

156 © 1969, Hope Publishing Co., Carol Stream, IL 60188. All rights reserved. Used by permission.

160 © 1988, 1989, Christopher Walker. Published by OCP. 5536 NE Hassalo, Portland, OR 97213. All rights reserved. Used by permission.

161 © 1986, GIA Publications, Inc.

162 Text: © Desmond Tutu. Tune: © 1996, Iona Community, GIA Publications, Inc., agent.

163 © 1984, Les Presses de Taizé, GIA Publications, Inc. agent

164 Spanish text and tune: © 1973, Kiko Argüello. Tr. © 1988, OCP. Published by OCP, 5536 NE Hassalo, Portland, OR 97213. All rights reserved. Used by permission.

166 Text: © 1983, 1987, Hope Publishing Co., Carol Stream, IL 60188. All rights reserved. Used by permission. Tune: © 2003, GIA Publications, Inc.

167 © 1981, 1982, 1987, GIA Publications, Inc.

168 Tune: © 1988, Bob Hurd. Published by OCP. 5536 NE Hassalo, Portland, OR 97213. All rights reserved. Used by permission.

169 Text tr.: © 1971, John W. Grant

170 © 1989, GIA Publications, Inc.

173 © 2002, GIA Publications, Inc.

174 Harm.: © Downside Abbey, Bath, BA3 4RH, UK

Acknowledgments/*continued*

175 © 1972, CCCM Music/Universal Music–Brentwood Benson Publishing (admin. CapitolCMGPublishing.com). All rights reserved. Used by permission.

176 Text adapt. and tune: © 2008, GIA Publications, Inc.

177 Text: © 1962, World Library Publications. wlpmusic.com. All rights reserved. Harm.: © 1958, Ralph Jusko Publications, Inc.

178 Text: © 1966, 1982, Rev. Willard F. Jabusch. Published by OCP. 5536 NE Hassalo, Portland, OR 97213. All rights reserved. Used by permission. Harm.: © 1986, GIA Publications, Inc.

179 © 1988, GIA Publications, Inc.

180 © 1986, Bernadette Farrell. Published by OCP. 5536 NE Hassalo, Portland, OR 97213. All rights reserved. Used by permission.

182 © 1994, Iona Community, GIA Publications, Inc., agent

184 © 1979, 2011, Manuel José Alonso and José Pagán. Exclusive agent in US, Canada and Mexico: OCP. 5536 NE Hassalo, Portland, OR 97213. All rights reserved. Used by permission.

185 © 1984, Peace of Music Publishing AB, admin. Walton Music Corp., a div. of GIA Publications, Inc.

187 © 1986, 1991, Les Presses de Taizé, GIA Publications, Inc. agent

188 Text: Sts. 2, 3, © 1987, Faith Alive Christian Resources, Grand Rapids, MI 49650. All rights reserved. Used by permission. Acc.: © 2000, GIA Publications, Inc.

189 © 1979, Les Presses de Taizé, GIA Publications, Inc., agent

190 Acc.: © 2000, GIA Publications, Inc.

191 Acc.: © 2000, GIA Publications, Inc.

192 © 1975, New Spring Publishing, Inc. (admin. CapitolCMGPublishing.com). All rights reserved. Used by permission.

194 Arr.: © 1998, Iona Community, GIA Publications, Inc., agent

195 Sts. 1–4: © 1982, The Jubilate Group (admin. Hope Publishing Co., Carol Stream, IL 60188). All rights reserved. Used by permission.; sts. 5, 6, © 1993, GIA Publications, Inc. Harm.: © 1992, GIA Publications, Inc.

196 Text: © 1973, Hope Publishing Co. Tune: © 1973, The Jubilate Group (admin. Hope Publishing Co., Carol Stream, IL 60188). All rights reserved. Used by permission.

197 Arr.: © 1990, Iona Community, GIA Publications, Inc., agent

199 © 1989, Universal Music—Brentwood Benson Publishing (admin. CapitolCMGPublishing.com). All rights reserved. Used by permission.

200 © 1990, GIA Publications, Inc.

203 © 2011, Worshiptogether.com Songs/Sixsteps Music/Said and Done Music/Shout! Music Publishing/Thankyou Music (admin. CapitolCMGPublishing.com). All rights reserved. Used by permission.

204 © 1993, GIA Publications, Inc.

205 Text: Verses, © 1963, The Grail, GIA Publications, Inc., agent; refrain, © 1985, Paul Inwood. Tune: © 1985, Paul Inwood. Published by OCP. 5536 NE Hassalo, Portland, OR 97213. All rights reserved. Used by permission.

206 Text and acc.: © 1978, 1990, Les Presses de Taizé, GIA Publications, Inc., agent

207 © 2001, Thankyou Music (admin. CapitolCMGPublishing.com). All rights reserved. Used by permission.

208 Text: © 1972, Hope Publishing Co., Carol Stream, IL 60188. All rights reserved. Used by permission. Tune: © 1989, GIA Publications, Inc.

209 © 1985, GIA Publications, Inc.

213 © 1980, GIA Publications, Inc.

214 © 1986, Hope Publishing Co., Carol Stream, IL 60188. All rights reserved. Used by permission.

215 Text: © 1992, Hope Publishing Co., Carol Stream, IL 60188. All rights reserved. Used by permission. Tune: © 2007, GIA Publications, Inc.

216 Text and tune: © 1970, 1975, Celebration. Acc.: © 1987, GIA Publications, Inc.

217 Harm.: © 1992, Horace Clarence Boyer

218 Tune: © 1987, GIA Publications, Inc.

219 Text of verses and tune arr.: © 1996, Carey Landry. Published by OCP. 5536 NE Hassalo, Portland, OR 97213. All rights reserved. Used by permission.

220 © 1984, Peace of Music Publishing AB, admin. Walton Music Corp., a div. of GIA Publications, Inc.

221 © 1988, GIA Publications, Inc.

222 Text: © 1992, GIA Publications, Inc. Harm.: © 1985, GIA Publications, Inc.

223 © 1981, OCP. 5536 NE Hassalo, Portland, OR 97213. All rights reserved. Used by permission.

224 © 1985, tr. 2005, GIA Publications, Inc.

225 © 1984, Peace of Music Publishing AB, admin. Walton Music Corp., a div. of GIA Publications, Inc.

226 © 1990, Bernadette Farrell. Published by OCP. 5536 NE Hassalo, Portland, OR 97213. All rights reserved. Used by permission.

227 Text and tune adapt.: © 1963, Stainer & Bell Ltd., London, England (admin. Hope Publishing Co., Carol Stream, IL 60188). All rights reserved. Used by permission.

229 © 1989, GIA Publications, Inc.

230 © 2001, 2011, Les Presses de Taizé, GIA Publications, Inc., agent

Acknowledgments/*continued*

Acknowledgments/*continued*

286 Text: Reproduced by permission of Oxford University Press.

287 Text: Vss. 2-4, © 1973, James E. Byrne. Arr.: © 1978, Songs of the Sword of the Spirit/The Word of God Music (admin. The Copyright Company, Nashville, TN) All rights reserved. International copyright secured. Used by permission. Acc.: © 1989, GIA Publications, Inc.

288 Text: © 1994, World Library Publications. Acc.: © 1984, World Library Publications. wlpmusic.com. All rights reserved.

289 © 2010, ICEL

290 Arr.: © 2000, GIA Publications, Inc.

293 © 1974, Hope Publishing Co., Carol Stream, IL 60188. All rights reserved. Used by permission.

294 Text: Estate of Roland F. Palmer. Harm.: © 1986, GIA Publications, Inc.

295 © 1993, GIA Publications, Inc.

296 © 1989, GIA Publications, Inc.

297 Text: Sts. 2–7, © 1971, Faber Music Ltd., London, WC1B 3DA. Reprinted from *New Catholic Hymnal* by permission of the publishers.

302 Harm.: © Willis Music Co.

304 © 1979, Les Presses de Taizé, GIA Publications, Inc., agent

306 © 1976, Crouch Music/Bud John Songs (admin. CapitolCMGPublishing.com). All rights reserved. Used by permission.

307 Harm.: © 1975, GIA Publications, Inc.

309 ©1988, GIA Publications, Inc.

310 Tune: © 1977, ICEL

311 Text: © 1982, The Jubilate Group (admin. Hope Publishing Co., Carol Stream, IL 60188). All rights reserved. Used by permission. Acc.: © 1987, GIA Publications, Inc.

312 © 1999, GIA Publications, Inc.

313 Harm.: © 1994, GIA Publications, Inc.

314 © 1983, GIA Publications, Inc.

315 © 1966, 1970, 1986, 1993, GIA Publications, Inc.

316 Tr.: © 2011, GIA Publications, Inc. Harm.: © 1986, GIA Publications, Inc.

317 © 1978, John B. Foley, SJ. Published by OCP. 5536 NE Hassalo, Portland, OR 97213. All rights reserved. Used by permission.

318 © 1988, Bob Hurd and Pia Moriarty. Published by OCP. 5536 NE Hassalo, Portland, OR 97213. All rights reserved. Used by permission.

319 © 1983, GIA Publications, Inc.

320 Verse text: © 1989, James Quinn, SJ, Selah Publishing Co., Inc., North American agent. www.selahpub.com. Refrain text and tune: © 1989, GIA Publications, Inc.

321 © 1973, OCP. 5536 NE Hassalo, Portland, OR 97213. All rights reserved. Used by permission.

322 © 1989, tr. © 2004, GIA Publications, Inc.

323 © 1977, Archdiocese of Philadelphia. Published by International Liturgy Publications, PO Box 50476, Nashville, TN 37205. www.ILPmusic.org

324 © 1984, OCP. 5536 NE Hassalo, Portland, OR 97213. All rights reserved. Used by permission.

325 © 2001, GIA Publications, Inc.

326 © 1984, tr. 2005, Les Presses de Taizé, GIA Publications, Inc., agent

327 Text and Tune: © 2008, 2010, GIA Publications, Inc. Verses text: © 1963, 2000, The Grail, GIA Publications, Inc., agent. Spanish tr.: © 1970, 1972, Conferencia Episcopal Española

328 Tune: © 1992, World Library Publications. wlpmusic.com. All rights reserved.

329 © 2010, GIA Publications, Inc.

330 © 1984, Les Presses de Taizé, GIA Publications, Inc., agent

331 Text tr.: © 1969, James Quinn, SJ, Selah Publishing Co., Inc., North American agent. www.selahpub.com.

332 © 1987, GIA Publications, Inc.

333 © 1978, Stainer & Bell, Ltd. & Methodist Church (UK) Division of Education and Youth (admin. Hope Publishing Co., Carol Stream, IL 60188). All rights reserved. Used by permission.

334 Text: Sts. 2, 3, © 1994, Faith Alive Christian Resources, Grand Rapids, MI 49650. All rights reserved. Used by permission. Acc.: © 2000, GIA Publications, Inc.

335 Text and tune adapt.: © 1997, GIA Publications, Inc.

336 © 1976, Hinshaw Music, Inc. Printed with permission.

337 Acc.: © 2000, GIA Publications, Inc.

338 Tune adapt.: © 1983, Abingdon Press (admin. The Copyright Company, Nashville, TN) All rights reserved. International copyright secured. Used by permission. Acc.: © 1993, GIA Publications, Inc.

13   A Ti, Señor / To You, O Lord - Psalm 25
24   Acompáñame / Be with Me - Psalm 91
131   Adeste Fideles / O Come, All Ye Faithful / Venid, Fieles Todos
301   Adiós, O Queen of Heaven / Adiós, Reina del Cielo
301   Adiós, Reina del Cielo / Adiós, O Queen of Heaven
137   Again We Keep This Solemn Fast
184   Alabaré
275   All Are Welcome
210   All Creatures of Our God and King
285   All Night, All Day
280   All People That on Earth Do Dwell
26   All the Ends of the Earth - Psalm 98
211   All Things Bright and Beautiful
276   All Who Hunger, Gather Gladly
153   Alleluia, Alleluia, Give Thanks
151   Alleluia! Sing to Jesus
255   Amazing Grace!
197   Amen Siakudumisa / Amen, We Praise Your Name
197   Amen, We Praise Your Name / Amen Siakudumisa
121   Angels We Have Heard on High
222   As a Fire Is Meant for Burning
284   At Evening
329   At the Table of Jesus
295   Ave Maria
223   Awake from Your Slumber
110   Awake Now, Friends
117   Awake to the Day
120   Away in a Manger

311   Baptized in Water
299   Be Joyful, Mary
18   Be Merciful, O Lord / Señor, Misericordia - Psalm 51
250   Be Not Afraid (Dufford)
158   Be Not Afraid (Taizé)
24   Be with Me / Acompáñame - Psalm 91
324   Behold the Lamb
182   Behold, I Make All Things New
224   Benditos los Pobres / Blest Are They
203   Bless the Lord, O My Soul
266   Bless the Lord / Tengo Sed de Ti
242   Blessed Are the Poor in Spirit
33   Blessed Are They - Psalm 119
291   Blessed Feasts of Blessed Martyrs
224   Blest Are They / Benditos los Pobres
325   Bread of Life from Heaven / Pan de Vida Eterna

239   Bring Forth the Kingdom
322   Canción del Cuerpo de Cristo / Song of the Body of Christ
198   Cantad al Señor / Sing Praise to the Lord
8   Canticle of Mary (Magnificat)
213   Canticle of the Sun
200   Canticle of the Turning
4   Canticle of Zachary (Now Bless the God of Israel)
205   Center of My Life
166   Christ Is Alive
286   Christ Is the King!
156   Christ the Lord Is Risen!
154   Christ the Lord Is Risen Today
309   Christ Will Be Your Strength
223   City of God
124   Cold Are the People
326   Coman de Este Pan / Eat This Bread
331   Come Adore This Wondrous Presence / Tantum Ergo
281   Come All You People / Uyai Mose
110   Come, Emmanuel
221   Come! Live in the Light!
167   Come Lord Jesus
118   Come Now, O Prince of Peace
209   Come, O God of All the Earth
312   Come to the Water
113   Contemplaré / Wait for the Lord
246   Contigo Estoy / You Are Mine
119   Creator of the Stars of Night

6   Day Is Done
141   Deep Within
300   Desde el Cielo / From the Heavens
229   Digo "Sí," Señor / I Say "Yes," Lord
22   Do Not Forget - Psalm 78
258   Dona Nobis Pacem
245   Donde Hay Amor / Where True Charity / Ubi Caritas
328   Draw Near

161   Easter Alleluia
326   Eat This Bread / Coman de Este Pan
230   El Reino de Dios / The Kingdom of God
29   El Señor Es Compasivo / The Lord Is Kind and Merciful - Psalm 103
187   El Señor Es Mi Fortaleza / In the Lord I'll Be Ever Thankful
168   Envía Tu Espíritu

Index of First Lines and Common Titles/*continued*

32   Éste Es el Día / Let Us Rejoice - Psalm 118
171   Every Time I Feel the Spirit
155   Ewe, Thina / We Walk His Way

175   Father, I Adore You
335   Final Blessing
23   For Ever I Will Sing - Psalm 89
334   For Health and Strength
212   For the Beauty of the Earth
111   For You, O Lord, My Soul in Stillness Waits
337   For Your Gracious Blessing
225   Freedom Is Coming
300   From the Heavens / Desde el Cielo

278   Gather Us In
277   Gather Your People
321   Gentle Jesus, Risen Lord
257   Give Us Your Peace
125   Gloria, Gloria
240   Go Make a Difference
336   Go Now in Peace
31   Go Out to All the World - Psalm 117
126   Go Tell It on the Mountain
226   God Has Chosen Me
283   Good Morning, God
162   Goodness Is Stronger than Evil
228   Guide My Feet
7   Guiding Me, Guarding Me - Psalm 121
327   Gusten y Vean / Taste and See

302   Hail, Holy Queen Enthroned Above
295   Hail Mary, Full of Grace
154   Hail the Day That Sees Him Rise
185   Halleluya! We Sing Your Praises
130   Hark! The Herald Angels Sing
127   He Came Down
332   Healer of Our Every Ill
231   Here I Am, Lord
207   Here I Am to Worship
278   Here in This Place
176   Holy and Blessed Three
186   Holy God, We Praise Thy Name
296   Holy Is Your Name
172   Holy Spirit, Come to Us / Ven, Espíritu

315   I Am the Bread of Life / Yo Soy el Pan de Vida
279   I Come with Joy
227   I Danced in the Morning
253   I Heard the Voice of Jesus Say
192   I Just Came to Praise the Lord

254   I Love the Lord
39   I Praise You, O Lord - Psalm 139
316   I Receive the Living God
229   I Say "Yes," Lord / Digo "Sí," Señor
231   I, the Lord of Sea and Sky
216   I Want to Walk as a Child of the Light
246   I Will Come to You in the Silence
3   I Will Praise the Lord - Psalm 146
40   I Will Praise Your Name for Ever - Psalm 145
267   If You Believe and I Believe
297   Immaculate Mary
265   In Christ There Is No East or West
248   In Every Age
214   In the Bulb There Is a Flower
144   In the Cross of Christ
187   In the Lord I'll Be Ever Thankful / El Señor Es Mi Fortaleza
206   In the Lord Rejoicing! / Jubilate Deo
20   In the Morning I Will Sing - Psalm 63
37   In the Sight of the Angels - Psalm 138
43   Isaiah 12: You Will Draw Water

307   Jerusalem, My Happy Home
232   Jesu, Jesu / Jesús, Jesús
179   Jesucristo Ayer / Jesus Christ, Yesterday, Today, and Forever
330   Jesus Christ, Bread of Life
157   Jesus Christ Is Risen Today
179   Jesus Christ, Yesterday, Today, and Forever / Jesucristo Ayer
257   Jesus, Give Us Your Peace
181   Jesus in the Morning
232   Jesús, Jesús / Jesu, Jesu
143   Jesus Kneels, in Sorrow
128   Jesus Our Brother, Kind and Good
147   Jesús, Recuérdame / Jesus, Remember Me
147   Jesus, Remember Me / Jesús, Recuérdame
122   Joy to the World
183   Joyful, Joyful, We Adore You
206   Jubilate Deo / In the Lord Rejoicing!
189   Jubilate Deo Omnis Terra
189   Jubilate, Servite / Raise a Song of Gladness
42   Judith 13: You Are the Highest Honor

261   Ki Ri Su To No / May the Peace of Christ Be with You
202   Know That God Is Good / Mungu ni Mwema

Index of First Lines and Common Titles/*continued*

269 Lead Me, Guide Me
242 Lead Me, Lord
176 Let There Be Light
275 Let Us Build a House
 35 Let Us Go Rejoicing / Vamos Todos Alegres - Psalm 122
 32 Let Us Rejoice / Éste Es el Día - Psalm 118
235 Let Us Talents and Tongues Employ
293 Lift High the Cross
207 Light of the World
112 Light One Candle
289 Litany of the Saints
248 Long Before the Mountains Came to Be
199 Lord, I Lift Your Name on High
 16 Lord, Let Your Mercy - Psalm 33
271 Lord of All Hopefulness
 38 Lord, On the Day I Called - Psalm 138
 30 Lord, Send Out Your Spirit / Señor, Envía Tu Espíritu - Psalm 104
244 Lord, When You Came / Pescador de Hombres
233 Lord, You Give the Great Commission

  8 Magnificat (My Heart Sings Out)
304 Magnificat / Sing Out, My Soul
259 Make Me a Channel of Your Peace
303 Mañanitas a la Virgen de Guadalupe / Morning Praises to the Virgin of Guadalupe
220 Marcharemos / We Are Marching / Siyahamba
335 May God Bless and Keep Us
338 May the Lord, Mighty God
261 May the Peace of Christ Be with You / Ki Ri Su To No
140 Mercy, O God
282 Morning Has Broken
303 Morning Praises to the Virgin of Guadalupe / Mañanitas a la Virgen de Guadalupe
263 Muchos Miembros Hay / We Are Many Parts
202 Mungu ni Mwema / Know That God Is Good
  8 My Heart Sings Out (Magnificat)
  9 My Shepherd Is the Lord - Psalm 23
200 My Soul Cries Out
111 My Soul in Stillness Waits
296 My Soul Is Filled with Joy
 19 My Soul Is Thirsting - Psalm 63

247 Nada Te Turbe / Nothing Can Trouble
124 Night of Silence
123 Noche de Paz / Silent Night, Holy Night
247 Nothing Can Trouble / Nada Te Turbe
  4 Now Bless the God of Israel (Canticle of Zachary)
237 Now I Know
284 Now It Is Evening
193 Now Thank We All Our God
319 Now We Remain

174 O Breathe on Me, O Breath of God
131 O Come, All Ye Faithful / Venid, Fieles Todos / Adeste Fideles
109 O Come, O Come, Emmanuel
225 O Freedom
268 O God, Keep Me Safe
262 O God of Love, O King of Peace
169 O Holy Spirit, by Whose Breath
149 O How Good Is Christ the Lord! / ¡Oh, Qué Bueno Es Jesús!
274 O Lord, Hear My Prayer / Señor, Ten Piedad
205 O Lord, You Are the Center of My Life
298 O Queen of Heaven / Regina Caeli
135 O Sun of Justice
290 O When the Saints Go Marching In
149 ¡Oh, Qué Bueno Es Jesús! / O How Good Is Christ the Lord!
251 On Eagle's Wings
317 One Bread, One Body
272 Open My Eyes
 12 Open Wide Your Gates - Psalm 24
 34 Our Help Comes from the Lord - Psalm 121
194 Over My Head

318 Pan de Vida
325 Pan de Vida Eterna / Bread of Life from Heaven
114 Peace Before Us
114 People, Look East
244 Pescador de Hombres / Lord, When You Came
188 Praise and Thanksgiving
280 Praise God from All Blessings Flow
 41 Praise the Lord, My Soul - Psalm 146
180 Praise to You, O Christ, Our Savior
260 Prayer of Peace
116 Prepare the Way of the Lord
 25 Proclaim to All the Nations - Psalm 96

Index of First Lines and Common Titles/*continued*

9 Psalm 23: My Shepherd Is the Lord
252 Psalm 23: Shepherd Me, O God
10 Psalm 23: The Lord Is My Shepherd
12 Psalm 24: Open Wide Your Gates
11 Psalm 24: We Long to See Your Face
14 Psalm 25: Teach Me Your Ways
13 Psalm 25: To You, O Lord / A Ti, Señor
15 Psalm 27: The Lord Is My Light
16 Psalm 33: Lord, Let Your Mercy
17 Psalm 34: Taste and See
18 Psalm 51: Be Merciful, O Lord / Señor, Misericordia
20 Psalm 63: In the Morning I Will Sing
19 Psalm 63: My Soul Is Thirsting
22 Psalm 78: Do Not Forget
21 Psalm 78: The Lord Gave Them Bread
23 Psalm 89: For Ever I Will Sing
24 Psalm 91: Be with Me / Acompáñame
25 Psalm 96: Proclaim to All the Nations
26 Psalm 98: All the Ends of the Earth
27 Psalm 98: Sing to the Lord a New Song
28 Psalm 100: We Are God's People
29 Psalm 103: The Lord Is Kind and Merciful / El Señor Es Compasivo
30 Psalm 104: Lord, Send Out Your Spirit / Señor, Envía Tu Espíritu
31 Psalm 117: Go Out to All the World
32 Psalm 118: Let Us Rejoice / Éste Es el Día
33 Psalm 119: Blessed Are They
7 Psalm 121: Guiding Me, Guarding Me
34 Psalm 121: Our Help Comes from the Lord
35 Psalm 122: Let Us Go Rejoicing / Vamos Todos Alegres
36 Psalm 126: The Lord Has Done Great Things
37 Psalm 138: In the Sight of the Angels
38 Psalm 138: Lord, On the Day I Called
39 Psalm 139: I Praise You, O Lord
40 Psalm 145: I Will Praise Your Name for Ever
3 Psalm 146: I Will Praise the Lord
41 Psalm 146: Praise the Lord, My Soul
234 Pues Si Vivimos / When We Are Living

256 Rain Down
189 Raise a Song of Gladness / Jubilate, Servite
298 Regina Caeli / O Queen of Heaven
190 Rejoice in the Lord Always
139 Remember You Are Dust

164 Resucitó
136 Return to God / Volvamos Hoy a Nuestro Dios

270 Seek Ye First
170 Send Down the Fire
167 Send Us Your Spirit
30 Señor, Envía Tu Espíritu / Lord, Send Out Your Spirit - Psalm 104
18 Señor, Misericordia / Be Merciful, O Lord - Psalm 51
274 Señor, Ten Piedad / O Lord, Hear My Prayer
308 Shall We Gather at the River
252 Shepherd Me, O God
195 Shout for Joy
123 Silent Night, Holy Night / Noche de Paz
152 Sing a New Song
196 Sing a New Song to the Lord
201 Sing Alleluia to the Lord
204 Sing, O People, Sing Our God Together
294 Sing of Mary, Pure and Lowly
204 Sing Our God Together
209 Sing Out, Earth and Skies
304 Sing Out, My Soul / Magnificat
177 Sing Praise to Our Creator
198 Sing Praise to the Lord / Cantad al Señor
191 Sing, Sing, Praise and Sing!
27 Sing to the Lord a New Song - Psalm 98
165 Sing with All the Saints in Glory
220 Siyahamba / We Are Marching / Marcharemos
138 Somebody's Knockin' at Your Door
322 Song of the Body of Christ / Canción del Cuerpo de Cristo
306 Soon and Very Soon
173 Spirit of God
143 Stations Hymn
115 Stay Awake, Be Ready
148 Stay Here and Keep Watch
305 Steal Away to Jesus
163 Surrexit Christus / The Lord Is Risen
312 Sweet Refreshment

320 Take and Eat
273 Take, O Take Me As I Am
331 Tantum Ergo / Come Adore This Wondrous Presence

Index of First Lines and Common Titles/*continued*

314 Taste and See (Moore)
17 Taste and See - Psalm 34
327 Taste and See / Gusten y Vean
14 Teach Me Your Ways - Psalm 25
203 Ten Thousand Reasons
266 Tengo Sed de Ti / Bless the Lord
159 That Easter Day with Joy Was Bright
133 The First Nowell
213 The Heavens Are Telling the Glory
178 The King of Glory
230 The Kingdom of God / El Reino de Dios
21 The Lord Gave Them Bread - Psalm 78
36 The Lord Has Done Great Things - Psalm 126
29 The Lord Is Kind and Merciful / El Señor Es Compasivo - Psalm 103
15 The Lord Is My Light - Psalm 27
10 The Lord Is My Shepherd - Psalm 23
163 The Lord Is Risen / Surrexit Christus
243 The Servant Song
238 The Summons
129 The Virgin Mary Had a Baby Boy
2 This Day God Gives Me
160 This Day Was Made by the Lord
166 This Is a Day of New Beginnings
217 This Little Light of Mine
324 Those Who Were in the Dark
236 'Tis the Gift to Be Simple
229 To the God Who Cannot Die
13 To You, O Lord / A Ti, Señor - Psalm 25
215 Touch the Earth Lightly
145 Tree of Life
139 Turn Away from Sin

245 Ubi Caritas / Where True Charity / Donde Hay Amor
281 Uyai Mose / Come All You People

35 Vamos Todos Alegres / Let Us Go Rejoicing - Psalm 122
172 Ven, Espíritu / Holy Spirit, Come to Us
131 Venid, Fieles Todos / O Come, All Ye Faithful / Adeste Fideles
136 Volvamos Hoy a Nuestro Dios / Return to God

313 Wade in the Water
113 Wait for the Lord / Contemplaré
219 Walk, Walk in the Light
112 Watch for Messiah
221 We Are Called
28 We Are God's People - Psalm 100
263 We Are Many Parts / Muchos Miembros Hay
220 We Are Marching / Siyahamba / Marcharemos
218 We Are Walking in the Light
322 We Come to Share Our Story
321 We Come to Your Table
319 We Hold the Death of the Lord
11 We Long to See Your Face - Psalm 24
287 We See the Lord
264 We Shall Overcome
288 We Sing of the Saints
134 We Three Kings of Orient Are
241 We Walk by Faith
155 We Walk His Way / Ewe, Thina
150 Were You There
132 What Child Is This
146 What Wondrous Love Is This
208 When in Our Music God Is Glorified
333 When Jesus the Healer
290 When the Saints Go Marching In
234 When We Are Living / Pues Si Vivimos
245 Where True Charity / Ubi Caritas / Donde Hay Amor
238 Will You Come and Follow Me
243 Will You Let Me Be Your Servant
249 With a Shepherd's Care

292 Ye Watchers and Ye Holy Ones
315 Yo Soy el Pan de Vida / I Am the Bread of Life
246 You Are Mine / Contigo Estoy
239 You Are Salt for the Earth
42 You Are the Highest Honor - Judith 13
310 You Have Put on Christ
323 You Satisfy the Hungry Heart
250 You Shall Cross the Barren Desert
251 You Who Dwell in the Shelter
43 You Will Draw Water - Isaiah 12